Third Edition

Children's Literature in the Reading Program

An Invitation to Read

Edited by Deborah A. Wooten & Bernice E. Cullinan

INTERNATIONAL
Reading Association
800 BARKSDALE ROAD, PO BOX 8139
NEWARK, DE 19714-8139, USA
www.reading.org

The International Reading Association attempts, through its publications, to provide a forum for a wide spectrum of opinions on reading. This policy permits divergent viewpoints without implying the endorsement of the Association.

Executive Editor, Books   Corinne M. Mooney
Developmental Editor   Charlene M. Nichols
Developmental Editor   Tori Mello Bachman
Developmental Editor   Stacey L. Reid
Editorial Production Manager   Shannon T. Fortner
Design and Composition Manager   Anette Schuetz

Project Editors   Stacey L. Reid and Christina M. Terranova

Cover   Design, Six Red Marbles

Library of Congress Cataloging-in-Publication Data

Children's literature in the reading program : an invitation to read / edited by Deborah A. Wooten & Bernice E. Cullinan. -- 3rd ed.
      p. cm.
   Includes bibliographical references and index.
   ISBN 978-0-87207-699-0
   1. Reading (Elementary)--United States. 2. Children's literature--Study and teaching--United States. 3. English language--Study and teaching (Elementary)--United States. I. Wooten, Deborah A. II. Cullinan, Bernice E.
   LB1573.C455 2009
   372.64--dc22

2009020234

I dedicate this book to Bee Cullinan, who has so graciously invited me to be a part of editing and contributing to the third edition of *Children's Literature in the Reading Program: An Invitation to Read*. The contributors to this book have all somehow experienced her influence in making sure teachers and children read wonderful books. Bee's enthusiasm about children's literature is contagious, and our bookshelves are filled with magnificent work by broad cross-sections of authors as a result.

—Deborah A. Wooten

CONTENTS

ABOUT THE EDITORS   vii

CONTRIBUTORS   ix

FOREWORD   xi
Richard L. Allington

PREFACE   xv
Deborah A. Wooten and Bernice E. Cullinan

SECTION ONE   1
Genre Studies

CHAPTER 1   3
Exploring Visual Images in Picture Books
Cyndi Giorgis

CHAPTER 2   15
Graphic Novels in Education: Cartoons, Comprehension, and Content Knowledge
Stergios Botzakis

CHAPTER 3   24
Using Postmodern Picture Books in the Classroom
Elizabeth A. Swaggerty

CHAPTER 4   37
Discovering the Many Layers in Nonfiction Books: An Author's View
James Cross Giblin

CHAPTER 5   45
Yes, Poetry Can!
David L. Harrison

CHAPTER 6   57
Series Books for Young Readers:
Seeking Reading Pleasure and Developing Reading Competence
Anne McGill-Franzen

CHAPTER 7   66
Learning Through Literature That Offers Diverse Perspectives:
Multicultural and International Literature
Junko Yokota

SECTION TWO   75

The Role of Children's Literature in the Classroom

CHAPTER 8   77
The Surreptitious Role of Children's Literature in Classrooms That Aim to Be "Exemplary"
Nancy Roser, Audra K. Roach, and Michelle D. Horsey

CHAPTER 9   88
Young Writers Use Mentor Texts
Jane Hansen

CHAPTER 10   99
Responding and Comprehending: Reading With Delight and Understanding
Lauren Aimonette Liang and Lee Galda

CHAPTER 11   110
Enhancing Learning: Implementing Content Area Children's and Young Adult Literature
Carole S. Rhodes and Janice Smith

CHAPTER 12   121
Inviting All Students Into the Literacy Arena Through Writing and Sharing Connections
Deborah A. Wooten and Patricia W. White

CHAPTER 13   130
So Many Books—How Do I Choose?
Colleen P. Gilrane

SECTION THREE   141

Reaching Beyond the Classroom Walls to Support Literacy and Learning

CHAPTER 14   143
Teacher and School Librarian Collaboration: Imagine a Partner
Gail Bush

CHAPTER 15   156
Using Literature to Build Home and School Connections
Sophie C. Degener

INDEX   167

CHILDREN'S LITERATURE AUTHOR INDEX   174

CHILDREN'S LITERATURE TITLE INDEX   177

ABOUT THE EDITORS

 **Deborah A. Wooten** is an associate professor of reading in the Theory and Practice in Teacher Education Department at the University of Tennessee in Knoxville, Tennessee, USA. Before joining the university faculty in 2002, she taught elementary school for 23 years. Her résumé includes experience in the rural schools of Mississippi and in the urban classrooms of New York City. After earning her PhD at New York University in New York, USA, in 1992, she used her final 10 years in the elementary classroom to research practical new methods of using children's literature to foster connections across curriculum boundaries while scaffolding students to think metacognitively. Results are published in her book *Valued Voices: An Interdisciplinary Approach to Teaching and Learning.*

Deborah is currently serving as a board member for the Children's Literature Assembly. She has served as cochairperson and regional coleader of the International Reading Association's (IRA) Children's Choices as well as a reviewer for the Children's and Young Adult Book Awards and Paul A. Witty Short Story Award. She was a member of the review board for IRA's Kids InSight book publications and is a member of the review board for *The New Educator*. She is a reviewer of professional books, videos, and DVDs for *School Library Journal's* Curriculum Connections. She is an author and editor of numerous books, chapters, and articles, including coediting and contributing to *The Continuum Encyclopedia of Young Adult Literature.*

Deborah and her husband, Gene, and their two children, Matt and Katie, enjoy the outdoors and especially reading rich, thick books while sitting in the sun at the beach.

 **Bernice E. Cullinan**, professor emerita of New York University, New York, USA, is both nationally and internationally known for her work in children's literature. She has written more than 30 books on literature for classroom teachers and librarians, including *Literature and the Child* (6th edition), *Language Arts: Learning and Teaching*, and *Language, Literacy and the Child*. Bee is known for her books about poetry, which include *Easy Poetry Lessons That Dazzle and Delight* and *Three Voices: Invitation to Poetry Across the Curriculum*. She has written books for parents as well, including *Read to Me: Raising Kids Who Love to Read* and *Family Storybook Reading.*

Bee is chief editor of Wordsong, the poetry imprint of Boyds Mills Press, and has collected poems written by the recipients of the National Council of Teachers of English (NCTE) Award for Poetry in *A Jar of Tiny Stars*. Bee is the coeditor of *The Continuum Encyclopedia of Young Adult Literature.*

Bee served as president of the International Reading Association, was inducted into the Reading Hall of Fame and The Ohio State

University Hall of Fame, and was selected as the recipient of the NCTE Arbuthnot Award for Outstanding Teacher of Children's Literature.

Bee and her husband Kenneth enjoy traveling nationally and internationally, attending Broadway productions, and reading books especially. They reside in New York City.

CONTRIBUTORS

Stergios Botzakis
Assistant Professor of Education
University of Tennessee
Knoxville, Tennessee, USA

Gail Bush
Professor, Reading and Language
    Department and Director, Center for
    Teaching Through Children's Books
National-Louis University
Skokie, Illinois, USA

Bernice E. Cullinan
Professor Emerita
New York University
New York, New York, USA

Sophie C. Degener
Assistant Professor, Reading and Language
    Department
National-Louis University
Skokie, Illinois USA

Lee Galda
Professor, Children's and Adolescent
    Literature
University of Minnesota
Minneapolis, Minnesota, USA

James Cross Giblin
Children's Book Author
New York, New York, USA

Colleen P. Gilrane
Associate Professor of Theory and Practice
    in Teacher Education
University of Tennessee
Knoxville, Tennessee, USA

Cyndi Giorgis
Professor of Literacy Education
University of Nevada—Las Vegas
Las Vegas, Nevada, USA

Jane Hansen
Professor of Literacy
University of Virginia
Charlottesville, Virginia, USA

David L. Harrison
Poet Laureate
Drury University
Springfield, Missouri, USA

Michelle D. Horsey
Response to Intervention Specialist
Austin Independent School District
Austin, Texas, USA

Lauren Aimonette Liang
Assistant Professor, Department of
    Educational Psychology
University of Utah
Salt Lake City, Utah, USA

Anne McGill-Franzen
Professor and Director of the Reading Center
University of Tennessee
Knoxville, Tennessee, USA

Carole S. Rhodes
Professor and Literacy Education Director
Queens College
Flushing, New York, USA

Audra K. Roach
Doctoral Candidate, Language and Literacy
 Studies
The University of Texas at Austin
Austin, Texas, USA

Nancy Roser
Professor of Education
The University of Texas at Austin
Austin, Texas, USA

Janice Smith
Undergraduate Coordinator for Music
 Education
Queens College
Flushing, New York, USA

Elizabeth A. Swaggerty
Assistant Professor of Reading Education
East Carolina University
Greenville, North Carolina, USA

Patricia W. White
Educator
Jefferson County Schools
Knoxville, Tennessee, USA

Deborah A. Wooten
Associate Professor of Reading
University of Tennessee
Knoxville, Tennessee, USA

Junko Yokota
Professor, Reading and Language
 Department and Director, Center for
 Teaching Through Children's Books
National-Louis University
Skokie, Illinois, USA

FOREWORD

I grew up in the country. As in, on a small dairy farm in the Midwest, roughly six miles from the nearest small town (population 800). I also attended a one-room country school from kindergarten through sixth grade. I had the same teacher every year but kindergarten. Likewise, I had the same classmates for seven years, all four of them. At the same time I attended Pioneer Elementary School so did another 30–35 students. It may be some sort of record, but 40% of my classmates earned PhDs ($n = 2$).

I mention this because it was in that one-room school where I became a reader. So did lots of other kids. But I cannot recall a single feature of a reading lesson I participated in. Not one! I guess we used some core reading program, but there were no dittos or workbooks. The first was because there were no copying machines back then and the second, I suppose, was because they cost money. But if I cannot remember anything about the reading lessons, and there were no workbook pages to do, how did I learn to read?

That's the question that still drives my work. I was not from a well-to-do family. Nor was I from a family that bought children's books. I do remember my mom reading paperback books, and I remember my dad reading comic books to me and my brothers (my memory strengthened by a photo of my brothers and I sitting on and around my dad as he reads a comic book to the four of us) and him reading the *Farm Journal* for his purposes. However, I do remember reading for myself as an important part of my childhood.

The first book I remember reading was Walter Edmonds's (1941) *The Matchlock Gun*. That was probably in third grade but perhaps in second grade. I recall being transported into history by that French and Indian War novel. The basic story is that the father leaves his family, on the small farm in the wilderness outside what is now Albany, New York, USA, as he goes off with other settlers to battle Native Americans who are attacking the white settlements. The young son is left with his mother and the old matchlock gun that laid on the rack above the fireplace. It was an ancient weapon. Suffice it to say that everything works out for the family, and the boy becomes a hero (at least from a white settler's point of view). I recall reading and rereading that book and being simply enthralled with the story.

That book deserves more credit than I've ever given it for turning me into reader. I got that book from the bookmobile that visited our school. The bookmobile crew came to our school every other week to offer us books to read. I took them up on the offer. Soon I had permission to check out 10 books every two weeks! But 10 books weren't enough reading for the whole two weeks, so I had my friends borrow books I really wanted but couldn't check out because of the 10-book limit.

Now I'm not sure why it was I had time to read a book literally every day in elementary school. Perhaps it was the fact that with at least five subjects to teach to each group of students at each grade level (or 35 separate lessons every day), everyone but the teacher simply had a lot of down time during the

Children's Literature in the Reading Program: An Invitation to Read (third edition), edited by Deborah A. Wooten and Bernice E. Cullinan. © 2009 by the International Reading Association.

school day and I filled mine with independent reading. I recall reading every biography that the bookmobile brought. One set of biographies I began with was a childhood series that imagined what it had been like to grow up as Abe Lincoln or Abigail Adams. Then came the Landmark series of biographies, covering people from all of history and focusing on the adult lives of famous people. I recall also reading juvenile novels and mysteries but what stands out to me is how much I learned, not just about reading, but about history.

Today, I still read biographies (at the moment I'm finishing *American Lion* [Meachem, 2008], a book about Andrew Jackson's presidency) and historical fact and fiction primarily (I was a history major as an undergraduate). I do like the occasional mystery or thriller and consider myself a devotee of Tony Hillerman, whose mysteries set in modern day Navajo culture take me to worlds I've never visited much less been a part of. Every once in a while I read the latest trendy or award-winning book but generally stay happily in books about the past. This brief journey into my reading habits may leave you wondering, "Where is he going with this?" and "Why?"

The question I pose to teachers is, How many hours each day do you expect your students to read? How much reading do your kids do during the school day? And how much more time is spent reading outside the school day? I'm not sure what answer makes me happy, but it is hard for me to believe that when I ask these questions to many teachers they assume I am from some distant planet or somewhere else outside their known universe.

"There is no time in the school day to just read," I too often hear. "Why not?" I ask. "What do kids do all day every day if not lots of independent reading?" What I hear is that kids have schoolwork to attend to instead of just spending time in independent reading. I

don't doubt these teachers' reports, but I wonder whether we have put the cart before the horse. Is it possible that "just reading" could be good for you? Maybe as good as "schoolwork"? Children do need explicit reading instruction if they are to learn to read. But they also need time, lots of time I'd argue, to just read, if we expect that they will become readers. Although we are currently witnessing a burgeoning emphasis on testing and on test scores, I suggest that test scores may tell who *might* read but they are not reliable predictors of who *will* read.

There may be another, less admirable side to all this testing and schoolwork as well. Although the reading performances of the United States' fourth graders have risen modestly on the National Assessment of Educational Progress during the past 40 years, the performances of twelfth graders has dropped just about the same amount that fourth-graders' scores increased. In other words, the most recent forms of schooling in the U.S. have not resulted in improved reading proficiencies for graduates of our K–12 school system.

Most recently, the federal National Institute for Literacy (Armbruster, Lehr, & Osborn, 2001) recommended against having children spend time during the school day just reading and, instead, argued for greater amounts of explicit reading instruction. I suggest that the best teachers we have observed provided both useful and explicit reading instruction while ensuring their students read widely during the school day and beyond it. These exemplary teachers created readers— not just kids with good test scores (though they were that as well).

In this third edition of *Children's Literature in the Reading Program: An Invitation to Read*, edited by my friend and colleague, Deb Wooten, and my friend, Bee Cullinan, reading to and reading by children is the focus. Such an emphasis should be part and parcel of every undergraduate's teacher education program. Being able to read is a critical skill but being able to and deciding not to bother reading is really no better than never having developed the ability to read. And it is books like *The Matchlock Gun* that can create readers.

This volume offers a myriad of wonderful chapters—chapters on the power of series books or the newest genre, graphic novels, to entice kids into becoming readers. In addition, other chapters provide clear direction for fostering literate conversations, a research-based key to improving children's reading comprehension. All in all, this is one of those books we could give as a gift to any and all of our colleagues and children would benefit.

In the end, I think we need to spend as much time and energy helping children find books that they can't wait to read as we now spend working with children on their reading skills development. This book will help us toward that goal. So read it and then get busy turning kids into readers.

—Richard L. Allington
University of Tennessee

REFERENCES

Armbruster, B.B, Lehr, F., & Osborn, J. (2001). *Put reading first: The research blocks for teaching children to read*. Washington, DC: National Institute for Literacy.

LITERATURE CITED

Edmonds, W. (1941). *The matchlock gun*. New York: Dodd, Mead, & Co.

Meachem, J. (2008). *American lion: Andrew Jackson in the White House*. New York: Random House.

PREFACE

My first teaching job, 30 years ago at this writing, was in a middle school in rural Mississippi, USA. My remedial reading class consisted mainly of boys who were intimidatingly taller than me. It was a disaster. On my second day, the boys locked me out of the classroom. I (Deborah) had to get the principal to make the students let me back in. I learned two valuable truths that year: I was not cut out for teaching middle school at that young age, and I should always read books aloud with my students. I eventually learned that reading aloud to a group of students had the power to lure them into an authentic literacy experience, and I learned that reading aloud was as important for students as it was for a new teacher. Reading aloud with my students saved my life and career.

Five years later I moved to New York City and got a job teaching fifth grade at Public School 11. Most Friday afternoons would find me standing on top of my desk reading aloud a book like *The Z Was Zapped: A Play in Twenty-Six Acts* (Van Allsburg, 1987), with the students predicting which disaster would strike the next letter of the alphabet. We were loud, and we were engaged under the spell of a book. My passion had become finding the right book for the right students at the right time.

I set forth collecting books that would lure my students to engage in the act of reading. I wanted students to want to read so that they would learn to read by reading. The search for literary treasures took me to every new and used bookstore, garage sale, library, and book order form I could find. Librarians became my dearest friends, and teachers who shared my passion for children's literature became my fellow crusaders. We formed book clubs. We read aloud books that would breathe life into our curriculum, and we even read aloud for fun. And we noticed that many of the books we introduced would mysteriously disappear from the shelves, only to be found in the hands of eager students who wanted to experience them again on their own. We learned right beside the students, encouraging them to make connections to the books we shared so that together we would weave a tapestry of literary experiences.

I was fortunate that Bee Cullinan became my academic mother. She adopted me right after she mentored me through my PhD studies at New York University. When Bee would receive boxes of review copies of books, I would pack my two small children in the car with a frozen pizza and head to Bee's place. The following day my students would be in for some tasty new delights. I discovered that the books that won the hearts of my reluctant readers had strong emotional appeal and shocking details. Some were captivated by historical books about the plagues or the horrific circumstances explorers experienced seeking their dreams. Other students wanted to go to imaginary places, and still others wanted realistic fiction.

Today, as a professor at the University of Tennessee, Knoxville, Tennessee, USA, I am

Children's Literature in the Reading Program: An Invitation to Read (third edition), edited by Deborah A. Wooten and Bernice E. Cullinan. © 2009 by the International Reading Association.

still known as the "book lady." My classrooms are filled primarily with graduate students who are teachers plagued with today's emphasis on testing. Most still find time to read aloud and market excellent books to their students. I find that my students are especially drawn to books with strong characters who overcome huge obstacles in life, books with shocking, grotesque, and even macabre details, books that take us to imaginary places and books that make us laugh.

An overcoming spirit is exemplified in *A Woman for President: The Story of Victoria Woodhull* (Krull, 2004). Victoria Woodhull rose from poverty to riches and fought for women's rights, running for president against Ulysses S. Grant 48 years before women gained the right to vote. *Sequoyah: The Cherokee Man Who Gave His People Writing* (Rumford, 2004) tells the true story of the Native American who created the first Cherokee writing system. Physically handicapped, Sequoyah also had to overcome the scorn of his fellow tribespeople who burned down his house, destroying all of his work. Sequoyah developed another writing system, better than the original, which ultimately was accepted by his tribespeople, bringing the opportunity for literacy to thousands of Cherokees.

A hush falls on my classroom when I share the shocking, sorrowful *Erika's Story* (Vander Zee, 2003). Erika's Jewish family was herded onto one of the death trains of the Holocaust during World War II. In a desperate bid to save her daughter's life, Erika's mother threw her tiny baby from the train. A German woman found her in the grass by the train track and raised Erika as her own. Recounting the horror that her mother must have endured, Erika summarizes that when her mother was on her way to death, she threw her daughter to life. Plenty of shock and surprise is found in *Something Out of Nothing: Marie Curie and Radium* (McClafferty, 2006). This biography of Marie Curie includes description of some of the radium-containing products that were produced during Curie's days, such as suppositories and a cigarette holder filled with the deadly element. Kathleen Krull's Giants of Science series includes true stories of scientists whose experiments went beyond human logic. *Isaac Newton: Giants of Science* (Krull, 2006) tells of Newton's explorations of light and sight, including probing the back of his eyeball with a hook-type device. Macabre details like that can keep readers turning pages.

Books that take us to imaginary places include *Arrival* (Tan, 2007). This wordless graphic novel creates a story about a man who immigrates to a new country, foreign to all readers. This story fosters a forum for discussion about the challenges one must overcome to adapt to new surroundings. Readers are transported to another world in *Dali and the Path of Dreams* (Obiolis, 2003). Dalí, or Salvi, is depicted as a young boy on a surreal quest that begins with him lifting the ocean shore and discovering a key. All of the illustrations are whimsical versions of some of Dalí's masterpieces.

My classes laugh heartily, if a little uncomfortably, when I read aloud *Flush: The Scoop on Poop Throughout the Ages* (Harper, 2007). Told through humorous poetry with informative sidebars, the book starts with the historical uses of urine and concludes with "waste in space." Reactions are predictably hilarious when my students are introduced to the Smelly Old History series by Mary Dobson. These scratch-and-sniff books are filled with historical facts and poetry about various time periods and the smells that go with them. Titles include *Reeking Royals* (Dobson, 1999), *Vile Vikings* (Dobson, 1998b), *Greek Grime* (Dobson, 1998a), *Victorian Vapours* (Dobson, 1997), and others. Almost every page smells awful. Your students will laugh and laugh again.

In *Imagine a Place* (Thomson, 2008), the following quote appears next to a surreal piece of artwork by Rob Gonsalves, depicting an enormous labyrinth of rooms with domed ceilings and arched passageways supported by tall columns: "Imagine a place...where words shelter you, ideas uphold you to the secret inside the labyrinth" (n.p.). The entire structure is made of books, one stacked atop another. Poised in the center is a man standing on the top of a ladder holding a lit candle and inserting the final book into the ceiling. The hues are a host of warm, brown shades. These books are closed because their function is to serve as physical building blocks for this literary labyrinth. Our function as educators is to open books, thus opening the minds of students to the vast array of hues inside.

When students make connections with themselves, the world, and with other books, the building blocks to literacy fall into place. Rosenblatt's (1978, 2005) mantra was for readers to have the opportunity to transact with text aesthetically so that they could make sense of their world through books. This book promotes reading so that students transact with text both aesthetically (reading for pleasure) and efferently (gaining knowledge). The teaching strategies and host of children's literature herein have been implemented successfully with students from around the nation. This book has been woven as a literacy tapestry for the taking. Our hope is that you will transact with it both aesthetically and efferently.

How to Use This Book

In the planning stages of this book, we asked teachers what would best help them in their classroom practices. The top requests were for practical, efficient, and effective teaching strategies, and lists of excellent children's and young adult literature that has been tried and proven effective with students from various backgrounds. These requests became the foundation for developing the third edition of *Children's Literature in the Reading Program: An Invitation to Read*. We have attempted to ensure that every chapter contains a rich collection of children's and young adult literature along with strong teaching and learning strategies ready for implementation.

Section One: Genre Studies features seven genres, five of which are long-established. These are picture books, nonfiction, poetry, series books, and multicultural and international books. This section also explores two budding genres, graphic novels and postmodern picture books, which are quickly gaining notoriety in our new millennium. Graphic novel sales continue to rise with both male and female readers, and postmodern picture books appeal to a wide range of readers because of their lack of conformity when compared with other genres.

Section Two: The Role of Children's Literature in the Classroom invites you into actual classroom settings where children's and young adult literature is the centerpiece of the literacy curriculum. The strategies and methods described not only satisfy mandated curriculum requirements but also exceed those requirements. Literacy strategies featured in this section encourage students to make literacy connections to themselves, other texts, and the world. This section shares how celebrating literature and students' responses breeds enthusiasm and enjoyment for reading while sharpening critical thinking skills.

Section Three: Reaching Beyond the Classroom Walls to Support Literacy and Learning is intended to make life easier for teachers by offering real strategies that help motivate the classroom beyond the confines of its walls. Explained in this section are two invaluable resources to literacy learning: librarians and students' parents or guardians. Practical, well-organized strategies show how librarians and parents can work with teachers with the goal of making the process of educating more effective for teachers, students, and parents alike.

An Invitation to Read

Today's emphasis on accountability and high-stakes testing seems to continue to gain momentum. Rosenblatt (2005) believed that if the traditional method of teaching and learning continues, our democratic society is in jeopardy. Bearing Rosenblatt's concern in mind, this book is designed to identify children's and young adult books, promote critical thinking, cultivate deeper understanding of text, and create better understanding of and appreciation for diversity. The methods of instruction in this handbook are differentiated so as to ensure that all students are invited into the literacy-learning arena. The third edition of *Children's Literature in the Reading Program* is an invitation that we hope will make your teaching lifestyle more enjoyable, purposeful, and profitable. We extend our hand for you to accept our invitation and be sure to send us an RSVP—which means that you will Respond, Stretch, Venture, and Pass on the love of literacy to another generation (Cullinan, 1992, p. xii).

Acknowledgments

We first want to acknowledge our editor, Stacey Reid, for her noteworthy work ethic. I (Deborah) appreciate the kindness that was extended with cards and prayers from Stacey Reid as well as Executive Editor Corinne Mooney when my dad passed away suddenly during the development of this book. Their compassion served to bring us all closer.

We thank our husbands, Gene and Kenneth, and our children, Katie, Matt, Janie, and Webb, for their support that came in many ways, such as ordering out dinner and having an understanding attitude when we were not free to go and play during the weekends. We also thank Rich and Revanna for their consistent friendship and prayers.

—Deborah A. Wooten and
Bernice E. Cullinan

REFERENCES

Cullinan, B.E. (1992). *Invitation to read: More children's literature in the reading program*. Newark, DE: International Reading Association.

Rosenblatt, L.M. (1978). *The reader, the text, the poem: The transactional theory of the literary work*. Carbondale: Southern Illinois University Press.

Rosenblatt, L.M. (2005). *Making meaning with texts: Selected essays*. Portsmouth, NH: Heinemann.

CHILDREN'S LITERATURE CITED

Dobson, M. (1997). *Victorian vapours*. Oxford, England: Oxford University Press.

Dobson, M. (1998a). *Greek grime*. Oxford, England: Oxford University Press.

Dobson, M. (1998b). *Vile Vikings*. Oxford, England: Oxford University Press.

Dobson, M. (1999). *Reeking royals*. Oxford, England: Oxford University Press.

Harper, C.M. (2007). *Flush: The scoop on poop throughout the ages*. New York: Little, Brown.

Krull, K. (2004). *A woman for president: the story of Victoria Woodhull*. New York: Walker.

Krull, K. (2006). *Isaac Newton*. New York: Viking.

McClafferty, C.K. (2006). *Something out of nothing: Marie Curie and radium*. New York: Farrar, Straus and Giroux.

Obiolis, A. (2003). *Dali and the path of dreams*. London: Frances Lincoln.

Rumford, J. (2004). *Sequoyah: The Cherokee man who gave his people writing*. Boston: Houghton Mifflin.

Tan, S. (2007). *The arrival*. New York: Scholastic.

Thomson, S. (2008). *Imagine a place*. New York: Atheneum.

Van Allsburg, C. (1987). *The Z was zapped: A play in twenty-six acts*. Boston: Houghton Mifflin.

Vander Zee, R. (2003). *Erika's story*. Mankato, MN: Creative Editions.

Genre Studies

The idea of organizing literature into genres is traced to Aristotle, who believed that organizing the way we look at anything helps us understand it better. Section One explores seven different genres that will provide useful information for teachers when looking for books to share with students. Whether you are teaching your students about the power of poetry or how picture books can help your students become better writers and readers, this section is designed to make your job easier.

Chapter 1 deepens our understanding of the impact that elements such as line, color, space, texture, and perspective have in picture books. As we progress further into the 21st century, new genres are added to the landscape of children's literature. Two of these are graphic novels and postmodern literature. In Chapter 2 we learn that the appeal of graphic novels continues to grow. This genre inspires students to make inferences by connecting panels together in order to comprehend the story. Chapter 3 defines postmodern picture books and explains how they promote critical thinking skills.

Despite the fact that 60% to 70% of our school libraries contain nonfiction literature, many say this is a neglected genre. Focused on teaching in the upper elementary grades, Chapter 4 explores the layers of information that can be mined from nonfiction chapter books. This mining process is metaphorically akin to separating and lifting the layers of a rock formation. Chapter 5 celebrates poetry through interactive teaching lessons that are ready to use with your K–5 students. The poetry selections range from whimsical to content related. Chapter 6 explains the history of series books, what draws readers to read them, and why we need to make sure they are available for our students. Chapter 7 emphasizes that the United States is more diverse than ever before and, as teachers, we need to make sure that cultural diversity is well represented in our reading programs. This chapter provides guidance for making wise decisions when selecting multicultural and international literature along with instructional teaching strategies for using them.

CHAPTER 1

Exploring Visual Images in Picture Books

Cyndi Giorgis

Although the picture book may look like a typical book—paper pages between two pieces of cardboard—it's unique in many ways. A picture book is not just a container for text and illustrations. When you make a picture book, you use words, images, and the book form—the book's shape and heft and physical quality—to suggest the reader's path of movement through the story: right to left, up and down, in and out, page to page.... Reading a picture book involves the eye, the mind, and the hand. When you turn the pages, your imagination—your thinking, feeling mind—fills the moments between page one and page two.... If the image is well made and the story is well told, the reader is curious, anticipating and wondering, what's next?

—Eric Rohmann, 2003 Caldecott Medal acceptance speech

As Eric Rohmann points out in his Caldecott Medal acceptance speech for *My Friend Rabbit* (Rohmann, 2002), the picture book is a unique format that presents story through words and images. For many children, a picture book is often their first introduction to art. Carol Hurst emphasizes, "we can't afford to make that introduction with mediocre or poorly conceived books" (www.carolhurst.com/newsletters/21bnewsletters.html). Parents, teachers, and librarians should make informed choices when selecting books to share with children. Fortunately, there are numerous visually appealing picture books being published today that warrant and deserve a child's rapt attention. Children are generally visually literate; however, adults can extend children's appreciation and understanding of visual images by being knowledgeable about art elements and physical characteristics of a picture book.

Children's Literature in the Reading Program: An Invitation to Read (third edition), edited by Deborah A. Wooten and Bernice E. Cullinan. © 2009 by the International Reading Association.

Today, there is so much emphasis placed on text that illustrations in picture books are often overlooked with regard to their importance in the storytelling process. Children are immediately drawn to the illustrations when reading picture books. Just as skills are taught in the reading of text, this same objective can be applied to reading illustrations to interpret the numerous images that students encounter in books as well as in the world around them. Julie Cummins (1992) states that the world of children's book illustrations, particularly picture books, continues to grow and evolve. Children's book illustrators are designing wonderfully exciting and appealing art in children's books. Becoming literate in reading images enhances children's visual literacy and appreciation of picture book art.

What Is a Picture Book?

A picture book is one in which text and illustration work in concert to create meaning (Serafini & Giorgis, 2003). Often, picture books are viewed as literature for young children. However, it is important to consider the picture book as a format that is not always indicative of reader ability or interest level. The interplay of narrative and illustration is fundamental to the book as a whole. In the best picture books the illustrations extend and enhance the written text, providing readers with an aesthetic experience that is more than the sum of the book's parts.

Elements of Visual Design

Picture book illustrators use a variety of visual elements such as line, color, space, shape, texture, and perspective. When these elements come together, they create the composition of the illustration and of the page. And, in turn, the use of these visual elements assists readers in generating meaning from the story. Recognizing how elements of design are used by illustrators provides opportunities for discussions with children about what they see and how they interpret these visual images. This knowledge also gives all readers a reason for slowing down and lingering over each page in the picture book they are reading.

Line

Line is the most commonly found element of design in picture books (Kiefer, 1995). Horizontal lines suggest peace or relaxation while vertical lines indicate stability. Diagonal lines imply motion and movement such as when a plunging diagonal line signifies falling, a loss of control, or speed. Circular lines convey serenity, contentment, or safety, but disorganized lines signal disorder, chaos, or frenetic feelings. The use of thin lines creates an elegant quality or indicates fragility, while thick or bold lines show strength or provide emphasis.

Uri Shulevitz's (1969) *Rain, Rain Rivers* is a lyrical portrait of rain from the drips on the windowpane to rushing rivers. Shulevitz uses thin, diagonal blue and green lines to show the rain coming down and thicker, circular lines to illustrate the puddles being formed. In contrast, *Wolf! Wolf!* by John Rocco (2007) uses bold, black brush strokes on the book cover to set the stage for the story. In this variation of the Aesop fable, thin lines are used for the interior illustrations to provide detail to each character and to suggest eye movement across the page. In another example, Laura Vaccaro Seeger's thick, black lines outline the characters of *Dog and Bear: Two Friends, Three Stories* (Seeger, 2007) in this book about an unusual but profound friendship. These lines also highlight objects that are colored with bright, variegated hues and are set against white backdrops.

Color

Color is one of the most expressive elements of visual design, as it conveys the mood or tone of a story. Color can range from a full spectrum, to various shades of gray, to black and white. Illustrators make a conscious choice in the hue, tone, and saturation of a color. Red is an attention-getting color that can signify excitement and happiness or danger and courage. Yellow denotes happiness, as in the color of sunshine, but it can also urge caution like a street sign. Blue is a restful color expressing calmness and tranquility, coldness, and sometimes sadness. Green is often related to nature, whereas warm and cheerful orange hints at the changing leaves and the coming of the fall season. Purple is associated with royalty and can be a color that suggests power and importance.

Author and illustrator Molly Bang is known for her successful use of art elements, especially color. In *When Sophie Gets Angry—Really, Really Angry...* (Bang, 1999) Sophie's changing moods are depicted through the use of intense orange and red hues to show her anger and soothing blues and greens to envelop her as she "cools" down. Illustrator Don Wood uses a monochromatic color scheme in Audrey Wood's (1984) *The Napping House* to illustrate this cumulative tale of people and animals engaged in slumber. The blues and purples increase in brightness as the slew of sleepers is awakened by a restless flea. Patricia Polacco celebrates make-believe friends in *Emma Kate* (Polacco, 2005) through the use of expertly rendered black-and-white graphite drawings depicting backgrounds scenes and an enormous elephant alongside an imaginative girl in a brightly colored red dress. Red is also the color choice for Ian Falconer's precocious pig *Olivia* (Falconer, 2000). Polacco's and Falconer's protagonists are the focal points of the story, and the eye goes directly to them

before moving across the page to discover other unique aspects of the illustrations.

Space and Shape

Space and shape, two of the elements of design, work together to form a finished work of art. There are two kinds of space that artists use: positive and negative. Positive spaces are those occupied by the main subjects of the illustration. Negative space is the area around and behind the positive spaces and is often referred to as the background. The shapes of positive spaces are generally determined by the shapes of the main subjects of the work. However, negative spaces have shapes as well. If the subjects are removed from a piece of art, the negative spaces are left with a blank space in the shapes of the parts removed. Therefore, the shapes of the negative spaces are determined by the shapes of the positive spaces. Ann Jonas's classic book *Round Trip* (Jonas, 1983) presents a wonderful example of optical illusions where the space that appears to be under the figure is considered the negative space while the space on top of the figure becomes the positive space. *The Very Hungry Caterpillar* by Eric Carle (1986) provides endpapers that highlight the book's color scheme and an apparently random display of white dots. However, the three-dimensional illusion starts with overlapping dots of color using negative and positive space.

Texture

Texture is another design element that is found in illustrations and provides the illusion that something feels hard or soft, smooth or rough. Often texture is created through collage and invites readers to "feel" the pages. Lois Ehlert uses everyday objects and materials to create a layered effect in her books *Top Cat* (Ehlert, 1998) and *Pie in the Sky* (Ehlert, 2004). Denise

Fleming creates her own vivid paper with unique coloring for her picture book illustrations in *Mama Cat Has Three Kittens* (Fleming, 1998) and *The First Day of Winter* (Fleming, 2005). Readers will want to touch the pages of these books in an attempt to feel the illustrations and the texture they exhibit.

Perspective

One of the most interesting elements that an artist uses is perspective or point of view. Perspective is the place or angle for viewing the picture. Readers might be given a bird's-eye view, which provides a sense of looking down on a scene, such as in Jane Yolen's *Owl Moon* (Yolen, 1987) as child and parent go "owling" on a crisp winter's night. Chris Van Allsburg's *Two Bad Ants* (Van Allsburg, 1988) allows readers to experience a worm's-eye view as small insects invade what they believe is a bizarre world, but which is actually a kitchen. The middle third of an illustration is considered the middle ground. Readers' eyes are often drawn to the middle of the page in an illustration and move either up or down. Artists use the foreground or the bottom third of an illustration to place items or characters that appear closer, hence drawing more attention. In the background, aspects of the illustration are smaller in size because they are further away.

Characteristics in the Design of Picture Books

Children's book illustrators make conscious decisions about the design and layout of each page in a picture book. In addition to the elements discussed previously, the characteristics outlined in the following section are part of the storytelling process in creating meaning for the reader.

Framing

Framing is an important characteristic in picture book art. Sipe (2001) indicates that the frames give illustrations a "window in the book" (p. 33). In wordless picture books such as Barbara Lehman's *The Red Book* (Lehman, 2004) in which a child finds a red book in the snow, each illustration is framed with a striking black border against a white background. David Wiesner effectively uses framed vertical and horizontal panels in *Sector 7* (Wiesner, 1999) to depict various scenes and action when a boy is befriended by a jolly cloud and whisked away to a cloud factory in the sky. *My Friend Rabbit* (Rohmann, 2002) has thick, black borders around each single- and double-page illustration. However, not even the borders can contain the various animals, particularly the elephant, as they assist rabbit in his attempt to retrieve a toy airplane from a tree. However, framing doesn't always have to involve lines around an illustration. Jon J. Muth's *Zen Shorts* (Muth, 2005) shows white space around each illustration that features a Zen approach to the world in this story about three siblings and their new neighbor, a panda.

When an illustration is not framed and hence extends to the edges of the page, it is called a bleed. A full-bleed illustration is one that is printed to the very edge of the page. In *Tupelo Rides the Rails* (Sweet, 2008), a story of a dog abandoned by the side of the road with only his sock toy, Mr. Bones, to comfort him, a full-bleed illustration shows Tupelo alone holding Mr. Bones in his mouth, the huge night sky above with the constellation Sirius shining in the distance. Illustrator Brian Lovelock uses full-bleed artwork in *Roadwork* (Sutton, 2008) to accompany Sally Sutton's rhyming text about how seven machines function in the building of a road.

Artists may also use a border to frame their illustrations. Jan Brett uses her trademark borders in *Honey...Honey...Lion!* (Brett, 2005), the story of a greedy honey badger who is taught a lesson by his feathered friend. Side panels contained within the border reveal myriad African animals spreading the news through the plains of Badger's betrayal via "bush telegraph," from elephant to hippo, hippo to warthog, and warthog to hyena. These borders add another layer to the narrative story and pique children's interest as they lean in to further examine each page.

Page Turns

As Rohmann (2003) pointed out in his acceptance speech, each picture book page should prompt the reader to wonder, "What will happen next?" and want to turn the page to continue the story. Has the author or illustrator given the reader any reason to keep turning pages, or does each page stand alone? Once a book is opened, the reader has complete control over whether a page is turned. In his 2008 Caldecott Medal speech, Brian Selznick (2008) talked about the importance of the page turns in his book *The Invention of Hugo Cabret* (Selznick, 2007). This unique and suspenseful 550-page award-winning picture book set in Paris in the 1930s relies heavily on the page turns to move the reader through engaging text and stunning black-and-white pencil illustrations. His inspiration was Remy Charlip's *Fortunately* (Charlip, 1984) that alternates between Ned "fortunately" getting an invitation to attend a surprise party in Florida, but "unfortunately" having a series of mishaps in getting there from New York. Selznick referred to an earlier essay by Charlip in which he compared a book to a swinging door and the element of delight and surprise that is felt "when we move that page or door to reveal a change in everything that has gone before, in

time, place, or character" (Selznick, 2008). This is the essence of the page turn.

Maurice Sendak's *Where the Wild Things Are* (Sendak, 1963) also effectively uses page turns through sentence fragments and illustrations that grow larger on each page until the wild rumpus covers two double-page spreads. *Brown Bear, Brown Bear, What Do You See?* (Martin, 1967) and *What Do You Do With a Tail Like That?* (Jenkins, 2003) ask questions that pique readers' interest into wanting to turn the page to discover the answer. The illustrations in Denise Fleming's books *Lunch* (Fleming, 1992) and *Beetle Bop* (Fleming, 2007) seem to spill over the edges of the paper right onto the next page prompting the reader to uncover each subsequent illustration.

Page turns can create suspense and drama, confirm or thwart readers' predictions, or provide gaps in the narrative that the reader must bridge (Sipe, 2001). It is the narrative progression of a story that engages readers' desire to keep going as they experience "the drama of the turning of the page" (Bader, 1976, p. 1).

Physical Aspects of a Picture Book

Each component or part of a book contributes to the overall meaning. As readers hold a picture book, it is important for them to have the opportunity to explore its physical aspects—to linger over the book cover, explore the endpapers, and examine the title page.

Book Cover

Before reading aloud a story, teachers will often hold up a picture book and ask children what they think the story might be about. The predictions children will make are based on their interpretation of the art featured on the book cover. The purpose of a book cover, however, extends beyond predicting to setting the story's mood or tone, visually introducing one or more characters, or highlighting a dramatic or climactic scene in the book. And of course, a cover also provides the title and the names of the author and illustrator. Children do judge a book by its cover (don't we all?), which is their first invitation for taking a closer look and to begin the reading experience.

The cover of David Wiesner's *Flotsam* (Wiesner, 2006) intrigues readers with a close-up of a large, red carp's eye. Once the story has begun, readers will discover that this eye is similar in appearance to the eye of the Melville Underwater Camera that a boy discovers on the beach. When the wrap-around book cover of *Flotsam* is laid flat, a larger portion of the carp is revealed along with smaller fish that appear to be swimming toward the eye. *Detective LaRue: Letters From the Investigation* by Mark Teague (2004) depicts a different illustration on the back than the one featured on the front cover. Canine sleuth Ike LaRue is shown peering through a magnifying glass at paw prints that undoubtedly belong to the feisty felines popping out of the trash can behind him. The front cover is in shades of blue and gray while the full-color back cover shows Ike busily typing as a police officer reads a newspaper and consumes his daily doughnut. Neither of these illustrations appears in the book itself, but the reader will definitely ponder what Ike is up to now.

Endpapers

The endpapers of a picture book are often ignored. Artist and illustrator Will Hillenbrand (Sipe, 2001) compares endpapers to the stage curtains for a play, which are the first thing the audience sees when it enters the theater as well as the last thing seen when the play is over. Endpapers serve as a structural bond between the body of a book and the casing. They are glued down to hold the book together. Endpapers are often white but may also be a solid color such as the dark green in *Muncha! Muncha! Muncha!* (Fleming, 2002). This color isn't a random choice but is seen throughout the pages of this story in which Mr. McGreely tries to find a way to keep persistent bunnies from eating his vegetables. Other times, the endpapers contain a design such as in Mo Willems's *Knuffle Bunny: A Cautionary Tale* (Willems, 2004) where the beloved bunny is being tossed around inside a washing machine. This picture also gives a hint as to the climax of the story.

The front and back endpapers are often the same, but occasionally they may be different for a significant reason. In *Hey, Al* (Yorinks, 1986), the opening endpapers are a tan color that is drab just like Al's life. The final endpapers are a bright yellow to signify the changes that have occurred in the now exuberant janitor's life. A pastel blue background with pink, fluffy clouds greets the reader as they open *Don't Let the Pigeon Stay Up Late!* (Willems, 2006) while the navy blue sky with lighter blue clouds at the end is evidence of the persistent (and obnoxious), now dozing, pigeon.

Many times, the narrative of the story begins on the endpapers. Such is the case with those of *The Friend* (Stewart, 2004), which show a young girl, Belle, sitting in a massive bed situated in an expansive bedroom. Subsequent pages illustrate Belle as she climbs out of bed and ventures downstairs holding her stuffed bear. This is a significant part of the story that sets the mood and introduces the main protagonist. This transition between the exterior and interior of the book is used to welcome the reader into the story. Such is also the case in *Duck, Duck, Goose* (Hills, 2007), in which the endpapers illustrate the small figures of duck and goose against the expansive, lush green background. Observant readers will realize, once the story is read, the significance of the soccer ball that is barely visible by the bushes.

Title Page

The title page is another part of the picture book that readers should not ignore. After turning to the title page of *Car Wash* (Steen & Steen, 2001), readers are greeted with "Hop in/Lock the doors,/Buckle up./Let's go." On this page, the seemingly ordinary car hits a huge mud puddle, "Splatter! Splosh!" and so it's off to the car wash and readers along with it. There's Ike the dog at the base of a tree where a bag of cat treats reside on the title page of *Detective LaRue: Letters From the Investigation* (Teague, 2004). High up in the tree branches sits a feisty white cat and a black scaredy cat. The next page reveals a newspaper article stating that Ike is suspected of feline foul play and displays a photo with the misunderstood pooch (who just happens to be holding the bag of cat treats in his mouth) being nabbed by a police officer. In both of these books, skipping over the title page would leave out valuable, if not comical, story elements.

The Creation of a Picture Book: A "Walk" Through *A Kitten Tale*

Picture book author and illustrator Eric Rohmann received the 2003 Caldecott Medal for his ingenious and delightful story *My Friend Rabbit* (Rohmann, 2002). This award for the most distinguished picture book published in the preceding year is one of the most well-known and prestigious book awards given in the United States.

To fully understand the thought processes of illustrators as they create a picture book, it is fitting to go directly to the source. In this case the source was Eric Rohmann, who graciously agreed to discuss the artistic process for his most recent book, *A Kitten Tale* (Rohmann, 2008). *A Kitten Tale* tells the story of four kittens who become concerned about snow and the coldness that comes with it. The fearless yellow kitten appears to be undaunted by the prospect of the cold and remarks repeatedly, "I can't wait." Although Rohmann's story, the text for which appears in a large font, may appear to be for younger readers, it becomes evident that his artistic process is anything but simple.

Exploring the Front and Back Covers

We begin our walk through *A Kitten Tale* with the cover illustration depicting the four kittens (see Figure 1.1). This illustration introduces readers to the four felines but doesn't appear in the story. When Rohmann initially planned the cover, he thought about it as a

FIGURE 1.1
Cover for *A Kitten Tale*

wrap-around cover. He envisioned the kittens in the middle of the book cover when it was laid flat as he explained,

> If you take the cover and imagine a line going through the middle of the kittens and fold it, those kittens would wrap around the book. The problem was that if you do that, it becomes too much about the yellow kitten because all you see is tails of the other kittens. (personal communication, September 7, 2008)

If Rohmann had used that initial idea and made the yellow kitten the only one on the cover where the face was showing, it would "kill the point of the story that the kittens were separated at the beginning but they are all together at the end (personal communication, September 7, 2008). So Rohmann took the full illustration and put it all on one page.

The title of the book and the placement of Rohmann's name also became an aesthetic decision. The publisher initially wanted the words, "from Caldecott Medal winning illustrator" below Rohmann's name but he felt that it would be "complicated visually to have all those words in there because the eye goes to words before it goes to images. That's how we've trained ourselves. This works so much better [printing only the author and title] because there's cleanliness to the cover" (personal communication, September 7, 2008). The background of *A Kitten Tale* is a crisp, bright white, heavy stock paper. There is also a varnish layer applied to the kittens that is glossy and gives them a "little more punch" (personal communication, September 7, 2008).

When readers view the back illustration, they will see half of the yellow kitten clinging to the mailbox. This illustration does appear later in the book. However, there is a circle around this illustration that is something that Rohmann incorporates into several of his picture books, including *My Friend Rabbit*. Rohmann explains, "There's a circle on the

back, like with the Warner Brothers cartoons where they say 'That's All Folks' and it goes from a big circle to a dot. It's a way to show what might be happening inside" (personal communication, September 7, 2008). Rohmann also believes that "the cover draws you in," which supports the previous statements in this chapter about the importance of the book cover to entice readers into picking up the book.

Creative Endpapers

Rohmann believes that the endpapers are the first introduction or "the sherbet course that cleanses the palate and turns your eye to the world of the book, away from what's going on outside of the story to give a feeling of what is going on in the story" (personal communication September 7, 2008). Originally, the endpapers in *A Kitten Tale* were a mustard color that was the same color as the rambunctious kitten. However, Rohmann wanted a pale yellow so that it didn't draw more attention to that particular kitten. The brighter, warmer color cools and grays the blue-violet snow at the book's end and tends to dull the image. This again, is one of the decisions that illustrators make as part of the process in creating a picture book.

When readers turn to the next page in *A Kitten Tale*, the page that appears right before the title page, Rohmann envisioned this as

> the one picture that you want the reader to be most involved in. There are no words that tell you what to think or what the kittens are doing. So it's an essential picture and initially I was afraid that kids weren't going to get it. But, of course they always do. (personal communication, September 7, 2008)

The next page provides the lead up to the story that allows readers to understand why the kittens turned to one another and smile. Rohmann explains,

I did have words there as the kittens were talking and telling each other how they were feeling, but the picture was doing it. There was no need to have text. That is the whole thing about trying to decide what to leave in and what to leave out. (personal communication, September 7, 2008)

Inside the Book

Rohmann has worked in a variety of artistic media over the years and was faced with the decision of how to create the illustrations for *A Kitten Tale*. He explains that the story always dictates the technique:

> Imagine something like *The Cat in the Hat* [Seuss, 1957] done by Chris Van Allsburg in black-and-white like *Jumanji* [Van Allsburg, 1981]. The story always dictates the way you make the pictures. I tried a couple of techniques such as watercolor, but I realized that what I wanted was to have the playful quality of woodcuts. I tried a couple of woodcuts, but woodcuts are opaque and you get this thick color that goes on top of another color that goes on top of another color. That wasn't working. So I went back to a technique called monotype. In this technique, there are layers and layers of transparent color that build up yet allow the white of the paper to come through. (personal communication, September 7, 2008)

When determining the colors, Rohmann knew that this book was going to be done in soft colors and would have a vaguely Japanese feeling. He explains:

> You have the seasons and cats and those are often subjects depicted in Japanese printmaking. Initially, I wasn't sure what the kittens were going to look like or what color they were going to be. That's the process of figuring things out a little at a time. Something always emerges that is unexpected. (personal communication, September 7, 2008)

Rohmann also determined sometime during the process that he should frame each illustration with a black line border:

> The border helps to hold them in and gives them a feeling that they are framed prints. Originally there were full bleeds all the way to the outside of the page, but through experimentation, I found the borders worked better. (personal communication, September 7, 2008)

Perspective is also used effectively by Rohmann when he shows all four kittens and the spring environment at the beginning of the story:

> When you get to the scene with the mailbox, we see it more at a ground level, which sets up the next page. When looking at this scene, you give all your attention to the kitten on the mailbox. When you turn the page, you give the other kittens equal footing by showing them from up above. Also, you see the yellow kitten's perspective—you see the yellow kitten first then you turn the page and see what he sees. (personal communication, September 7, 2008)

Rohmann believes that the picture book is a unique art form. He explains,

> You have very few images to tell a complex story. *A Kitten Tale* has the repeated line, 'I can't wait', but there's a lot going on in between. If you look at the first three pages, there are no words except for the title. Those pages set up the story. On the first page the kittens are separate and the only two we see together are fighting. You turn the page and all of them are together except the yellow one. Then you turn the page and all of them are doing the same thing—drinking out of the bowl—except for the yellow one. Right away, without any words, the pictures tell something about those cats' personalities. Those three hang out and conform with one another while the yellow one is looking away. He's an individual. So, it's no surprise to turn the page and see the yellow one in the mailbox. Just those pictures without words reveal the personality. I don't know of any other

art form that does this. What's great about picture books is that it allows the reader to fill in things that aren't necessarily blatantly shown. (personal communication, September 7, 2008)

Page turns are very important for Rohmann in telling a story. According to Rohmann,

> During the page turn, your imagination and your anticipation of what's going to happen fill in the unknowns. I always use the example that I'm standing next to an elephant and I'm holding a can of green paint. When you turn the page, I'm flat as a pancake and the elephant is covered with green paint. This makes you wonder, what happened between those two pages? I have to make it clear what could happen, but I don't have to spell it out. In picture books the page turns allow our imagination to become involved and to fill in what just happened. That is the hardest part for me about picture books—trying to figure out what to leave out. A bad picture book is one that gives you too much information. It tells you everything in words and pictures. There's always this feeling that there's someone talking at you. (personal communication, September 7, 2008)

However, a successful picture book that will engage children is one that allows readers to bring something of themselves to the reading of the text and illustrations.

When working on a picture book, Rohmann will create a book dummy in order to better understand the impact of the page turns. He says that

> you can put the pages on the wall and look at them as a storyboard, but that's different because you are seeing them all at the same time. The glory of a picture book is that when you turn the page, you remember the image that came before and that informs the next image. Good picture book artists think about how the story moves. When students ask me what they need to learn to be a picture book artist, I tell them there are two things: first, give your characters personality, and second, learn how to tell a sequential story visually (personal communication, September 7, 2008)

Extending the Understanding of Picture Book Illustrations Through Illustrator Studies

Invite children to "step into the shoes" of their favorite illustrator. Read numerous books illustrated by that individual and conduct research on his or her background and career. Students can become their favorite illustrators and prepare presentations for the class about their media and techniques. For older students (particularly those in intermediate grades) presentations can include displays exhibiting the illustrator's work, question-and-answer sessions, interviews, and press releases on the illustrators' most recent books.

Consider the developmental stage of students when building illustrator studies. First, determine what they already know. Based on this knowledge, what skills should they develop? Are there minilessons that could be used to introduce the story and be incorporated throughout? For example, how can the elements of design such as line, shape, color, texture, and perspective be introduced through picture books? Using sticky notes is an excellent strategy for writing down observations as students read the book and placing the notes on that page. Teachers and parents can slow down while reading a book and discuss how the text works with illustrations to create meaning. Also, reading and rereading picture books provides greater access to illustrations in order for students to have the opportunity to do some self-exploration.

When students engage in illustrator studies, they develop an awareness of visual images and expressive elements. Children of all ages can use vocabulary when describing illustrations they encounter in picture books. Terms such as *gutter*, *endpapers*, and *page turns* are understood and articulated once they are introduced and expanded upon when sharing literature with children.

REFERENCES

Bader, B. (1976). *American picturebooks from Noah's ark to the beast within.* New York: Macmillan.

Cummins, J. (1992). *Children's book illustration and design.* New York: PBC Intl.

Kiefer, B. (1995). *The potential of picturebooks: From visual literacy to aesthetic understanding.* Englewood Cliffs, NJ: Merrill.

Rohmann, E. (2003). Caldecott Medal acceptance. *The Horn Book Magazine, 79*(4), 393–400.

Selznick, B. (2008). Caldecott Medal acceptance. *The Horn Book Magazine, 84*(4) 393–406.

Serafini, F., & Giorgis, C. (2003). *Reading aloud and beyond: Fostering the intellectual life with older readers.* Portsmouth, NH: Heinemann.

Sipe, L.R. (2001). Picturebooks as aesthetic objects. *Literacy Teaching and Learning, 6*(1), 23–42.

CHILDREN'S LITERATURE CITED

Bang, M. (1999). *When Sophie gets angry—really, really angry...* New York: Scholastic.

Brett, J. (2005). *Honey...honey...lion!* New York: Putnam.

Carle, E. (1986). *The very hungry caterpillar.* New York: Putnam.

Charlip, R. (1984). *Fortunately.* New York: Simon & Schuster.

Ehlert, L. (1998). *Top cat.* San Diego, CA: Harcourt.

Ehlert, L. (2004). *Pie in the sky.* San Diego, CA: Harcourt.

Falconer, I. (2000). *Olivia.* New York: Atheneum.

Fleming, D. (1992). *Lunch.* New York: Henry Holt.

Fleming, D. (1998). *Mama cat has three kittens.* New York: Henry Holt.

Fleming, C. (2002). *Muncha! Muncha! Muncha!* New York: Atheneum.

Fleming, D. (2005). *The first day of winter.* New York: Henry Holt.

Fleming, D. (2007). *Beetle bop.* San Diego, CA: Harcourt.

Hills, T. (2007). *Duck, duck, goose.* New York: Schwartz & Wade.

Jenkins, S. (2003). *What do you do with a tail like this?* Boston: Houghton Mifflin.

Jonas, A. (1983). *Round trip.* New York: Greenwillow.

Lehman, B. (2004). *The red book.* Boston: Houghton Mifflin.

Martin, B., Jr. (1967). *Brown bear, brown bear, what do you see?* New York: Holt, Rinehart and Winston.

Muth, J.J. (2005). *Zen shorts.* New York: Scholastic.

Polacco, P. (2005). *Emma Kate.* New York: Philomel.

Rocco, J. (2007). *Wolf! Wolf!* New York: Hyperion.

Rohmann, E. (2002). *My friend rabbit.* New York: Roaring Brook.

Rohmann, E. (2008). *A kitten tale.* New York: Random House.

Seeger, L.V. (2007). *Dog and Bear: Two friends, three stories.* New Milford, CT: Roaring Brook.

Selznick, B. (2007). *The invention of Hugo Cabret.* New York: Scholastic.

Sendak, M. (1963). *Where the wild things are.* New York: Harper.

Seuss, Dr. (1957). *The cat in the hat.* New York: Random House.

Shulevitz, U. (1969). *Rain, rain rivers.* New York: Farrar, Straus and Giroux.

Steen, S., & Steen, S. (2001). *Car wash.* New York: Putnam.

Stewart, S. (2004). *The friend.* New York: Farrar, Straus and Giroux.

Sutton, S. (2008). *Roadwork.* Cambridge, MA: Candlewick.

Sweet, M. (2008). *Tupelo rides the rails.* Boston: Houghton Mifflin.

Teague, M. (2004). *Detective LaRue: Letters from the investigation.* New York: Scholastic.

Van Allsburg, C. (1981). *Jumanji.* Boston: Houghton Mifflin.

Van Allsburg, C. (1988). *Two bad ants.* Boston: Houghton Mifflin.

Wiesner, D. (1999). *Sector 7.* New York: Clarion.

Wiesner, D. (2006). *Flotsam.* New York: Clarion.

Willems, M. (2004). *Knuffle Bunny: A cautionary tale.* New York: Hyperion.

Willems, M. (2006). *Don't let the pigeon stay up late!* New York: Hyperion.

Wood, A. (1984). *The napping house.* San Diego, CA: Harcourt.

Yolen, J. (1987). *Owl moon.* New York: Philomel.

Yorinks, A. (1986). *Hey, Al.* New York: Farrar, Straus and Giroux.

SUGGESTED BOOKS ABOUT PICTURE BOOK ILLUSTRATIONS AND ILLUSTRATORS

Artist to Artist: 23 Major Illustrators Talk to Children About Their Art. (2007). New York: Philomel.

This remarkable and beautiful anthology features artists such as Maurice Sendak, Robert Sabuda, Rosemary Wells, Eric Carle, and 19 other of the most honored and beloved artists in children's literature. All of the artists talk informally to children—sharing secrets about their art and how they began their adventures into illustration. Fold-out pages featuring photographs of artists' early work, their studios and materials, as well as their sketches and finished art create an exuberant feast for the eye that will attract both children and adults.

Evans, D. (2008). *Show & Tell: Exploring the Fine Art of Children's Book Illustration.* San Francisco: Chronicle.

Dilys Evans highlights the work of 12 contemporary illustrators such as David Wiesner, Denise Fleming, Brian Selznick, and Betsy Lewin. Looking at the wide variety of artistic genius in children's books, *Show & Tell* teaches the reader how to look for the perfect marriage of art and text.

Gonyea, M. (2005). *A Book About Design: Complicated Doesn't Make It Good.* New York: Holt.

Gonyea, M. (2007). *Another Book About Design: Complicated Doesn't Make It Bad.* New York: Holt.

Both of these colorful books contain brief, chatty chapters that present principles of composition, line, color, and contrast, as well as techniques for drawing attention to what's important on a page. The text, set against pure white backdrops, is easy to read, and the artwork's elemental shapes and bright colors illustrate the theories in ways that children will readily grasp.

Marcus, L. (2006). *Pass It Down: Five Picture Book Families Make Their Mark.* New York: Walker.

Leonard Marcus presents the events and circumstances that have resulted in five picture-book dynasties. Each chapter includes biographical information about each of the featured families, photographs, preliminary sketches, and final art. Other books by Marcus such as *A Caldecott Celebration: Seven Artists and Their Paths to the Caldecott Medal* (Walker, 2008) and *Side by Side: Five Picture-Book Teams Go to Work* (Walker, 2001) also look at picture book illustrators and their process.

CHAPTER 2

Graphic Novels in Education: Cartoons, Comprehension, and Content Knowledge

Stergios Botzakis

In past decades, comic books were strictly taboo in classrooms, stuck between the pages of a textbook and read when the teacher was not paying attention. In more recent times, these types of texts have been expanded upon and called graphic novels. They have lost some of their contraband status, and some even have come to be merited. Art Speigelman's (1986) *Maus* began this trend when it won the Pulitzer Prize Special Award in 1992, and it was more recently continued when Gene Yang's (2006) *American Born Chinese* was a finalist of the 2006 National Book Award in the category of Young People's Literature. Librarians have been advocating their inclusion in school libraries (American Library Association, 2006; Weiner, 2004), and states such as Maryland (Mui, 2004) have taken up these texts and built initiatives around them to engage with struggling or reluctant readers. No longer considered objects to be hidden, graphic texts have come into prominence in educational settings.

Graphic novels have also come into more prominence in bookstores and in the buying habits of young readers. *Manga*—Japanese comics translated into English—have become particularly popular with young readers, especially girls (Glazer, 2005). The sales numbers for graphic novels in general and manga in particular have been growing quickly in the United States (Goodnow, 2007). Past research has shown that what students prefer to read is typically not included in the curriculum (Worthy, Moorman, & Turner, 1999), and other research (Alvermann, Moon, & Hagood, 1999; Norton, 2003) indicates that students could become more motivated and successful when their interests are included in instruction.

Because graphic novels have become a top reading choice of many young readers, it makes sense to look at how they might fit into an educational setting. With this growing attention to graphic novels, the point of this chapter is to introduce more about what graphic novels can do in general, to demonstrate some uses of particular graphic novels, and to provide information about where you might find appropriate and appealing graphic novels for your students.

Children's Literature in the Reading Program: An Invitation to Read (third edition), edited by Deborah A. Wooten and Bernice E. Cullinan. © 2009 by the International Reading Association.

Why Use Graphic Novels in Class?

Popularity alone is not reason enough to include graphic novels in a curriculum, but there are a number of features unique to the medium that lend themselves well to instruction. Three of these features are transitions, contextual information, and visual permanence.

Transitions

Reading graphic novels, like reading comics in general, requires the reader to make connections between images set apart by panels and gutters—the empty spaces between panels (McCloud, 1994). Such reading requires constant inference making, as readers have to assume that actions are occurring between the panels. When students assume action takes place in the time it takes them to move from one panel to another, they are engaged in higher level thinking skills oftentimes without even knowing it. Making inferences from images is typically easier for students, and that skill can be introduced and taught using graphic novels (Frey & Fischer, 2004) and later revisited for more traditional text reading. What can be difficult for students to do with simple text can be more easily accomplished when reading visually oriented materials.

Contextual Information

Along with transitions that foster inference making, the illustrations in graphic novels provide contextual information that can assist or enhance readers' abilities to engage with text. This contextual information has been used successfully to engage with English-language learners (Cary, 2004) and also struggling readers, because the use of images along with words provides clues for comprehension. Such learning need not only be limited to concrete facts but also can be applied to more abstract learning. For example, the images in graphic novels can be used much in the same way that more print-based text features are discussed in language arts classes. Examining how an author draws a particular scene or character can extend the discussion to symbolism that authors create in poems and prose. For example, the way that Art Spiegelman uses imagery to convey character traits in *Maus* offers an avenue for teachers to speak about how Nathaniel Hawthorne does the same thing in *The Scarlet Letter* or any of his other works. Exploring the interactions between text and image can open up doors to further academic discussions.

Visual Permanence

One other feature of graphic novels that makes them useful to readers of varying ability is their "visual permanence" (Yang, 2008, p. 188). The words and pictures contained in graphic novels do not move and are fixed on a page, allowing readers to choose how fast or slow they wish to read it and also the degree to which they should attend to the words and pictures. Graphic novels give the illusion of time passing, but they leave the rate of change up to the reader. Yang likens this feature of the graphic novels to being able to rewind and revisit information (or conversely to keep on going), which is not unrelated to the rereading students can do with more traditional print-based texts. The major difference lies in the presence of images, which can be more attention-getting and unthreatening to more visually oriented youth. In short, Yang espouses that graphic novels make it easier for students to read at a rate appropriate to them.

Three Graphic Novels to Use in the Classroom

Just as putting students in front of a computer does not guarantee that learning is taking place, having students read graphic novels does not necessarily mean that they are reading and understanding them. The ease associated with reading graphic novels and comic strips can be deceiving. Just because graphic novels are popular doesn't mean that people know how to produce or even talk about them. Therefore, the following section describes three different graphic novels along with ways that teachers can use them with their students.

Yotsuba&!

Yotsuba&! (Azuma, 2003) is a manga series about a young girl who moves into a new neighborhood with her father, complete with the misadventures that happen when she gets to know her new neighbors and surroundings. With her green hair and unique outlook on the world, Yotsuba learns about a variety of subjects from cicadas to air conditioning to global warming. She also gets into a lot of mischief.

Understanding the Format. Because not all students are familiar with the conventions of sequential art, it may be helpful to have them read a small selection first and then explain how they make meaning of the text. Ask students to look at a page from the book in pairs. Have students attend to the pictures and text, and ask them what they think happened. Be sure to have them make a list of evidence from the text that helps them justify their responses: How do they know they are right? After the pairs complete this task, have them report to the class about what happened and what on the page made them think that. Creating a list of text features, such as the word bal-

loons, panels, facial expressions, symbols, and characters' positions, can help novice readers pick up on visual clues that will help them understand these kinds of texts. It would also be important for the teacher to point out that manga read from right to left, in contrast to how English is typically read. Posting this list in the classroom can also be a great resource for students to revisit when looking at other graphic texts. Ideally, this exercise would be done a few times with a variety of texts, because graphic novels are done in multiple styles just as are more text-centered works, such as short stories, novels, or poems.

Making Inferences. Moving from the understandings of text conventions, students can also be asked questions about finer details of what they've read. Using the combination of words and images, teachers can encourage students to make inferences about what they are reading (Jacobs, 2007). Students can be asked more detailed questions about what they've read, such as how old they think Yotsuba is or why the girl in the background thinks she is a foreigner. Moving on to predictions, students can be asked what they think will happen on the next page.

Teachers can also ask about the design and layout of the page. Why does Yotsuba crouch as she does? Why did the artist depict her as she is? How does the story flow? What is the sequence of action? The artist has to make choices about how depict the characters and actions. Discussing how the author uses text features and art to compose a message is an important step in getting students to write and draw on their own.

Journey Into Mohawk Country

A unique collaboration across centuries, *Journey Into Mohawk Country* is composed of a series of journal entries written by the

Dutchman H.M. Van den Bogaert (2006) during his visits to the Iroquois nation in the winter of 1634 and illustrations by present-day artist George O'Connor. The story involves a round-trip journey from Fort Orange where Van den Bogaert and two associates travel to meet and trade with various Native American clans. The combination of cultures lends insights into the lives and daily routines of 17th-century European settlers and the peoples they met on the North American continent. Also, there is a great deal of drama involved in travel during harsh winter conditions without many of the technical advances we might take for granted. This graphic novel would be a great addition in either a language arts or a social studies class.

Illustrated Journals. Illustrated journals are a great way to motivate students who like to draw, and graphic texts can be used to bolster instruction of the writing process. After students have had the chance to look at a range of texts and observe the features that help convey meaning (the activity described in the discussion of what could be done with *Yotsuba&!*), they can make their own illustrated narratives. A teacher could assign students to write about almost any kind of autobiographical experience, such as their own winter travels or an encounter when they felt like an outsider. To accompany the print story, students can extend their stories into graphic form using the conventions they have seen used by graphic novel authors. This need not be a huge endeavor, and some teachers may want to consider parsing the assignment into a smaller one by limiting the length of the story to six panels, typical of a Sunday comic strip (Botzakis, 2005). Students would have to make decisions about what aspects and details of their story should be included and also about how to best show

them using the conventions of panel size and shape, body positions, facial expressions, sound effects, and balloon placement. This activity can be related to the draft work and planning that is done in a more visible way than in most print-text centered assignments (Bitz, 2004). Additionally, the drawing may help motivate reluctant writers to take part so they can show off their artistic abilities (Khurana, 2005).

Content Learning. Not just an example of a survival story, *Journey Into Mohawk Country* also contains many historical and cultural references that can be used to enhance learning about the U.S. colonies. Not only can students get a glimpse into life in the 17th century, including a look at the contemporary trading, tools, and technology, but they can also observe the social situation of the time. Students could be given a graphic organizer to draw attention to the different Native Americans they encountered on their trek (see Figure 2.1). By drawing attention to how the visitors were treated, how or if they were welcomed, what was asked of them, or to any customs observed, teachers can engage students in learning about peoples from the past on a concrete level. Additionally, their behavior can be contrasted in another assignment where the students look at what the Dutch people do, expect, and say during the trip. From there, more abstract questions might be asked about how the Mohawks viewed the Dutch and vice versa, what they thought each group wanted from the other, and whether either group felt like they were taking advantage of the other. This narrative gives a rich picture of a historical moment from the viewpoint of a person who was there, and it also portrays a complex situation where the Mohawks are not simply cast as savages or the Dutch as colonial conquerors.

FIGURE 2.1
Sample Graphic Organizer of Native American Clans
in *Journey Into Mohawk Country*

Who did they visit?	What customs did they see?	Did they trade?
1.		
2.		
3.		
4.		

Clan Apis

Graphic novels can be used in other content areas as well, and some of these texts are listed at the end of this chapter. Jay Hosler's *Clan Apis* (Hosler, 2007) is a text that would fit in nicely with a science unit on insects. This story of bees is centered on Nyuki, a larva who grows into a productive member of the hive community. Nyuki is very inquisitive and as the reader follows her along her life cycle much is explained about bee development, hive behavior, and the very social lives bees lead. The adventurous Nyuki ventures away from the hive where she encounters other insect species, some of which are unfriendly to say the least, and in the end she learns to contribute as much as she can to the good of the hive. Aside from being an often humorous and compelling story, *Clan Apis* abounds with information within the narrative and a concluding facts section.

Sequence Maps. The story of *Clan Apis* can be read as an interesting, imaginative account of the life cycle of a bee. Nyuki begins the tale as a larva but quickly moves into being a pupa before maturing into an adult bee. This process is visually represented on page 33 (see Figure 2.2), but along the way much is explained about how a bee takes on many roles throughout its life. Teachers could take advantage of the twin narratives of Nyuki and Dvorah, her older sister and mentor. As students are reading this book, a parallel sequence map could be used to document

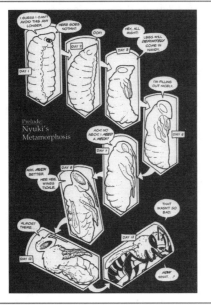
help people realize what words do and do not mean. The variety of creatures Nyuki encounters on her journeys offers students opportunities for comparing and contrasting, and a great way to get at this knowledge is a semantic feature analysis (Johnson & Pearson, 1984). For this activity, the teacher begins with a category, in this case creatures from *Clan Apis*, and then lists some members of this group and features attributed to them in table form (see Figure 2.4). Students then either work individually or in groups to determine whether each feature applies to each creature, and they can be encouraged to add further features to help them make connections and differentiate between words.

Putting It All Together

There is much about graphic novels that make them appealing to students as well as teachers. Both groups may be surprised to find that the characters they enjoyed reading about in the story also provided them with content information that tied in with what they learn in their classes. Teachers may be surprised to find material that can be used to drive, bolster, or supplement their instruction. Many graphic novel authors have taken time and care to include many accuracies and details in their work through historical or scientific research; there is often much more to a graphic novel than comical scenes and one-liners.

In recent years, the increased attention on graphic novels from consumers and producers is leading to a surge in titles, series, and the amount of remarkable literature becoming available. The amount of graphic novels, however great, should also give one pause. Although there is much that graphic novels offer in terms of attractiveness and academic usefulness, I am not advocating here that every graphic novel is a treasure trove or should be used in

specific information about the various physical features and roles a bee takes in a lifetime (see Figure 2.3). At the end, students would have practice in identifying important or relevant types of information as well as a record of what occurs as a bee ages. This activity can be helpful for students to see how to visually group information, and it also extends into a note-taking activity (Topping & McManus, 2002) that can be used in a variety of content area classes.

Compare and Contrast. Learning vocabulary requires that students take time to visit and revisit words in a number of contexts so that they can attribute meanings with them (Schwanenflugel, Hamilton, Kuhn, & Stahl, 2004). These various interactions with words

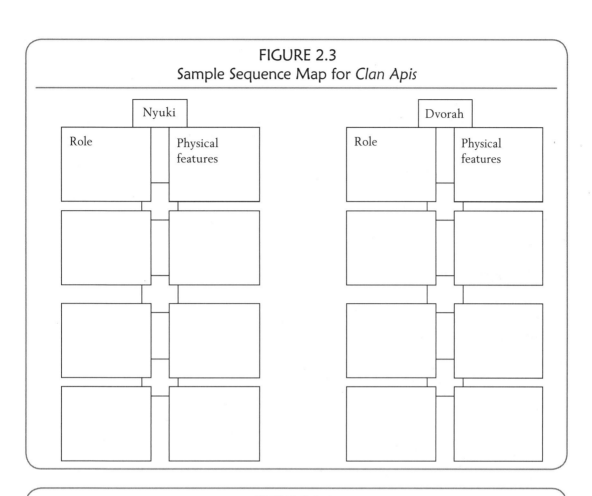

FIGURE 2.3
Sample Sequence Map for *Clan Apis*

Nyuki

| Role | Physical features |

Dvorah

| Role | Physical features |

FIGURE 2.4
Sample Semantic Feature Analysis for *Clan Apis*

Character	Lives socially	Predator	Gathers food	Can fly	Uses camouflage	Is an insect
Nyuki	+	-	-	+	-	+
"Nobody"	-	+	-	-	+	+
Thom	-	+	-	-	+	-
Sisyphus	-	-	+	-	-	+

school. Just as not every novel or textbook is appropriate for every class, so it is with graphic novels. Teachers should be informed about the content of graphic novels and also about where to find further information that may help them find appropriate resources. To that end I have provided a list of titles that can give a start to teachers interested in the possibilities of graphic novels. There are more elaborate resources, such as Stephen Weiner's *101 Best* *Graphic Novels* (Weiner, 2006) and the Comics in the Classroom website (comicsintheclassroom.net; Tingley, 2008), and the University of Wisconsin-Madison's Cooperative Children's Book Center website (www.education.wisc.edu/ccbc/books/graphic novels.asp; 2008). These contain many links for inquisitive teachers or students. Graphic novels can offer students and teachers an invitation to engaging, educational reading.

REFERENCES

Alvermann, D.E., Moon, J.S., & Hagood, M.C. (1999). *Popular culture in the classroom: Teaching and researching critical media literacy.* Chicago: National Reading Conference.

American Library Association. (2006). *Graphic novels: Suggestions for librarians.* Retrieved April 17, 2009, from www.ncac.org/graphicnovels.cfm

Bitz, M. (2004). The comic book project: Forging alternative pathways to literacy. *Journal of Adolescent & Adult Literacy, 47*(7), 574–586.

Botzakis, S. (2005, February). *Just 'kids' stuff?' Comic books in the classroom.* Paper presented at the meeting of the Georgia Council of Teachers of English, Jekyll Island, GA.

Cary, S. (2004). *Going graphic: Comics at work in the multilingual classroom.* Portsmouth, NH: Heinemann.

Cooperative Children's Book Center. (2008). *Graphic novels.* Retrieved May 23, 2008, from www.education.wisc.edu/ccbc/books/graphicnovels.asp

Frey, N., & Fischer, D. (2004). Using graphic novels, anime, and the Internet in an urban high school. *English Journal, 93*(3), 19–25. doi:10.2307/4128804

Glazer, S. (2005, September 18). Manga for girls. *The New York Times Book Review,* 16–17.

Goodnow, C. (2007, March 8). Teens buying books at fastest rate in decades. *Seattle Post-Intelligencer.* Retrieved May 23, 2008, from seattlepi.nwsource.com/books/306531_teenlit08.html

Jacobs, D. (2007). More than words: Comics as a means of teaching multiple literacies. *English Journal, 96*(3), 19–25.

Johnson, D.D., & Pearson, P.D. (1984). *Teaching reading vocabulary* (2nd ed.). New York: Holt, Rinehart and Winston.

Khurana, S. (2005). So you want to be a superhero? How the art of making comics in an afterschool setting can develop young people's creativity, literacy and identity. *Afterschool Matters, 1*(4), 1–9.

McCloud, S. (1994). *Understanding comics: The invisible art.* New York: HarperPerennial.

Mui, Y.Q. (2004). *Schools turn to comics as trial balloon.* Retrieved May 23, 2008, from www.washingtonpost.com/ac2/wp-dyn/A59964-2004Dec12?langauge=printer

Norton, B. (2003). The motivating power of comic books: Insights from *Archie* comic readers. *The Reading Teacher, 57*(2), 140–147.

Schwanenflugel, P.J., Hamilton, A.M., Kuhn, M.R., & Stahl, S.A. (2004). Becoming a fluent reader: Skill and prosodic features in the oral reading of young children. *Journal of Educational Psychology, 96*(1), 119–129. doi:10.1037/0022-0663.96.1.119

Tingley, S. (2008). *Comics in the classroom.* Retrieved May 23, 2008, from comicsintheclassroom.net/

Topping, D., & McManus, R. (2002). *Real reading, real writing: Content-area strategies.* Portland, ME: Stenhouse.

Weiner, S. (2004). *The rise of the graphic novel: Faster than a speeding bullet.* New York: Nantier Beall Minoustchine.

Weiner, S. (2006). *101 best graphic novels* (2nd ed.). New York: Nantier Beall Minoustchine.

Worthy, J., Moorman, M., & Turner, M. (1999). What Johnny likes to read is hard to find in school. *Reading Research Quarterly, 34*(1), 12–27. doi:10.1598/RRQ.34.1.2

Yang, G. (2008). Graphic novels in the classroom. *Language Arts, 85*(3), 185–192.

CHILDREN'S LITERATURE CITED

Azuma, K. (2003). *Yotsuba&!* (Vol. 1). Houston, TX: ADV Manga.

Hosler, J. (2007). *Clan apis.* Columbus, OH: Active Synapse.

Spiegelman, A. (1986). *Maus: A survivor's tale.* New York: Pantheon.

Van den Bogaert, H.M., & O'Connor, G. (2006). *Journey into Mohawk country.* New York: First Second.

Yang, G. (2006). *American born Chinese.* New York: First Second.

SUGGESTED GRAPHIC NOVELS FOR GRADES K–3

Barks, C. (2006). *Disney presents Carl Barks' greatest Ducktales stories* (Vol. 1). York, PA: Gemstone.

Gownley, J. (2003). *Amelia rules! The whole world's crazy.* New York: IBooks.

Hayes, G. (2008). *Benny and Penny: Just pretend.* New York: RAW Jr.

Holm, J. (2005). *Babymouse #1: Queen of the world!* New York: Random House.

Kitchen, A. (2006). *Drawing comics is easy! (Except when it's hard!).* Amherst, MA: Denis Kitchen.

Kochalka, J. (2008). *Johnny Boo: The best little ghost in the world* (Vol. 1). Marietta, GA: Top Shelf Productions.

Lynch, J., & Cammuso, F. (2008). *Otto's orange day.* New York: RAW Jr.

Soo, K. (2008). *Jellaby* (Vol. 1). New York: Hyperion.

Spiegelman, A., & Mouly, F. (Eds.). (2003). *Big fat little lit.* New York: Puffin.

Varon, S. (2007). *Robot dreams.* New York: Roaring Brook Press.

SUGGESTED GRAPHIC NOVELS FOR CONTENT AREA LEARNING

Biographies

Kinney, J. (2007). *Diary of a wimpy kid: A novel in cartoons.* New York: Amulet Books.

Schrag, A. (Ed.). (2007). *Stuck in the middle: Seventeen comics from an unpleasant age.* New York: Viking.

Siegel, S.C., & Siegel, M. (2006). *To dance: A ballerina's graphic novel.* New York: Atheneum.

Yang, G. (2006). *American born Chinese.* New York: First Second.

Science

Abadzis, N. (2007). *Laika.* New York: First Second.

Hosler, J. (2003). *The sandwalk adventures.* Columbus, OH: Active Synapse.

Ottaviani, J. (2003). *Dignifying science: Stories about women scientists* (2nd ed.). Ann Arbor, MI: G.T. Labs.

Ottaviani, J., & Attic, B.T. (2005). *Bone sharps, cowboys, and thunder lizards: A tale of Edwin Drinker Cope, Othniel Charles Marsh, and the gilded age of paleontology.* Ann Arbor, MI: G.T. Labs.

Science Fiction/Fantasy

Guibert, E., & Sfar, J. (2006). *Sardine in outer space.* New York: First Second.

Petersen, D. (2007). *Mouse guard: Fall 1152.* Kearny, NJ: Archaia Studios.

Runton, A. (2004). *Owly: Just a little blue.* Marietta, GA: Top Shelf Productions.

Smith, J. (2004). *Bone: The complete cartoon epic in one volume.* Columbus, OH: Cartoon Books.

Social Studies

Gonick, L. (1997). *Cartoon history of the universe* (Vol. 1). New York: Main Street Books.

Lutes, J., & Bertozzi, N. (2008). *Houdini: The handcuff king.* New York: Hyperion.

Sfar, J., & Guibert, E. (2007). *The professor's daughter.* New York: First Second.

Sturm, J., & Tommaso, R. (2007). *Satchel Paige: Striking out Jim Crow.* New York: Jump at the Sun.

CHAPTER 3

Using Postmodern Picture Books in the Classroom

Elizabeth A. Swaggerty

Today's children are growing up in a world that differs a great deal from the one in which their parents and teachers grew up; a world that is influenced by a digital media culture and is characterized by connectivity, interactivity, nonlinearity, and instantaneous access to information and social networks. Termed *digital natives*, the current generation of children is growing up with exposure to—and often the ability to simultaneously use—multiple technological devices such as computers, MP3 players, and cell phones (Prensky, 2001). Digital natives typically have the ability to control information flow, and they prefer to be in control of what they engage in (Veen & Vrakking, 2006). To this generation, school is not *the* focal point of their lives; rather it is one of many (Veen & Vrakking, 2006). To engage students who are comfortable multitasking, socializing, and working at "twitch speed" (Prensky, 1998) in literacy learning, it is necessary to consider new tools and tasks that take into consideration the learning styles of this new generation.

Acknowledging that children of today are digital natives does not mean that books should be replaced by laptops and MP3 players in classroom settings. Instead, the implication is that teachers should consider the learning preferences of "Net-generation" students and get creative in imagining ways to engage them in meaningful experiences with text. Postmodern picture books offer great potential to engage children across grade levels in reading and to promote critical thinking about text.

Authors and illustrators of postmodern picture books employ a variety of alternative literary and illustrative characteristics that can be compared with digital genres such as the Internet (Dresang & McClelland, 1999; Labbo, 2004). Some postmodern picture books have a nonlinear format, consisting of multiple storylines, which requires readers to decide how to read the text on each page. Similarly, surfing the Internet requires users to make choices about which link they click on and which part of the screen they will read first.

Dresang and McClelland (1999) use the term *radical change* to describe the ways in which interactivity, connectivity, and access are incorporated into the design of contemporary books such as postmodern picture books.

Children's Literature in the Reading Program: An Invitation to Read (third edition), edited by Deborah A. Wooten and Bernice E. Cullinan. © 2009 by the International Reading Association.

Perhaps children who are drawn to the interactive nature of the digital world are attracted to many of the same qualities present in postmodern picture books. For example, many of these books feature characters who speak directly to the reader. Some books require readers to make choices about how they will navigate the text by presenting multiple texts. Some children are drawn to the absurdity and humor often found in postmodern picture books, or they may enjoy stories that poke fun at fairy tales with which they are familiar. Whatever the reason, postmodern picture books are surfacing in bookstores and libraries and in the hands of children, justifying the attention of educators.

Given that postmodern picture books often deviate from traditional narrative structure and elements, traditional comprehension strategies may not be effective in assisting students' understandings of the stories. So how might teachers support students in reading these unique texts? This chapter will introduce the reader to postmodern picture books and then outline how teachers might thoughtfully integrate them into the reading curriculum.

What Is a Postmodern Picture Book?

The word *postmodern* has a number of different meanings, depending on whether you ask an artist, minister, architect, fashion designer, or singer. Generally speaking, postmodernism emerged in the mid-20th century and is characterized by the mocking of traditional art forms. Today, many creators of picture books are experimenting with ways of mocking the traditional picture book, designing books that employ a variety of alternative characteristics and, as a result, are pushing the boundaries of what readers expect to encounter when they pick up a picture book.

Many readers can relate to the feeling of inhabiting a book, or "losing themselves" in a story. When readers are really "into" a story, they sometimes forget that they are even reading a book. Postmodern picture books, on the other hand, tend to have the opposite effect on readers. Authors of this nontraditional genre work to bring the readers' attention to the fictional state of the book, or the book as a physical object (Goldstone, 2002). For example, Michaela Muntean (2006) and illustrator Pascal Lemaitre bring the act of creating a book to the readers' attention in *Do Not Open This Book!* This picture book features a pig working in a cluttered workshop, surrounded by tools and boxes of punctuation marks, letters, and words. He greets the reader with angry eyes and a serious warning against entering the book because *it is not written yet.* Throughout the book, the reader continues to annoy the main character by turning the pages before the pig has written the story. This unique story brings attention to the fact that the book in the reader's hands is a physical object and that the reader is a coconstructor of the story.

Postmodern Picture Book Characteristics

Postmodern picture books employ any number of alternative literary and illustrative characteristics, including techniques for accentuating the fictional state of the book, nonlinear plots, ambiguity, parodic characteristics, and intertextual references (McCallum, 1996, Pantaleo, 2002). Some of these individual characteristics may not necessarily indicate a postmodern picture book when employed alone, but when used in combination with other devices they have the potential to accentuate the fictional state of the book (McCallum, 1996). Pantaleo and Sipe

(2008) explain that picture books can fall on a continuum in terms of the degree of postmodernism. For example, *The Stinky Cheese Man and Other Fairly Stupid Tales* (Sciezska & Smith, 1992) is often considered an exemplary postmodern picture book because it exhibits many postmodern characteristics. Next, consider a picture book that is a parody of a traditional fairy tale, such as *Falling for Rapunzel* (Wilcox, 2003). Aside from parody, this fractured fairy tale does not employ additional postmodern picture book devices that work to bring attention to the fictional state of the book, so it would fall on the opposite end of the continuum.

The sections that follow briefly describe postmodern picture book characteristics. These devices include self-conscious writing and illustrations that emphasize the fictional state of the book, nonlinear plots, ambiguity, parodic characteristics, and intertextual references.

Emphasis on the Fictional State of the Book

Open postmodern picture books and you are likely to see strange things—objects sliding off of pages, characters jumping in and out of the surface of pages, and strange, hidden, illustrative details. Pantaleo (2004) notes that many postmodern picture books employ devices that accentuate the fictional state of the book with both verbal and visual text. Illustrations (independently of and sometimes in conjunction with the text) in picture books often reveal the fictional reality of the story. For example, *The Three Pigs* by David Wiesner (2001) begins like the familiar story of the three pigs, but readers quickly realize that the story with which they are familiar has gone awry when the first little pig gets blown out of the story frame by the big bad wolf (see Figure 3.1). As the pig exits the story frame, his appearance changes from a flat cartoon-like illustration to a three-dimensional, more realistic drawing. The pig suddenly appears to be standing *on top* of the page. Several times throughout the story, characters appear in half-cartoon and half-realistic form as they step out of the book and into reality or into another story frame. By employing this illustrative technique, Wiesner brings attention to the picture book as a physical object, causing the reader to question the boundaries of the story.

In another example, *The Red Book* by Barbara Lehman (2004) is a wordless postmodern picture book that relies solely on illustrations to portray the plot, in which a little girl enters the book she is reading and is magically transported to another place. The girl finds a red book in the snow as she is walking to school. She is intrigued by the friend she observes in the pages of the book and actually enters the book to journey to meet him. The illustrations in this picture book cause the reader to ponder the idea of the red book, wondering if the red book in their hands has the magical power to emulate the story in the fictional red book.

In addition to unique illustrative style, unusual or original design layouts are commonly present in postmodern picture books. When the design layout differs from what readers expect to see, readers do not "get lost" in the story as they read. Rather, the readers' attention is brought to the book as a physical object; an object that that can be visually manipulated in novel and unique ways. Additionally, when the design layout differs from traditional text, the readers' expectations of reading a book from top to bottom and left to right is challenged (Anstey, 2002). For instance, on the first page spread of David Macaulay's (1990) *Black and White* the reader encounters a two-page spread that is divided

into four panels, each of which displays words and illustrations that are seemingly separate and unconnected (see Figure 3.2). Throughout the story, readers must determine how to read the four panels and may find that they return to previous pages in an effort to make meaning.

Another common device that reminds readers of the fictional reality of the story portrays the story narrator directly addressing readers or commenting on the book. McCallum (1996) describes narrator and author intrusion as, "overly obtrusive narrators who directly address readers and comment on their own narrations" (p. 397). *The Stinky Cheese Man* *and Other Fairly Stupid Tales* (Sciezska & Smith, 1992), a collection of humorous parodies, exemplifies this phenomenon. Jack (the narrator) addresses readers on the dedication page, which is upside-down: "I know. I know. The page is upside down. I meant to do that. Who ever looks at that dedication stuff anyhow? If you really want to read it—you can always stand on your head." Readers are alerted in a humorous way that the book is a physical object when Jack talks about his part in constructing the book.

In a more recent postmodern picture book, *Wolves*, Emily Gravett (2006) acknowledges the reader by inserting a message from

the author to the reader. In this story, a rabbit checks out a book about wolves from the library. Illustrations depict the rabbit reading the book, but as the book progresses, the rabbit is shown *inside* the illustrations of the book and in danger of being eaten by wolves. The story closes with two endings, one of which is a happy ending, provided by the author for sensitive readers.

Finally, text formatting is another device that creators of postmodern picture books experiment with to bring attention to the physical state of the book. In *Chester* (Watt, 2007), a cat named Chester attempts to control the story by using a red marker to cross out and add his own text and illustrations throughout. The mischievous cat and the book's creator, Mélanie Watt, struggle to gain control of the story until the very end when the disgruntled cat is portrayed in a tutu and crown and Mélanie Watt's photograph is doctored with red glasses, mustache, eyebrows, and beard (see Figure 3.3).

Nonlinearity

Goldstone (2002) explains that nonlinearity results when the story does not necessarily follow the traditional sequential story structure of beginning, middle, and end. The story parts may be mixed up or absent, readers may move forward or backward within the text, or multiple narratives may be present. Anthony Browne's (1998) *Voices in the Park* is a powerful example of this divergence from the traditional story grammar of beginning, middle, and end. This picture book tells the story of a day at the park from four very different perspectives in separate narratives that comprise four consecutive sets of a beginning, middle, and ending.

Who's Afraid of the Big Bad Book? by Lauren Child (2003) challenges readers' expectations of a traditional, linear text by presenting portions of text in various places across a two-page spread. For example, the main character, Herb, uses the words of the text as a ladder to attempt an escape and climb out of the story. The words are askew from Herb's hurried climbing. Readers of these texts find themselves making choices about which text they should read first. This book is also a good example of how postmodern picture books can remind readers of the fictional reality of the story.

FIGURE 3.3
Cover/Final Page From *Chester*

Cover from *Chester*, by Mélanie Watt, used by permission of Kids Can Press Ltd., Toronto. Cover illustration © 2007 Mélanie Watt.

Ambiguity

Many postmodern picture books have a high degree of indeterminacy in plot, characters, or setting, providing readers with too little information and often gaps and ambiguities that recur throughout the story. Readers are forced to construct their own meaning (Pantaleo, 2004). The books leave the readers wondering, What in the world does this book mean? Readers often reread the story, closely investigating the illustrations for clues to try to make more sense of the plot.

One example is *Flotsam* (Wiesner, 2006), a wordless picture book that capitalizes on detailed illustrations to produce ambiguity in meaning. Readers meet a boy at the beach who discovers a washed-up "Melville Underwater Camera." The developed film reveals strange surrealistic photographs of the ocean and portrayals of various children across time. Without text to explain the meaning of the illustrations, readers must create their own meaning of the plot.

Parody

Postmodern picture books often employ parodic devices, resulting in the mocking of traditional or familiar stories. *Wait! No Paint!* by Bruce Whatley (2001) tells an alternative version of the familiar story of the three pigs. In this tale, the pigs are at the mercy of an illustrator who accidentally spills juice on the pages of the story and runs out of red paint as he is illustrating the story, leaving the pigs feeling embarrassed by their pale appearance.

Intertextuality

Intertextuality is a literary term describing how authors are influenced by previous texts as they craft a book. Two or more familiar texts might be interwoven or connected to create a new narrative (Hellman, 2003), or the text might be characterized by a revision of a specific text (McCallum, 1996). When texts employ intertextuality, readers use their background knowledge to understand the text (Anstey, 2002). In *Who's Afraid of the Big Bad Book?* (Child, 2003), a boy named Herb falls asleep on one of his favorite old books. He awakens to find that he has entered the fairy tales of the book and has interesting encounters with various characters including Little Red Riding Hood, Rapunzel, Cinderella, and the Three Bears. Herb comes to realize that some of the characters are irritated with him because of his past mistreatment of the book, for example, the time he drew a mustache on the Queen from the story of Cinderella.

David Wiesner (2001) masterfully employs intertextuality in *The Three Pigs*. Readers enjoy trying to identify the stories that the three pigs journey through: familiar nursery rhymes, a medieval story with a dragon, and other storybook pages showing flying fish.

Thoughtfully Integrating Postmodern Picture Books With the Reading Curriculum

Much is known regarding the common strategies that children use when approaching traditional literature (Pearson, Roehler, Dole, &

Duffy, 1992; Pressley & Afflerbach, 1995). For example, looking for a familiar story structure; expecting a clear beginning, middle, and ending; or conceptualizing the story in terms of a sequence of events might aid students' understanding of the story.

Studies of story comprehension indicate that many individuals develop a sense of an idealized story, involving knowledge of structural features, called story schema (Mandler & Johnson, 1977; Rumelhart, 1978; Thorndyke, 1977) and that this knowledge facilitates understanding and recall (Fitzgerald & Spiegel, 1983; Fitzgerald, Spiegel, & Webb, 2001; Mandler & Johnson, 1977; Rumelhart, 1978; Thorndyke, 1977). Thus, if readers are familiar with the ways that authors commonly construct stories, then they are better equipped with the necessary background knowledge about what to expect when they hear and read similar stories, which contributes to story comprehension. When children build schema for story genres, they are better able to predict story structure. For example, if readers encounter a story that begins with the words *Once upon a time*, predicting that the story is fictional will aid comprehension of that particular text. Many teachers know that there is an underlying structure that all simple stories appear to have in common and provide instruction that focuses on developing this story schema.

Children encountering postmodern picture books, on the other hand, may find that these strategies are ineffective in assisting their understanding of the story. The presence of alternative literary characteristics challenges readers' expectations and requires access to alternative comprehension strategies. For example, predicting what might happen next, a common traditional comprehension strategy, may not be helpful in aiding readers' comprehension of postmodern picture books. Some postmodern picture books are nearly impossible to predict because the stories are ambiguous and end without resolution, leaving the reader to draw inferences. Sequencing events is another strategy that may or may not be effective in supporting comprehension of postmodern picture books because of the nonlinear nature of story lines and illustrations. Thus, teachers must explore alternative ways to support comprehension of postmodern picture books such as facilitating student talk about text, supporting students' negative reactions to alternative literary and illustrative characteristics, and valuing, supporting, and encouraging active engagement with texts.

The Importance of Talk

Student talk is a common feature of highly effective teachers' classrooms (Allington, 2002). There is potential for furthering comprehension of text through purposeful discussions and, because of the nontraditional characteristics common to postmodern picture books, discussion can be a particularly useful strategy to further understand these complex texts.

Because many postmodern picture books do not lend themselves to a read-aloud format because of nonlinear plots, complex illustrations, and other nontraditional features, most students can be encouraged to read the story the first time either independently or with a partner. The initial reading can be followed by a small-group discussion about the book so that students have the opportunity to gain more understanding of the story and a greater appreciation of its unique characteristics through interaction with peers. Book discussions should be primarily student-centered, but the teacher can and will likely need to interject more specific questions to guide understanding when students appear to be heading in the wrong direction or are unable to move the discussion forward.

In small-group discussions, teachers can model how students might work to problem solve various aspects of each plot. Students might ask one another questions, point out illustrative details, look to other textual features (such as the book cover, front and back flaps, copyright page, and so on) for clues about the plot, seek connections to other books and the media, and discuss the intertextual features in many of the books. For example, in the following vignette, a fourth grader named Lizzie (all names are pseudonyms) talks with her peers about *Black and White* (Macaulay, 1990).

Lizzie, a fourth grader, read *Black and White* (Macaulay, 1990) independently for the first time and was clearly frustrated as she attempted to make sense of its four simultaneous narratives. Throughout her reading of the book, she told her teacher that the book was "weird" and "scary" and she struggled to make sense of the story's plot. At the conclusion of the book, she stated that she "didn't get" the story. She turned to the book jacket flap and the "warning label" on the title page, seeming to search for clues that might shed some light on the plot.

Clearly, Lizzie was not comfortable with her initial understanding of *Black and White*. However, the following day, she participated in a book club discussion with six of her peers. The discussion revealed that Lizzie gained understanding of the story as a result of talking with her peers. For example, Lizzie asked her friends if they read the "warning label" on the title page of the book. When Samantha pointed out that the burglar in one quadrant was the same as the burglar from another quadrant, Lizzie exclaimed, "Oh! So that's who that is!" She then shared that she thought that the burglar was a woman. Cynthia and Samantha told her that the burglar was disguised as a woman. In the following conversation, Cynthia made a discovery about the plot that caused Lizzie to make her own discovery:

Cynthia: Oh! I just made a connection! Look! You know here they're wearing the stuff [newspapers]...now *they* are. (She points from one quadrant of the two-page spread to another quadrant.)

Lizzie: Yeah. And then they're...and then they're ripping it up.

Cynthia: I got something! I got something!

Lizzie: And then they're ripping...and then they're ripping it up!

Cynthia: Yeah.

Lizzie gained knowledge about the story from this interaction with Cynthia. The notion of learning through social interaction, or social constructivist learning theory (Vygotsky, 1978), is illustrated here as Lizzie built on Cynthia's comment about the plot and drew her own conclusion from the text.

Supporting Students' Negative Reactions to Alternative Literary and Illustrative Characteristics

Some students will likely experience negative feelings when they initially encounter the alternative devices in postmodern picture books. These students may be uncomfortable with ambiguity and might feel anxious as they search for the "right answer" in terms of discerning the story's plot. Students may also feel irritated when authors and illustrators challenge their background knowledge by modifying the stories with which they are familiar.

Teachers should be aware that children may have negative opinions of and feelings about the stories and should work to support students' negative reactions. Serafini (2005) suggests that teachers work to support readers' ability to "entertain ambiguity" (p. 60) by supporting their recognition and understanding of alternative literary devices and enjoyment of the challenges that they present.

For example, consider the following classroom vignette:

At the beginning of a book club session about *Who's Afraid of the Big Bad Book?* (Child, 2003) with fourth-grade students, Cynthia shared that she didn't like the story because it was difficult to read because of the different print conventions and wandering font. Later in that same session when participants were talking about the pages featuring upside-down font, Cynthia said that she thought the author was "smart" for inserting upside-down pages and admitted that she "got into it and thought it was funny." She continued to actively participate in the discussion about the book, gaining understanding about the plot. For example, she asked the group how Herb got out of the book. She wondered how he could fall on the floor as the text stated if he was already on the floor. A lengthy discussion ensued in which participants worked to understand this page, discussing various possibilities. Cynthia appeared to enjoy the book and gain understanding about the story's plot, but she shared that she "didn't like the book" at the conclusion of the book club session.

In a situation like this, a teacher might explain to Cynthia and her classmates that sometimes opinions of books can change as readers spend more time with them. Sometimes, the books that readers don't initially like eventually become the books that intrigue them the most and in hindsight are the books that they most enjoy.

Value, Support, and Encourage Active Engagement With Texts

Readers of postmodern picture books should be encouraged to become actively engaged with the text, and the classroom should be conceptualized as a place where active engagement with text is valued and encouraged. When reading, students who are actively engaged in the story might laugh out loud, talk for the characters in the story, and voice their critiques of the story (Sipe, 2002). Students can also become actively engaged in the story during discussions. An observer might see the same behaviors along with students working to problem solve and coconstruct the story with their classmates. Sipe (2002) recommends that teachers deepen students' understanding of text by encouraging expressive engagement during read-alouds, facilitating dramatization of the story, modeling, accepting and valuing talking back to the text, and encouraging critiquing or controlling of the text in which children actually take over the text and speak for the characters. When active engagement is modeled and encouraged in the classroom, the classroom environment becomes a place in which students can gain deeper understanding of text.

For example, consider the following classroom vignette that features a small group of intermediate readers talking about *The Red Book* (Lehman, 2004).

Readers of this book sometimes wonder where to draw the line between reality and fiction. Observing a book club group of fourth-grade students talking about this title, the discussion turned in this direction. Lizzie asked the group a compelling question, "Are we the reader or is somebody reading us?" Tyler responded, "Where's the person that's supposed to be watching us?" The students thoughtfully looked around the room and up at the ceiling.

Clearly, when readers' attention is drawn to the book as a physical object, they question the relationship between fiction and reality. Encouraging readers to become active participants in the story offers fertile ground for critical thinking as they co-construct the story with the book's creators.

Using David Wiesner's *The Three Pigs* to Encourage Students to Make Inferences

The Three Pigs (Wiesner, 2001) is an alternative to the traditional story of the three pigs. Within the first few pages of the story, when readers realize that the wolf blows the first pig right out of the story frame they are challenged to think about and make sense of this alternative story. The story is too unpredictable to consider when teaching children to make predictions. Many predictions will be left unconfirmed at the conclusion of the story. However, this text holds great potential for teaching students to make inferences, a strategy that is often difficult for students to understand and apply to their own independent reading. *The Three Pigs* requires that readers use their background knowledge, the text, and the illustrations to make inferences about the plot.

Reading skills improve through the teaching of comprehension strategies (Anderson, 1992; Brown, Pressley, Van Meter, & Schuder, 1996). The concept of making inferences could be introduced with an activity that helps children see that they make inferences regularly in their everyday lives. The following activity, which has been modified from Tanny McGregor's ideas in *Comprehension Connections* (McGregor, 2007), might be used to introduce students to making inferences. The teacher can bring in a purse or briefcase belonging to a fellow teacher, sharing items from the bag one at a time. For example, in sharing a receipt from a coffee shop, the teacher can write the item on a chart in the "evidence" column, and ask students what they can infer about the person from this receipt. "Coffee drinker" could be added to the "inference" column. If the teacher removed a pacifier from the bag, the students might infer that the mystery person has a child or even a grandchild. After analyzing all pieces of evidence and making inferences about the person to whom the contents belong, the students can make a guess as to which teacher the contents belong to. In other words, based on the evidence provided, students infer to whom the items belong.

Next, the teacher might guide students in making inferences with a story during a read-aloud of *The Three Pigs* (Wiesner, 2001). For example, in the book, the text on page 5 describes how the wolf huffed and puffed and blew the house down. The illustration, however, depicts the pig standing outside of the story frame and the confused wolf scratching his head. There is a discrepancy between the text and illustrations, leaving readers to infer what the author is implying in terms of the plot.

The teacher might then challenge students to make an inference at this point by asking, "What can you infer here? What is the author implying?" The teacher may point out to students that the text alone does not tell readers what is happening in the story. Readers must attend to the illustrations in combination with the text to understand the developing story. Students can be guided to think about the evidence in the text, the illustra-tions showing characters that are moving in and out of the storybook pages. Throughout the text, readers must draw on their background knowledge, the text, and the illustrations to make sense of this creative, ambiguous story. Even as the story concludes, readers are left to ponder what happened, how the story ends, and what the author's purpose was in writing this picture book. A postmodern picture book such as *The Three Pigs* (Wiesner, 2001) holds great potential for illustrating how *authors imply* and *readers infer* meaning because of its nontraditional story structure and ambiguity.

Conclusions

Although some postmodern picture books can be understood and enjoyed by younger readers, many are complex and ambiguous and may be better suited for older ones. Not only are these books often intended for older readers, but they hold potential for engaging today's "Net-generation" children in reading. By diverting from traditional linear formats and offering readers choices in terms of how to read and interpret them, postmodern picture books engage students, pique their curiosity, and encourage them to think. When asked why children should read postmodern picture books, a group of fourth-grade students explained that the books make readers think more creatively, are good for discussion, are mysterious, make the reader laugh, inspire the reader to write, and offer choices in terms of how to go about reading them.

If readers of this genre are provided with opportunities to talk about the text, support-ed in their reactions to the text, and encour-aged to actively engage with the text, they may come to appreciate and enjoy this com-plex genre that shares characteristics with their digital world.

REFERENCES

Allington, R.L. (2002). What I've learned about effective reading instruction from a decade of studying exemplary elementary classroom teachers. *Phi Delta Kappan, 83*(10), 740–747.

Anderson, V. (1992). A teacher development project in transactional strategy instruction for teachers of severely reading-disabled adolescents. *Teaching and Teacher Education, 8*(4), 391–403. doi:10.016/0742-051X(92)90064-A

Anstey, M. (2002). "It's not all black and white": Postmodern picture books and new literacies. *Journal of Adolescent & Adult Literacy, 45*(6), 444–457. doi:10.1598/JAAL.45.6.1

Brown, R., Pressley, M., Van Meter, P., & Schuder, T. (1996). A quasi-experimental validation of transactional strategies instruction with low-achieving second-grade readers. *Journal of Educational Psychology, 88*(1), 18–37.

Dresang, E.T., & McClelland, K. (1999). Radical change: Digital age literature and learning. *Theory Into Practice, 38*(3), 160–167.

Fitzgerald, J., & Spiegel, D.L. (1983). Enhancing children's reading comprehension through instruction in narrative structure. *Journal of Reading Behavior, 15*(2), 1–17.

Fitzgerald, J., Spiegel, D.L., & Webb, T.B. (2001). Development of children's knowledge of story structure and content. *The Journal of Educational Research, 79*(2), 101–108.

Goldstone, B.P. (2002). Whaz up with our books? Changing picture book codes and teaching implications. *The Reading Teacher, 55*(4), 362–370.

Hellman, P. (2003). The role of postmodern picture books in art education. *Art Education, 56*(6), 7–12.

Labbo, L.D. (2004). Seeking synergy between postmodern picture books and digital genres. *Language Arts, 81*(3), 207–216.

Mandler, J.M., & Johnson, N.J. (1977). Remembrance of things passed: Story structure and recall. *Cognitive Psychology, 9*(1), 111–151. doi:10.1016/0010-0285(77)90006-8

McCallum, R. (1996). Metafictions and experimental work. In P. Hunt (Ed.), *International companion encyclopedia of children's literature* (pp. 397–409). New York: Routledge.

McGregor, T. (2007). *Comprehension connections: Bridges to strategic reading.* Portsmouth, NH: Heinemann.

Pantaleo, S. (2002). Grade 1 students meet David Wiesner's *Three Pigs. Journal of Children's Literature, 28*(2), 72–84.

Pantaleo, S. (2004). Young children interpret the metafictive in Anthony Browne's *Voices in the Park. Journal of Early Childhood Literacy, 4*(2), 211–233. doi:10.1177/1468798404044516

Pantaleo, S., & Sipe, L.R. (2008). Introduction: Postmodernism and picturebooks. In L.R. Sipe & S. Pantaleo (Eds.), *Postmodern picturebooks: Play, parody, and self-referentiality* (pp. 1–8). New York: Routledge.

Pearson, P.D., Roehler, L.R., Dole, J.A., & Duffy, G.G. (1992). Developing expertise in reading comprehension. In S.J. Samuels & A.E. Farstrup (Eds.), *What research has to say about reading instruction* (pp. 145–199). Newark, DE: International Reading Association.

Prensky, M. (1998, January). Twitch speed: Reaching younger workers who think differently. *Across the Board.* Retrieved October 4, 2006, from www.twitchspeed.com/site/article.html

Prensky, M. (2001). Digital natives, digital immigrants. *On the Horizon, 9*(5). Retrieved October 4, 2006, from www.marcprensky.com/writing/Prensky%20-%20Digital%20Natives,%20Digital%20Immigrants%20-%20Part1.Pdf

Pressley, M., & Afflerbach, P. (1995). *Verbal protocols of reading: The nature of constructively responsive reading.* Hillsdale, NJ: Erlbaum.

Rumelhart, D.E. (1978). Understanding and summarizing brief stories. In D. Laberge & S.J. Samuels (Eds.), *Basic process in reading: Perception and comprehension* (pp. 265–303). Hillsdale, NJ: Erlbaum.

Serafini, F. (2005). Voices in the park, voices in the classroom: Readers responding to postmodern picture books. *Reading Research and Instruction, 44*(3), 47–64.

Sipe, L.R. (2002). Talking back and taking over: Young children's expressive engagement during storybook read-alouds. *The Reading Teacher, 55*(5), 476–483.

Thorndyke, P. (1977). Cognitive structures in comprehension and memory of narrative discourse. *Cognitive Psychology, 9*(1), 77–110. doi:10.1016/0010-0285(77)90005-6

Veen, W., & Vrakking, B. (2006). *Homo zappiens: Growing up in a digital age.* London: Network Continuum.

Vygotsky, L.S. (1978). *Mind in society: The development of higher psychological processes* (M. Cole, V. John-Steiner, S. Scribner, & E. Souberman, Eds. & Trans.). Cambridge, MA: Harvard University Press.

CHILDREN'S LITERATURE CITED

Browne, A. (1998). *Voices in the park*. New York: Dorling Kindersley.

Child, L. (2003). *Who's afraid of the big bad book?* New York: Hyperion.

Gravett, E. (2006). *Wolves*. New York: Simon & Schuster.

Lehman, B. (2004). *The red book*. Boston: Houghton Mifflin.

Macaulay, D. (1990). *Black and white*. Boston: Houghton Mifflin.

Muntean, M. (2006). *Do not open this book!* New York: Scholastic.

Sciezska, J., & Smith, L. (1992). *The stinky cheese man and other fairly stupid tales*. New York: Scholastic.

Watt, M. (2007). *Chester*. New York: Kids Can Press.

Whatley, B. (2001). *Wait! No paint!* New York: HarperCollins.

Wiesner, D. (2001). *The three pigs*. New York: Clarion.

Wiesner, D. (2006). *Flotsam*. New York: Clarion.

Wilcox, L. (2003). *Falling for Rapunzel*. New York: Putnam.

SUGGESTED POSTMODERN PICTURE BOOKS FOR CLASSROOM USE

Child, L. (2003). *Who's afraid of the big bad book?* New York: Hyperion.

Gravett, E. (2006). *Wolves*. New York: Simon & Schuster.

Jeffers, O. (2006). *The incredible book eating boy*. New York: Philomel.

Kanninen, B. (2007). *A story with pictures*. New York: Holiday House.

Lehman, B. (2004). *The red book*. Boston: Houghton Mifflin.

Lendler, I. (2005). *An undone fairy tale*. New York: Simon & Schuster.

Macaulay, D. (1995). *Shortcut*. New York: Houghton Mifflin.

Muntean, M. (2006). *Do not open this book!* New York: Scholastic.

Watt, M. (2007). *Chester*. New York: Kids Can Press.

Wiesner, D. (2001). *The three pigs*. New York: Clarion.

Wiesner, D. (2006). *Flotsam*. New York: Clarion.

CHAPTER 4

Discovering the Many Layers in Nonfiction Books: An Author's View

James Cross Giblin

A nonfiction book is like a rock formation: The deeper you dig into it, the more layers you find. In rock formations, the layers form a record of geological time, in a book, they reveal different aspects of the topic and different levels of meaning.

Sometimes the multiple layers of nonfiction texts are relatively easy to uncover, but other times the layers may not be so transparent. For instance, the layers may be more immediately apparent in a longer book directed toward upper elementary students. For example, in *The Life and Death of Adolf Hitler* (Giblin, 2002), at the surface layer, this book is a biography of the Nazi leader from his birth in a remote Austrian village to his suicide in a bunker deep under war-torn Berlin. However, at a deeper layer it's also a history of his times, including World War I, in which Hitler served as a private in the German army; the Weimar Republic, which proved a breeding ground for his Nazi party in the 1920s; and World War II, which Hitler launched in Europe, and persisted in fighting long after defeat was inevitable.

Another important layer in the book depicts the rising tide of German anti-Semitism under the Nazis, culminating in the horrors of the Holocaust.

In contrast, the textual layers may not be as obvious in a shorter book written for early elementary-age children. But all nonfiction books have layers; you just have to know how to look for them. In this chapter, I will explore in some detail the different layers in two books I've written for younger children, *Secrets of the Sphinx* (Giblin, 2004) and *The Many Rides of Paul Revere* (Giblin, 2007).

Finding the Layers in *Secrets of the Sphinx*

I was drawn to the first subject—as I've been with all of my nonfiction books—because I wanted to find out more about the Sphinx for myself. The gigantic statue with a lion's body and a man's head was pretty much of a mystery to me, and I figured it would also be a mystery to the book's readers.

Children's Literature in the Reading Program: An Invitation to Read (third edition), edited by Deborah A. Wooten and Bernice E. Cullinan. © 2009 by James Cross Giblin. Published by the International Reading Association.

The various layers in the topic emerged, as they always do, during the course of the research. The top layer, of course, is the overall history of the Sphinx. The chronicle begins when the statue was carved out of living rock more than 4,500 years ago, and continues down to the present day.

But as I delved deeper into the material, I realized there were many other layers I would need to explore—and many questions I would need to answer. Putting myself in the place of the reader, I asked, Who built the Sphinx, and why? What does it mean? And how did its builders, using primitive tools, manage to shape and carve such a towering monument?

To answer these questions and place the Sphinx in context, I began with a brief history of ancient Egypt up to the time the statue was carved. Next I introduced the idea that the lion had long been a symbol of strength in ancient art. But apparently the Egyptians were the first to combine the body of a lion with the head of a man. And not just any man—scholars believe it was the head of the pharaoh who ruled Egypt at the time the Sphinx was made. Perhaps the combination was meant to suggest the pharaoh possessed the power of a lion.

An investigation of the people who carved the statue and built the nearby pyramids provided another fascinating layer in the story. For a long time, people thought the workers must have been slaves. But archaeologists have recently unearthed the remains of a large settlement of mud brick houses near the monuments. The archaeologists estimate that as many as 1,000 skilled craftsmen lived with their families in the settlement.

The craftsmen weren't the only workers who labored on the Sphinx and the pyramids. Close by the settlement, the archaeologists have found the remains of barracks-like buildings. They believe these structures housed the unskilled laborers who carried out the instruc-

tions of the craftsmen. At any given time, it is thought there were 5,000–7,000 such laborers living in the military-style barracks.

The recent archaeological digs helped to answer other questions about who carved the Sphinx, how they did it, and injuries they suffered during the course of their work. In a cemetery near the workers' settlement, archaeologists have found well-preserved skeletal remains. Many of the skeletons showed evidence of fractures in the arms and legs. The scholars believe the fractures occurred as a result of falls from high platforms on which the laborers stood as they worked on the pyramids and the Sphinx.

What's especially interesting is that most of the fractures had healed completely, with full realignment of the broken bones. This indicates that the workers received good medical care, and that the fractures were set with splints. It's concrete details like this that nonfiction writers dream of finding. They not only enrich the text, but also help to bring the topic to life for readers.

Myths and legends often play a role in historical subjects. Several of them figure in the story of the Sphinx, adding another intriguing layer to the book. One of these legends involves Egyptian Prince Thutmose, who lived more than a thousand years after the statue was carved. One day the prince was hunting in the desert near the Sphinx and, fatigued by the hot sun, he decided to rest for a while in the shadow of the statue. The prince dozed off, and in his sleep he imagined he heard the voice of the Sphinx. Over the centuries, the statue had become half-buried in sand. Now it told the prince, "Behold, I am ailing in all my limbs and my entire body is in pain. For the sand of the desert presses in upon me from every side. I am waiting for you to do what must be done, for I know that you are my champion...." At that point, according to the legend, the prince woke up. But he was still conscious of the Sphinx's words, and determined to do something about its plight.

No one knows how much of this legend is true. But it *is* true that as soon as Thutmose became pharaoh in 1401 BCE, he ordered that the sand surrounding the Sphinx be cleared away. Now the giant creature was revealed once more in all of its strength and majesty.

Thutmose valued the Sphinx, but many others who encountered the statue in the centuries that followed did not. Some of these people threatened its very existence. They were aided by natural forces that menaced the statue in different, but no less destructive, ways. Together these human and environmental enemies injected a layer of suspense into the chronicle of the Sphinx.

For example, when Arabs from the Middle East conquered Egypt in the 7th century CE they tried to get the Egyptians to embrace the Muslim faith. The Sphinx was worshipped by the Egyptians as a symbol of the nation's power, so the Arabs tried to weaken the statue's influence—it was too big to dismantle, but some found other ways to attack it. They used hammers and chisels to knock off the Sphinx's nose and part of its upper lip. They thought the damage would make the Sphinx unrecognizable, but many Egyptians still came to bow in prayer before it.

Other challenges to the statue have occurred more recently, and one of them involves another legend—the story of the lost continent of Atlantis. The idea of a sunken continent somewhere in the Atlantic Ocean had been circulating for centuries. The ancient Greek philosopher Plato claimed it was a large island, bigger than North Africa and the Middle East combined. According to Plato, Atlantis was the home of a rich and powerful empire until disaster struck in about 10,000 BCE. The huge island was hit first by a tremendous volcanic eruption and then by a tidal wave and flood. Hundreds of thousands of its inhabitants were killed, and the entire continent sank beneath the sea.

Many scientific investigations have been conducted on the sea floor of the Atlantic Ocean, but no evidence of Atlantis has ever been found. However, that didn't stop an American eccentric, Edgar Cayce, from claiming not only that the continent existed, but that it had a strong connection to ancient Egypt. Cayce, who lived from 1877 to 1945, believed that well-educated refugees from Atlantis had somehow found their way to the Nile Valley and had laid the groundwork for Egypt's advanced civilization. Cayce, who also believed in reincarnation, was convinced that he himself was the reincarnation of the high priest of Atlantis, Ra-Ta.

What does this have to do with threats to the Sphinx today? Quite a lot, as a matter of fact. Cayce has been dead for more than 60 years, but he has a large band of followers who continue to believe in his ideas. One of the most potent is the notion that architects from Atlantis designed and constructed the pyramids and the Sphinx.

According to Cayce, the Sphinx was also chosen as the hiding place for the priceless documents the refugees had brought with them from the lost continent. These books and papers recounted the history of Atlantis, its religious beliefs, and the secrets of its advanced civilization. They were buried, Cayce said, in an underground chamber between the Sphinx's paws. Cayce left specific instructions on how to reach the chamber, and his followers have taken the instructions seriously. Starting in the 1970s, they conducted investigations of the area around the Sphinx and made exploratory drillings into the rock beneath its paws. In the mid-1990s, the Egyptian government stepped in. They put a stop to all the probes and drillings, fearing they might undermine the statue. Cayce's followers protested, but the government refused to lift the ban.

In addition, the Egyptian authorities had to contend with other, more long-range threats to the Sphinx. Most of them have to do with the environment. Fierce desert winds have torn chips and larger pieces off the statue's limestone surface. Erosion from sudden storms has eaten away at its base. Air pollution from the ever-growing city of Cairo is a serious new menace.

How Egyptian scientists have struggled to fight these threats and safeguard the future of the Sphinx provides the final layer in the narrative. As a result of their efforts, badly damaged sections on the flanks of the Sphinx have been replaced with new stone slabs. Today, the statue's future looks brighter that it has in years.

Finding the Layers in *The Many Rides of Paul Revere*

While some might call *Secrets of the Sphinx* (Giblin, 2004) the biography of a statue, *The Many Rides of Paul Revere* (Giblin, 2007) fits the more traditional description of a biography. It offers a rounded portrait of the Revolutionary War hero who was made famous by Henry Wadsworth Longfellow's renowned poem "Paul Revere's Ride." Each of the different layers in the biography adds to our understanding of Revere the man and the forces that shaped his character and actions.

The text does not begin with the focus on Revere, however. Instead, it opens with the story of his father, Apollos Rivoire. Apollos arrived in Boston in 1716 as a boy of 13, a young Protestant immigrant fleeing the conflict between Catholics and Protestants in his native France. Apprenticed to a silversmith, Apollos learned every aspect of his craft, and when his apprenticeship was over, he opened

his own shop. But he didn't use the name Apollos Rivoire in the newspaper ad that announced the opening. Instead, the ad listed the shop's owner as Paul Revere, the English equivalent of his French name. Like many other immigrants to America before and since, Apollos had adopted his new name because it was easier for his friends and customers to pronounce.

Besides providing background information about Paul Revere's father, Apollos's story introduces an important additional layer in the narrative—the fact that immigration played a key role in the growth of America from the very beginning. It also helps to explain why young Paul followed in his father's footsteps and became a silversmith.

However, before becoming a silversmith, Paul went to school, as discussed in the following passage:

> When it came time to send Paul to school, his father had two choices. Paul could go to a Latin, or grammar, school which prepared its students for Harvard and other colleges. Or, like most sons of craftsmen, he could go to a writing school which would teach him the basic skills he would need in business.
>
> Mr. Revere chose the second type, and enrolled six-year-old Paul in the North Writing School on Love Lane. There he attended reading classes on the first floor and writing classes on the second. His fellow students were all boys. In Paul's day, few girls went to school, and many women signed their names with just an "X."
>
> Paul's formal education ended when he was twelve. That was the age when most boys left school and became apprentices to master craftsmen. In Paul's case, that meant joining his father in his workshop and learning how to be a silversmith. (pp. 3–5)

These few paragraphs give readers a sense not just of Paul's basic education, but also of how schools in Boston and other cities were organized in pre–Revolutionary America. In doing so, they inject another layer into the narrative, and lead naturally to the next one: Paul's step-by-step training in how to make useful and beautiful objects of silver.

His training came in handy when Paul's father died suddenly in 1754, leaving Paul, age 19, and his younger brother, Thomas. to carry on the work of the shop. In the next few years, Revere married a young woman named Sara Orne, and they began to raise a family. In the evenings, Paul liked to get away for an hour or two, and he joined several men's clubs. One of them was the Long Room Club, a discussion group that met at a printing shop in one of Boston's narrow alleys, as discussed in the following passage:

> There Paul got to know some of the city's leading thinkers. Among them were John Hancock, the wealthy heir to his Uncle Thomas's fortune, and Samuel Adams, who wrote political articles for Boston newspapers.
>
> Most of the members of the Long Room Club were graduates of Harvard College, whereas Paul had only finished the North Writing School. But his fellow members did not look down on Paul because he had not gone to college. Instead, they appreciated his skill as a craftsman, his clear thinking, and his willingness to work hard at whatever task he was assigned. (pp. 12–14)

This passage enabled me to introduce another level into the narrative—the free-and-easy mixing of different social classes in colonial Boston and the contrast between that society and the one we know in the United States today. In the 1700s, it wasn't uncommon for a craftsman like Paul to mingle with the leading intellectuals of his time. Today, however, so-called "blue-collar workers" rarely socialize with members of the various professions—doctors, lawyers, college professors, and the like.

Revere's conversations with Hancock, Adams, and their ilk exposed him to the revolutionary ideas that were swelling up in Boston, especially the notion that the American colonies would be better off if they separated themselves from the mother country, Great Britain. This inevitably led him to join a revolutionary organization, the Sons of Liberty, and to be a part of such historic events as the Boston Massacre. Along the way, Paul continued to produce handsome silver objects—bowls, teapots, spoons—while learning new skills to aid the revolutionary cause. For example, he taught himself how to make copper engravings from which cartoons and illustrations could be printed. In Paul's day, there were no photographs, and newspapers ran few if any illustrations. If people wanted to see a picture of a news event, they had to buy an engraving of it. Revere was not an artist, so he would trace a watercolor of a scene like the Boston Massacre, painted by a friend. Then he would transfer the tracing to a copper plate to create his engraving.

Thousands of copies of Paul's engraving of the Boston Massacre were printed, and they sold quickly throughout the colonies. As people shared the engraving with friends and relatives, the vivid illustration helped generate support for a revolution. Before the Massacre, many Americans had been angry with their British rulers. Now, looking at an accurate picture of British guards firing at unarmed American civilians, they became downright furious.

Describing the Massacre in my book and accompanying it with a reproduction of Paul's engraving gave me an opportunity to weave yet another level into Revere's story—two levels, really. First, there was Paul's almost incredible ability to learn new skills and master one trade after another—a talent he would display throughout his life. And second, there was what we might call the primitive state of the media in Paul's day, when newspapers found it almost impossible to provide readers with visual impressions of current events.

As the drive toward revolution grew stronger, Paul's association with the Sons of Liberty pointed the way toward his most famous role in the oncoming conflict. At a time when there were no railroads, let alone automobiles, buses, or airplanes, and no form of wireless communication, the sole means of spreading the news from one place to another was a man or woman riding a fast horse. Paul Revere must have been a very good rider for, starting with the Boston Tea Party in December, 1773, he became known as the "Rider for the Revolution."

"Messenger for the Revolution" might have been a better name for him, for it was Revere who carried the news of key events like the Boston Tea Party to fellow revolutionaries in New York and Philadelphia. This gave me an opportunity to describe not only Paul's specific rides but also the more general travel conditions of the time. The following excerpt from the text provides a sample of the latter:

> Starting out before dawn on a hired horse, Paul followed a route mail riders—the mailmen of their day—had carved out over the years. The dirt roads he traveled were dusty in dry weather, muddy when wet, and always rough.
>
> Along the way, Paul was glad to find taverns in many of the towns and villages through which he rode. At them he could obtain food and drink for himself, and his horse could be rubbed down, watered, and replaced if necessary. If it was late in the day, Paul could rent a room for the night.
>
> He would be back in the saddle early the next morning, ready to ride on toward his next stop. On this trip, which was about 350 miles each way, he averaged more than 60 miles a day. He rode into Boston just eleven days after he had left. (pp. 27–28)

Revere made at least seven such long-distance rides before the one for which he is best known—the Midnight Ride of April 18, 1775. That was when he rode out of Boston to alert the militias in Lexington and Concord that British troops were on the way to seize the arms the militiamen had stored. And he made at least one more ride after the militiamen clashed with the British at Concord. He raced from one New England town to another, urging men to enlist in the army General George Washington was mobilizing to fight the Revolutionary War.

Paul made another contribution to the war—one that was uniquely his own. As the fighting continued, there was a danger that the army would run out of money to pay its soldiers. Britain had always supplied the colonies with silver currency, but there weren't enough coins to meet the army's needs. The colonists decided to use paper money, or "bills of credit," as a substitute. But who could make it? The rebel leaders remembered that Paul was a master engraver as well as a silversmith and asked him to take on the job. Working from several different designs, he cut copper plates similar to those he had made for his cartoons and printed enough paper money to fill the army's orders.

Most people don't know what happened to Paul Revere after the Revolution or what contributions he made to the new nation—the United States—that emerged from the struggle. I didn't either before I researched the book. What I discovered served to round out Revere's story. It also added a final layer of meaning to his biography.

Before the Revolution, Great Britain forbade the colonies from setting up factories to manufacture goods like stoves and firearms and plows. Instead, Americans had to import all such items from the mother country, while at the same time supplying Great Britain with agricultural products and timber.

After the war, American entrepreneurs moved quickly to build factories to replace the goods they had previously imported with products made in America. Paul Revere was in the forefront of this trend. During the war, he had learned to make armaments—gunpowder, cannons, and so forth—to supply Washington's forces with the weapons they needed in their fight against the British. Now he applied what he had learned to peacetime purposes.

First he studied how to make church bells, and within a few years he was supplying churches in Boston and throughout New England with bells from his foundry. Later he saw that there was a need for sheet copper, and he invested almost all of his savings in building a rolling mill to produce it. His gamble paid off, and soon sheet copper from his mill was being used in the manufacture of everything from the domes of public buildings to the bottoms of sailing ships.

Weaving the Layers Together

In this chapter, I've discussed the various layers embedded in *Secrets of the Sphinx* (Giblin, 2004) and *The Many Rides of Paul Revere* (Giblin, 2007), but my job as an author was not to single out the layers. As an author, my job is to weave those layers together in what I hope to be a seamless whole—a whole that would catch the attention of readers on the first page and hold it until the last.

That's not the end of the story, though, or the end of the discovery of new layers in the two books. Since their publication, many teachers of Social Studies and American History have introduced the books to their students. Some of the teachers have unearthed layers in the texts that I never suspected were there.

For example, one teacher wrote to tell me she had used the text of *Secrets of the Sphinx* (Giblin, 2004) in combination with Bagram Ibatoulline's brilliant illustrations to discuss the basic concepts of Egyptian art and architecture with her classes. Another teacher whom I met at a conference said she'd woven Paul Revere's experience as an engraver of paper money into a social studies unit on the history of money and banking in America.

As the books continue their travels, I expect to hear of more such discoveries. That's one of the special pleasures of writing nonfiction for children. The circle begins with what the author researches and writes. But it isn't complete until the books are published and go out to reviewers, librarians, teachers, parents, and young readers, each of whom may find different meanings in the material. When their findings reach the author in the form of feedback, the circle is finally complete.

CHILDREN'S LITERATURE CITED

Giblin, J.C. (2002). *The life and death of Adolf Hitler*. New York: Clarion.

Giblin, J.C. (2004). *Secrets of the sphinx*. New York: Scholastic.

Giblin, J.C. (2007). *The many rides of Paul Revere*. New York: Scholastic.

SUGGESTED NONFICTION BOOKS

Aronson, M. (2000). *Sir Walter Ralegh and the quest for El Dorado*. New York: Clarion.

Bolden, T. (2007). *M.L.K.: Journey of a king*. New York: Abrams.

Freedman, R. (2004). *The voice that challenged a nation: Marian Anderson and the struggle for equal rights*. New York: Clarion.

Freedman, R. (2007). *Who was first? Discovering the Americas*. New York: Holiday House.

Giblin, J.C. (2000). *The amazing life of Benjamin Franklin*. New York: Scholastic.

Hoose, P. (2004). *The race to save the Lord God bird*. New York: Farrar, Straus and Giroux.

Jenkins, S. (2007). *Living color.* Boston: Houghton Mifflin.

Lasky, K. (2003). *The man who made time travel.* New York: Farrar, Straus and Giroux.

McClafferty, C. (2006). *Something out of nothing: Marie Curie and radium.* New York: Farrar, Straus and Giroux.

Murphy, J. (2003). *An American plague: The true and terrifying story of the yellow fever epidemic of 1793.* New York: Clarion.

CHAPTER 5

Yes, Poetry Can!

David L. Harrison

"A Poem Begins"

A poem begins
with a question,
a thought about
whether to write it
(or whether to not),
but while you're engaged
in debating the whether,
words, like a current,
start flowing together.
Something is working:
A simile teases
a giggle that tickles,
a rhythm that pleases.
A metaphor roars
with delight at the thought
that you've written a poem—
ready or not!

—David L. Harrison

In his book of essays, *Can Poetry Matter?*, Dana Gioia (1992) reports that nearly a thousand new collections of verse are published each year and that public poetry readings are at an all-time high, probably numbering in the tens of thousands. Gioia, who is chairman of the National Endowment for the Arts, is speaking about poetry for adult audiences, but a parallel growth in poets and poetry is occurring in the realm of children's literature. In *Poetry People*, Sylvia Vardell

(2007) features 62 primarily contemporary poets who write for children, plus a number of emerging poets in the field. As surely as poetry influences our literature, it belongs in the classroom!

Why Poets and Why Poetry?

Poets love the challenge of seeking words that best convey their meaning. The poet's goal is to write big by writing small. Poets savor the taste and smell of words and love similes that bring together surprising comparisons to make a point. A metaphor, like a picture, may be worth a thousand words. Painting pictures with words, poets invite us to make our own associations. Every word carries in its genes— when used in the right way, the right time, the right place—the potential to stir the human spirit. A poem is proof that someone tried to get it right.

Karla Kuskin (in Cullinan, 1996, p. 17), writes, "If there were a recipe for a poem, these would be the ingredients: word sounds, rhythm, description, feeling, memory, rhyme and imagination. They can be put together a thousand different ways, a thousand, thousand...more." Wallace Stevens says that the purpose of poetry is to "contribute to man's happiness" (in Gioia, 1992, p. 16). Shel

Children's Literature in the Reading Program: An Invitation to Read (third edition), edited by Deborah A. Wooten and Bernice E. Cullinan. © 2009 by the International Reading Association.

Silverstein's (1981) *A Light in the Attic,* a *New York Times* best seller, attracted hundreds of authors to write children's poetry. Jack Prelutsky (1983) collected 572 favorite children's poems into *The Random House Book of Poetry for Children,* a high percentage of them humorous—a reminder that children (and adults) adore reading fun material that they can easily remember.

Putting Poetry to Work

Helping children develop skills that lead to successful reading is the goal of any reading program. Can poetry matter in our efforts? Yes, poetry can. Laura Robb (2000) writes, "Poetry helps students explore important issues in content areas, issues that extend beyond the classroom into their lives, communities, and the world" (p. 6).

Thanks to the rich variety of poems available today, teachers have never had more opportunities to harness the power of poetry in their classrooms. Kids like poetry for a lot of reasons. Many poems tell a story. Good ones often use surprising, vocabulary-stretching language. Poems explore feelings and situations that young people wonder and care about. Poems inspire. They amuse. They make kids think and help them learn to reason. They connect the new with what is already experienced and understood. And yes, poems make kids happy. David McCord's "Pickety Fence" (Cullinan, 1996, p. 5) rattles off the tongue and tickles the funny bone with its rollicking noise and rhythm.

> The pickety fence
> The pickety fence
> Give it a lick it's
> The pickety fence
> Give it a lick it's
> A clickety fence
> Give it a lick it's
> A lickety fence

> Give it a lick
> Give it a lick
> Give it a lick
> With a rickety stick
> Pickety
> Pickety
> Pickety
> Pick.

"A Pickety Fence" David McCord, from Cullinan, B. (Ed.).(1996). *A Jar of Tiny Stars.* Honesdale, PA: Boyds Mills. Reprinted with permission.

Reading Poetry to Students

Reading aloud to students improves fluency, vocabulary, and comprehension. The carefully crafted language of literature, even in poems for the very young, may introduce words in context that occur rarely or not at all in conversational language or that of television. Jim Trelease (1982) states,

> Literature's words, as opposed to those of the electronic media, offer a wealth of language for children to use. Because good literature is precise, intelligent, colorful, sensitive and rich in meaning, it offers the child his best hope of expressing what he feels. (pp. 18–19)

Poetry is at its best when read aloud. It provides the teacher with a varied menu of choices that demonstrate how intonation, expression, and timing play key roles in reading and understanding our language. Laura Robb (2000) stresses another important benefit of reading poems aloud: It helps students learn to form mental pictures when teachers model their own associations with a poem.

What Poems Do Kids Like?

Asking students what sort of poems they like helps set the stage for successful experiences with poetry. A study by Ann Terry (1974) found that children's preferences were as follows:

1. Contemporary poems

2. Poems they can understand

3. Narrative poems

4. Poems with rhyme, rhythm, and sound

5. Poems that relate to their personal experiences

It's important to note that children chose contemporary poems as their top preference. The same study found that children like humor (Who doesn't?). They do not prefer haikus, and, in fact, most professional poets writing in the English language skip them. David Crystal (2005) and Robert MacNeil and William Cran (2005) remind us that new words appear and old ones disappear from our language. For example, Merriam-Webster's 2007 Word of the Year was *w00t* (Agence France-Presse, 2007), a hybrid of letters and numbers invented by gamers to convey happiness or triumph. This illustrates that language is a living thing and children intuitively migrate toward the new.

Gary Knell (in Karaim, 2007), CEO of Sesame Workshop, says that in a world characterized as a digital universe, "adults are immigrants and kids are natives" (p. 6). If we insist on feeding students a diet of only the poems we think are good for them, we run the risk of repeating history by alienating young people to poetry the same way many of us were turned off by the poems read to us by our own teachers.

Everyone Likes to Be Asked

Marci Vogel (in Harrison & Cullinan, 1999) describes her sixth graders as "Enjoying the sense of freedom" (p. 19) through poetry. Vogel brings in poems printed in her local paper and shares them with her students. Each student receives a copy, and everyone sits in a circle while Vogel leads students in an open discussion of the poem. Even though the poem was not written for young people, the students generally demonstrate a good sense of the poem's meaning, and they love it that their teacher gives them a chance to discuss grown-up writing. When we ask students how they feel about a poem, or ask them to choose poems they like and explain why, they are more likely to enjoy poetry and look forward to reading and writing poems of their own.

Adults like to be asked, too. Sometimes at workshops I read poems for adult readers without identifying the poet. One of my favorite poets is former United States Poet Laureate Ted Kooser, and at workshops I might recite "The Necktie" from *Delights & Shadows* (Kooser, 2004, p. 31).

> His hands fluttered like birds,
> each with a fancy silk ribbon
> to weave into their nest,
> as he stood at the mirror
> dressing for work, waving hello
> to himself with his hands.

Ted Kooser, "The Necktie" from *Delights & Shadows*. Copyright © 2004 by Ted Kooser. Reprinted with the permission of Copper Canyon Press (www.copper canyonpress.org).

When I ask at what grades students would understand the poem and enjoy it, I'm nearly always told that kids in grades three, four, or five would like the poem. Most teachers are surprised to learn that the poet didn't have children in mind at all. Such is the value of poetry. People of all ages can relate to and enjoy the well-turned phrase, the telling metaphor, the fundamental conditions of being human.

Involving the Reader in a Two-Way Relationship

In E.B. White's (1966) opinion, "There are never more than two persons present in the act of reading—the writer and the reader. This gives the experience of reading a sublimity and power unequaled by any other form of communication" (p. 23). This two-way relationship between writer and reader was clearly evident when, while polishing the collection of autobiographical poems for *Connecting Dots: Poems of My Journey* (Harrison, 2004), I asked for student advice. At a school in New York, I received help from several key teachers and their students in grades three through six. The teachers read the poems aloud or provided time for students to read them. Following a general discussion, students thought about each poem, composed their feelings, decided on a rating from 1 to 4, and backed that up with personal comments. My critics at the school offered frank opinions (some not very subtle) to explain why they liked or disliked the poems:

> "Funny one, DH!"
>
> "I don't like the smells in this poem."
>
> "Ah, that's so cute!"
>
> "Yuck!"
>
> "You need to make this poem longer."

Some of my poems touched on moments in my youth when I experienced feelings such as guilt, embarrassment, or curiosity about the opposite sex. Many students confided that they had those feelings too. They identified with the poems, often strongly, because they matched their own experiences. Most contemporary poems are brief and focus on the subject so young readers can readily get the point and compare what they already know with what they are reading. What makes this approach appealing is that students can respond honestly without being required to analyze poems to within an inch of their lives. Instead, students read and think about words and meaning without destroying the poem or the pleasure of reading it. After all, literature is not normally created with classroom testing in mind. When children asked David Melton how long it took him to write a book, he quoted his age: It took him, he said, a lifetime to reach the point where that particular book became possible (Melton, 2000). Former United States Poet Laureate Billy Collins (2001) laments in his poem "Introduction to Poetry" that a poem should be held up to the light and enjoyed rather than tied to a chair and beaten to find out what it means. Nancy Larrick (in Cullinan, 1987) reminds us that there is more to be learned from the living poem than from its "vivisectioned" carcass. Jon Scieszka, (2008) the first U.S. National Ambassador for Young People's Literature, says, "There is nothing sadder than making books only a school project. Reluctant readers don't want to feel like they are stupid."

Establishing Oral Reading Time for Students

Many teachers establish a routine of inviting students to read poems aloud. When Ruth Nathan taught third grade, she encouraged her students to nominate poems they wanted to recite by writing the titles of the poems on paper fish and dropping them into the "Friday Fishbowl." Each Friday, fish were drawn from the bowl and lucky students got to stand and present their poems. The program became so popular that Ruth took her students up and down the hall, giving the entire school a "Poetry Break."

There is more than simple pleasure in this kind of activity. Richard Allington (2001) reminds us in *What Really Matters for Struggling Readers: Designing Research-Based Programs* that as readers progress they not only read faster and more accurately but also read with better phrasing and intonation. The short lines and phrases of poetry lend themselves especially well to developing phrasing and intonation skills. In a system that normally grades reading fluency by some factor of speed, poetry also offers students a chance to read according to the natural rhythm of the poem, which helps foster understanding.

In *Teaching and Assessing Spelling* (Fresch & Wheaton, 2002), the authors note that "The frequency of experiences with familiar poems and stories helps students formulate and organize their developing knowledge base" (p. 117). Vicki Ogden, (in Harrison & Holderith, 2003) ended every school day with "Poetry Time" (p. 21), a 5- or 10-minute period reserved for her fifth graders to stand and recite favorite poems. The only rule was that students had to practice reading their poems ahead of time and be prepared to do a good job. Students often repeated the same poems and never tired of reading and hearing them. The program became so entrenched that Vicki had to limit the number of times a student could recite in any given week. If she forgot to hold "Poetry Time," she was in trouble with her students!

Poetry Hams

Students are often so enthusiastic about poetry that they will eagerly take any opportunity to "ham it up." On my first visit to a school in New York, I was impressed when a student ran down the hall toward the principal yelling, "Listen to this poem!" A visiting poet to Pat Werner's third-grade room would hear students tell what they liked about selected poems and then read them aloud to see if the poet approved of their rendition. In another class, fifth-grade students were acting out poems from *The Purchase of Small Secrets* (Harrison, 1998). Given an opportunity to ham it up, students love to take on the characters in poems they read. Teachers sometimes provide background music, and some go further by piecing together costumes and props and even adding a few dance steps to the routine. By bringing together words, drama, music, and dance, teachers demonstrate the diversity and relationship of the ways in which humans communicate and encourage student efforts to connect what they know with new experiences.

In the fifth-grade class at Manhattan New School, two student actors were intrigued by the poem "Meeting on a Gravel Bar" (Harrison, 1998, p. 25). These were city kids with no experience of a riverbank. My editor for that book (Bernice Cullinan, coeditor of this book) and I had discussed the likelihood that not all readers would be familiar with some of the terms in my book. Wisely, Bee let the language stand. The result? Readers were in hot pursuit of meaning. They certainly "got" the poem, which is about personal courage and determination, and they learned something about what it's like to be a boy in rural southwest Missouri. The point of literature is to share experiences and expand horizons. Being puzzled about a gravel bar didn't discourage the students. They were intrigued by the poem and became involved in it. The resulting effort added new language and imagery to their vocabulary.

Poetry Jams

You may not think of poets as being competitive, but "poetry slams" routinely draw crowds to see poets compete against one another for top honors. A variation—called a "poetry jam"—works beautifully in the classroom.

Someone reads a poem aloud. The next poem read must be connected in some way to the first. The following poem should have something in common with the second, and so on. How each poem is connected is part of the fun and challenge. (Poetry jam rules should be kept loose and friendly.) It's also where students can enjoy the act of "seeing" how the message, voice, tone, rhyme, or subject of one piece of writing can have a relationship with another.

Divide your class into small groups of two to four students. Give each group one or two collections of poetry (the same or different ones), and let someone begin. The first volunteer after the initial reading gets to explain how their group's selection is related to the first, and then that person reads the poem. Depending on the grade, you can move your poetry jam quickly or stretch it out over more than one day; that is, on Tuesday someone responds to Monday's poem.

Pairing Readers

Timothy Rasinski (2003) writes, "Oral reading performance has the potential to transform a self-conscious student into a star performer—especially when he or she is coached and given opportunities to practice" (p. 23). I employed a version of this when I was poet-in-residence at an international school in Kuala Lumpur, Malaysia. One fifth-grade girl was shaking so much she could scarcely stand beside me to read her poem to the class. Her voice was weak, she stumbled over words, her delivery was wooden, and her knees were nearly knocking. But her poem was funny!

I asked another girl in the group—a strong reader and natural performer—to buddy with the poet by adding sound effects. The girls practiced that night, and the next morning they were ready. The poet demonstrated far more composure than before. She read with greater confidence and her voice carried to the back of the room. After each line, her buddy chimed in with dramatic (rather over the top) sound effects. The audience laughed at all the right places. I was charmed by the smile on the poet's face.

Poems for Two Voices

Performing two-voice poems is a powerful way to learn (Rasinski, 2003). They give stu-dents a chance to read their own parts aloud and also read the other voices silently to keep their place in the poem. Many two-voice poems provide dramatic short stories or events that lend themselves to reading and performing. Paul Fleischman's (1988) *Joyful Noise: Poems for Two Voices* is an excellent example. *Developing Fluency Through Poems for Two Voices* (Rasinski, Fawcett, & Harrison, 2009) provides a two-voice poem for each week of the school year, accompanied by activities suggested by the poems.

When Georgia Heard (2009) was compiling her book of list poems, I was reading about frogs and the variations on frog voices in various parts of the world. My resulting poem in her book, "Frog Chorus," (Harrison, 2009) takes place in four voices: greedeep, ribbet, peep-peep, and ker-plum. In classes or workshops, I divide the group into four sections and assign each a frog sound. Like a conductor I point at the appropriate time to each corner of the "pond." The performers discover that the sounds become a kind of metered tone poem. "Frog Chorus" begins like this:

Greedeep

                                        Ker-plum

Greedeep

                                        Ker-plum

Greedeep

            Ribbet ribbet

                        Peep-peep

                                        Ker-plum

From Harrison, D. (2009). *Falling Down the Page: List Poems.* New York: Roaring Brook Press.

Consider what a classroom teacher or music teacher can do with "Frog Chorus." For example, it can be used to "leapfrog" the class into a study of frogs. Why are frogs and other amphibians in danger of becoming extinct? Pursuing reasons for amphibians' peril leads to increased awareness of ecological and environmental issues. The class could also use the poem to explore the reason some frog voices in the same species are lower than others matters—if they have love on their minds. Teachers can also exchange words for each frog sound so that the chorus becomes a gossipy group of frogs chatting, bragging, asking questions, or maybe calling for mates.

The Versatility of Poems Across Content Areas

Almost any poem suggests numerous activities that will engage students' interest. Depending on the need for theme- or subject-related poetry, there are dozens of trade book anthologies, single-poet collections, and individual poems available. Many are listed at the end of this chapter. If you are studying math, you might try *Marvelous Math* (Hopkins, 1997). For language arts, you might try *Noisy Poems* (Bennett, 1987), *Joyful Noise: Poems for Two Voices*, (Fleischman, 1988), and *All the Small Poems* (Worth, 1991). There are many good books of poetry that lend themselves to social studies, including *My Name Is Jorge on Both Sides of the River* (Medina, 1999), *Sidewalk Chalk: Poems of the City* (Weatherford, 2001), and *The Distant Talking Drum: Poems From Nigeria* (Olaleye, 1995). *Castles: Old Stone Poems* (Lewis & Dotlich, 2006) takes us on a poetic tour of ancient castles. *Poems for Teaching in the Content Areas* (Lewis & Robb, 2007) introduces 75 poems that lend themselves to history, geography, science, and math lessons. *Pirates* (Harrison, 2008) is a collection of realistic poems about the lives of pirates. *Wild Country* (Harrison, 1999) reflects on the beauties and mysteries of nature. *Sounds of Rain: Poems of the Amazon* (Harrison, 2006) presents poems inspired by the Amazon rain forest of Peru, such as "Ambassadors":

> Upstream the jungle hovers,
> leans in from either side,
> hides secrets behind vines.
> Unexpectedly, three huts perch
> along a strip of clay.
> Men stand still as trunks,
> size us up as hunters do.
> Mothers pause, smile a little,
> a courtesy to strangers on the river.
> Children laughing with their eyes
> run the bank naked or not,
> good will grinning across the water.
> They wave and we wave back
> until we turn the bend,
> carrying away the memory. (p. 23)

From Harrison, D. (2006). *Sounds of Rain: Poems of the Amazon*. Honesdale, PA: Boyds Mills.

In *Using the Power of Poetry to Teach Language Arts, Social Studies, Science, and More* (Harrison & Holderith, 2003), activities are presented to help you use poetry across the curricula throughout the year. Experienced teachers work with school librarians to bolster their own personal and classroom libraries of poetry on core subject areas. When a new unit is on the horizon, such teachers gather books germane to their subject and marinate their students in good poetry related to the subject.

Writing to Read

So far this chapter has dealt primarily with reading poetry and responding to it. However, another important strategy is to provide students with opportunities to write poems of their own. In *Three Voices* (Cullinan, Scala, & Schroder, 1995), we are reminded, "Not only is poetry excellent material for reading, but it also serves as an excellent model for writing" (p. 41; for more information on mentor texts and using texts as models for writing, see Chapter 9). The writing process itself can be dealt with in greater detail elsewhere, such as in *How to Write Poetry* (Janeczko, 1999) and *Easy Poetry Lessons That Dazzle and Delight* (Harrison & Cullinan, 1999). The point here is that most students can easily be prepared to write poems, whether in response to poems from literature, or inspired by personal memories and experiences, or written as part of content area studies.

For example, when Kathy Holderith begins a unit on the rain forest with her third-grade students, she reads poems aloud and hands out poems and books on the subject. Over a period of days she carefully builds excitement into the lesson by telling her students that after they learn enough about the rain forest each of them will select a favorite creature to study and write about in a poem. Kathy hands out a rubric for the rain forest poems and goes over the details before her students begin. The rubric provides for self-evaluation on a scale of 0 to 3 (with 3 being the highest) on these aspects of the poem: physical characteristics of the animal, habitat, food, interesting facts, title, and strong verbs. The students can't wait to get started. They are going to "get" to write a poem! Can you imagine a roomful of students thinking that writing a poem is a treat? Such is the attraction of poetry when a teacher prepares students to love it.

One of the axioms of writing is to know your subject. Another is to write about what you love. A common query posed by young people is where to find ideas. When a teacher gives students a chance to write poems about favorite topics that they have been studying, all three elements—knowledge, love, and ideas of subject—merge into one creative writing experience. The resulting poems can be fresh and surprising.

Nancy Raider uses a similar technique with her fifth graders. Nancy's students complete their units in social studies and science by writing poems to show off their new knowledge. The following is a poem by one of Nancy's students:

"A Different Kind of Hero"

A vision of a hero
Is a strong and brave white knight.
Requirements include
A gleaming sword with which to fight.
They gallop on white stallions,
Save damsels in distress,
Shine up their shiny armor,
Never stopping for a rest.
While these visions are quite lovely,
If you open up your eyes
And take a little look around you,
You're sure in for a surprise.
For the real heroes don't wear armor
Or steal a dragon's hoard.
Instead, they're dressed in camouflage,
And the damsels have climbed aboard.
Dedicated to all our heroes in Iraq
—Lillian, grade 5

To Rhyme or Not to Rhyme?

I mention this because the rather Shakespearian dilemma (to rhyme or not to rhyme) comes up often, particularly when a teacher is uncomfortable with verse and tends to steer students toward free verse. It's worth noting that in *The Random House Book of Poetry for Children* (Prelutsky, 1983) about 95 of every 100 poems in the collection rhyme. Children love rhyme. For many children, a natural response to hearing poems that rhyme is to want to write their own poems that rhyme. One key benefit of writing poems in verse is its positive impact on spelling skills. Mary Jo Fresch and Aileen Wheaton (2002) point out in their research findings, "When designing activities for young spellers, rhyme and word play is an effective and fun way to reinforce letter/sounds within words" (p. 114). This is noteworthy because each skill reinforces the other. Poets often make lists of words with the same sound when they are seeking just the "right" one to complete their rhyme. Young poets employing this technique are at the same time reinforcing both their sense of sound and spelling.

The Picture Book Connection

A good way to model verse for the younger set is to read aloud from rhyming picture books. Some, such as *Brown Bear, Brown Bear, What Do You See?* (Martin, 1967), *When Cows Come Home* (Harrison, 2001), *Farmer's Garden* (Harrison, 2003), and *Farmer's Dog Goes to the Forest: Rhymes for Two Voices* (Harrison, 2005), are told in a series of rhyming verses. You can brainstorm with your class to compose additional verses to go with the story and then let students make up their own verses. I'm invariably impressed that primary-grade children can so quickly pick up the pattern, rhythm, rhyme, and idea of what they hear modeled.

Ruth Culham (2004; Culham & Coutu, 2008) relates that by passing out some of her favorite picture books, her class began to notice what made the writing in those books so powerful: "A great lead, delicious words, logical organization, powerful voice, fluid sentences, and fully developed ideas. Discovering the traits of writing in picture books breathed new life into our writing endeavors" (2004, p. 4).

Revising

I tell students that real writing takes place after the first rough draft. Anyone can slap something down. That's more or less how adult writers begin too. A draft can turn into writing only if the poet takes the time to revise and polish the effort. As Kathy Holderith (Harrison & Holderith, 2003) reminds us, "Creativity takes time" (p. 24).

I don't stress this point too heavily, but I assure students that it's important that they understand there is only one way to make writing get better: by revising. Something else is taking place as a student rereads his work, thinks about it, questions it, clarifies it, and refines it into a final poem. As Roger Rosenblatt (2002) says in his essay, *A Writer's Mind*, "A writer writes to discover what he or she thinks" (¶ 5). I tell kids that too. I tell them the more they revise, the smarter they sound.

A good way to help students learn to revise is to organize the process for them so that they have tangible goals. Students are more likely to buy in to the act of revision when you establish the expectation that their poems (and other writing) will be composed and improved in a series of steps. Here's one scenario:

1: Select a subject.
(Nearly *anything* will do!)

2: Write a rough draft.
(Get something down. The mind can't revise a blank page.)

3: Read the draft aloud; listen and think about how it sounds.
(Is it interesting? Does it need more "oomph"? Make notes.)

4: Substitute stronger or more specific nouns where possible.
("Finches singing" beats "birds singing.")

5: Search for interesting verbs.
("Finches trilling" beats "finches singing.")

6: Eliminate adverbs that add no meaning.
("Wet" beats "awfully wet.")

7: Keep only those adjectives that make a difference.
("Elephant" beats "gray elephant.")

8: Add language that creates images.
("Geese squabbling like kids at recess" beats "geese squabbling.")

9: Polish the rough spots where the reader stumbles or the meaning seems unclear.
(Reading aloud beats reading silently.)

10: Read the final poem to an audience.
(Celebrate the accomplishment!)

Modeling poetry by reading it aloud to students is endlessly fascinating, instructive, and informative. When students read good poetry, they improve their fluency, comprehension, and phonemic awareness skills while internalizing the elegance of well-phrased

written expression. The brevity of most poetry helps student writers focus on what they
want to say, and how. It took nine words to say
what I wanted in this poem from *bugs: poems
about creeping things* (Harrison, 2007, p. 10).

"A tick's friends"

A tick has
no
friends.
Therefore
my
story
ends.

From Harrison, D. (2007). *bugs: poems about creeping
things*. Honesdale, PA: Boyds Mills.

Can Poetry Matter?

A growing number of teachers are routinely using poetry to develop a range of student skills
from reading fluency and comprehension to a
greater appreciation and love of language. Few
forms of literature are as flexible, encouraging,
and forgiving to youthful efforts at reading and
writing poetry. To return to the beginning of
this chapter, as surely as poetry influences our
literature, it belongs in our classrooms. So, can
poetry matter? Yes, poetry can!

REFERENCES

Agence France-Presse. (2007, December 12). *"w00t"
voted Merriam-Webster's word of the year.* San
Francisco: Author. Retrieved May 7, 2009, from
afp.google.com/articleALeqM5ileUwltWfWTY4
wpRO8Ak67PixHfQ

Allington, R.L. (2001). *What really matters for struggling readers: Designing research-based programs.*
New York: Addison Wesley Higher Education.

Crystal, D. (2005). *How language works: How babies
babble, words change meaning, and languages live
or die.* London: Penguin.

Culham, R. (2004). *Using picture books to teach writing with the traits, grades 3 & up.* New York:
Scholastic.

Culham, R., & Coutu, R. (2008). *Using picture books
to teach writing with the traits, K–2.* New York:
Scholastic.

Cullinan, B.E. (Ed.). (1987). *Children's literature in
the reading program.* Newark, DE: International
Reading Association.

Cullinan, B.E., Scala, M., & Schroder, V. (1995).
*Three voices, an invitation to poetry across the cur-
riculum.* Portland, ME: Stenhouse.

Fresch, M.J., & Wheaton, A. (2002). *Teaching and
assessing spelling.* New York: Scholastic.

Gioia, D. (1992). *Can poetry matter? Essays on
Poetry and American Culture.* Saint Paul, MN:
Gray Wolf.

Harrison, D., & Cullinan, B. (1999). *Easy poetry lessons that dazzle and delight.* New York:
Scholastic.

Harrison, D., & Holderith, K. (2003). *Using the
power of poetry to teach language arts, social studies,
science, and more.* New York: Scholastic.

Janeczko, P. (1999). *How to write poetry.* New York:
Scholastic.

Karaim, R. (2007, December 16). *A new era in play.*
McLean, VA: USA Weekend.

Lewis, P., & Robb, L. (2007). *Poems for teaching in
the content areas.* New York: Scholastic.

Melton, D. (2000). *Speaking at the children's literature festival.* Warrensburg, MO: University of
Central Missouri.

Rasinski, T. (2003). *The fluent reader: Oral reading
strategies for building word recognition, fluency, and
comprehension.* New York: Scholastic.

Rasinski, T., Fawcett, G., & Harrison, D. (2009).
Developing fluency through poems for two voices.
New York: Scholastic.

Robb, L. (2000). *Teaching reading in middle school.*
New York: Scholastic.

Rosenblatt, R. (2002). *A writer's mind.* New York:
The New York Times. Retrieved May 7, 2009, from
www.pbs.org/newshour/essays/jan-june02writers
_1-17.html

Scieszka, J. (2008, March 30). Message posted to
www.englishcompanion.com/catenet/catenet.
html

Terry, C.A. (1974). Children's poetry preferences: A
national survey of upper elementary grades. Urbana,
IL: National Council of Teachers of English.

Trelease, J. (1982). *The read-aloud handbook*. New York: Penguin.

Vardell, S. (2007). *Poetry people: A practical guide to children's poets*. Westport, CT: Libraries Unlimited.

White, E.B. (1966). *An E.B. White reader*. New York: Harper & Row.

CHILDREN'S LITERATURE CITED

Bennett, J. (1987). *Noisy poems*. Oxford, England: Oxford University Press.

Collins, B. (2001). *Sailing alone around the room: New and selected poems*. New York: Random House.

Cullinan, B.E. (Ed.).(1996). *A jar of tiny stars*. Honesdale, PA: Boyds Mills.

Fleischman, P. (1988). *Joyful noise: Poems for two voices*. New York: Laura Geringer.

Harrison, D. (1998). *The purchase of small secrets*. Honesdale, PA: Boyds Mills.

Harrison, D. (1999). *Wild country*. Honesdale, PA: Boyds Mills.

Harrison, D. (2001). *When cows come home*. Honesdale, PA: Boyds Mills.

Harrison, D. (2001). *Farmer's garden*. Honesdale, PA: Boyds Mills.

Harrison, D. (2004). *Connecting dots: Poems of my journey*. Honesdale, PA: Boyds Mills.

Harrison, D. (2005). *Farmer's dog goes to the forest: Rhymes for two voices*. Honesdale, PA: Boyds Mills.

Harrison, D. (2006). *Sounds of rain: Poems of the Amazon*. Honesdale, PA: Boyds Mills.

Harrison, D. (2007). *bugs: poems about creeping things*. Honesdale, PA: Boyds Mills.

Harrison, D. (2008). *Pirates*. Honesdale, PA: Boyds Mills.

Harrison, D. (2009). *Falling down the page: List poems*. New York: Roaring Brook.

Heard, G. (2009). *Falling down the page: A book of list poems*. New York: Roaring Brook.

Hopkins, L.B. (1997). *Marvelous math: A book of poems*. New York: Simon & Schuster.

Kooser, T. (2004). *Delights & shadows*. Port Townsend, WA: Copper Canyon Press.

Lewis, J., & Dotlich, R. (2006). *Castles: Old stone poems*. Honesdale, PA: Boyds Mills.

MacNeil, R., & Cran, W. (2005). *Do you speak American?* New York: Doubleday.

Martin, B., Jr. (1967). *Brown bear, brown bear what do you see?* New York: Holt.

Medina, J. (1999). *My name is Jorge on both sides of the river*. Honesdale, PA: Boyds Mills.

Olaleye, I. (1995). *The distant talking drum: Poems from Nigeria*. Honesdale, PA: Boyds Mills.

Prelutsky, J. (1983). *The Random House book of poetry for children*. New York: Random House.

Silverstein, S. (1981). *A light in the attic*. New York: Harper & Row.

Weatherford, C. (2001). *Sidewalk chalk: Poems of the city*. Honesdale, PA: Boyds Mills.

Worth, V. (1991). *All the small poems*. New York: Sunburst.

SUGGESTED POETRY BOOKS

Bishop, R.S. (Ed.). (2000). *Wonders: The best children's poems of Effie Lee Newsome*. Honesdale, PA: Boyds Mills.

Ciardi, J. (2002). *Someone could win a polar bear*. Honesdale, PA: Boyds Mills.

Creech, S. (2001). *Love that dog*. New York: HarperCollins.

Dotlich, R.K. (2006). *What is science?* New York: Henry Holt.

Fletcher, R. (2005). *A writing kind of day: Poems for young poets*. Honesdale, PA: Boyds Mills.

Harley, A. (2001). *Leap into poetry: More ABCs of poetry*. Honesdale, PA: Boyds Mills.

Harrison, D. (2003). *The alligator in the closet: And other poems around the house*. Honesdale, PA: Boyds Mills.

Harrison, D. (2003). *The mouse was out at recess*. Honesdale, PA: Boyds Mills.

Heard, G. (1992). *Creatures of earth, sea, and sky*. Honesdale, PA: Boyds Mills.

Heard, G. (2002). *This place I know: Poems of comfort*. Somerville, MA: Candlewick.

High, L.O. (2004). *City of snow: The great blizzard of 1888*. New York: Walker & Company.

Marsalis, W. (2005). *Jazz A-B-Z*. Somerville, MA: Candlewick.

Micklos, J., Jr. (Ed.). (2001). *Mommy poems.* Honesdale, PA: Boyds Mills.

Scieszka, J. (2004). *Science verse.* New York: Viking.

Smith, C. (2004). *Hoop kings.* Somerville, MA: Candlewick.

Yolen, J. (2000). *Color me a rhyme: Nature poems for young people.* Honesdale, PA: Boyds Mills.

Yolen, J. (2007). *Shape me a rhyme: Nature's forms in poetry.* Honesdale, PA: Boyds Mills.

CHAPTER 6

Series Books for Young Readers: Seeking Reading Pleasure and Developing Reading Competence

Anne McGill-Franzen

For more than one hundred years, serialized fiction has hooked readers and kept them reading. Often considered anathema to teachers and librarians, or "light" reading at best, series books have been part of the literary landscape since the 1880s. Given the ubiquity of series books, it is surprising that few people have taken a serious look at what makes them attractive or their effects on readers. Catherine Sheldrick Ross (1995), a Canadian university professor in the library sciences and scholar of readers' preferences, is one of the few who has written extensively on "what makes readers and keeps them reading" (p. 201).

In this chapter, I first present a brief history of series books and the role that series books have played in the lives of avid readers, based in large part upon research by Ross (1995). Contrary to assumptions held by many librarians and educators, series books actually whet the appetite for reading and lead to deeper connections with the literary experience. Although the characters and authors have changed over the years, I present in sections that follow bookselling data that demonstrate

series books remain as popular as ever and speculate on reasons why that might be so. I identify several reasons why readers seek series books for pleasure—the comfort of the familiar and the desire to be part of a community of readers who share delight in particular stories, characters, or language. In seeking and reading series books for pleasure, novice readers consolidate word fluency and build vocabulary and comprehension skills, and I use as examples excerpts from several series popular today to demonstrate how these texts support the development of reading competence.

A Brief History of Series Books

"Dime novels" (Ross, 1995, p. 211), so-called because they were cheaply made and printed, were the predecessors of series books. Beadle and Adams, famous dime novel publishers of the era, published a new novel every couple of weeks in a numbered series. Similar to the experiences of series authors today, dime novelists would be given a title, plot, and other

Children's Literature in the Reading Program: An Invitation to Read (third edition), edited by Deborah A. Wooten and Bernice E. Cullinan. © 2009 by the International Reading Association.

specifications by the publisher and asked to quickly compose the story. In a historical review of the emergence of "reading for pleasure," Ross (1995) suggests that dime novels and other serialized materials democratized pleasure reading. Previously relegated to reading a few religious texts and the Bible, the "masses" obtained access to secular fiction materials because of the cheaper processes for printing and distribution during the latter part of the 19th century (p. 210). Ross cites several historical accounts of the way that "story papers," "dime novels," and "cheap libraries" opened up reading for pleasure to those who had not read before.

As Ross (1995) explains, this system was perfected by Edward Stratemeyer whose Stratemeyer Syndicate extended the audience for serialized fiction to juveniles. Stratemeyer and anonymous writers created dozens of series for children, including the long-running and still available Nancy Drew and Hardy Boys books, and provided a model for today's series books—formulaic school stories, family stories, science fiction, detective stories, and mysteries. Although librarians and literature experts of the day disparaged the literary quality of series books, an early 20th century American Library Association survey demonstrated that young readers—then as now—overwhelmingly preferred them (Soderbergh, 1980; cited in Ross, 1995, p. 219).

Reading for Pleasure

In an ethnography of reading recently published by Libraries Unlimited, Ross and her colleagues (Ross, McKechnie, & Rothbauer, 2005) explore avid readers' perceptions of the reading experience and what may have influenced them to become readers. Ross conducted more than 142 open-ended interviews with avid readers over several years, and she found that series books led almost every one of them into reading for pleasure. The following reader's response was typical of what Ross (1995) calls "committed readers"—those who identify reading for pleasure as a very important part of their lives (p. 216):

> The first book that I distinctly remember reading would probably have to be *The Enchanted Forest* by Enid Blyton. It's about these kids that go into a forest and they go up this tree, and there's different worlds at the top of this tree.... The next book would have been *The Magic Faraway Tree* which was a continuation of that story. My grandmother had a whole closet full of Enid Blyton books—the original hard cover, all dusty and yellow. (p. 218)

The story line of the Enid Blyton series evokes a familiar motif—both the Chronicles of Narnia series by C.S. Lewis and the Magic Tree House series by Mary Pope Osborne share plot and setting elements with Blyton's work.

Ross (1995) asked the adult readers in her study what made series books so pleasurable for them as children and adolescents. Two themes emerged from their responses. First was the "reassurance of the familiar" that supported novice readers, and the second, identification of the reader with not only the characters but also other readers of the series. Ross (1995) points out that although we think of reading as a solitary activity, readers describe series book reading "as a social activity embedded in the social relations of childhood. Series books have the cachet of something precious, to be collected, hoarded, discussed, and...'traded like baseball cards'" (p. 226). As one reader put it, "I read them just because everybody else was" (p. 224), and another, "I read [all the series books] I could get my hands on!"(p. 224).

Series Books Today— As Popular as Ever

R.L. Stine and his wildly popular Goosebumps series of the 1990s did much to rekindle interest in and arguments about the worth of series books and whether schools and libraries should permit children to read them. The Goosebumps series, with equal portions of humor and horror, made Stine the biggest selling author in America for three years in a row, at one point selling more than 4 million copies a month (Stelter, 2008).

The Maze of Bones (Riordan, 2008), the first book of a more recent series called 39 Clues, was released in early September 2008 and immediately appeared on *The New York Times* (2008) Children's Book List for the next seven consecutive weeks. Indeed, even a cursory examination of contemporary bestselling children's books demonstrates the enduring popularity of series books. Mary Pope Osborne's Magic Tree House series and Barbara Park's Junie B. Jones series have appeared in the top 10 best-selling children's books for close to 200 weeks, and Stephenie Meyer's Twilight Saga books are fast becoming the most popular books among preadoles-

cents since J.K. Rowling's Harry Potter series (see Table 6.1).

Because of the success of series that originally targeted children in grades 3–5, authors and publishers either have extended these books to students in higher grade levels, or more frequently, developed related series that are accessible to younger or struggling readers. Dav Pilkey, author of the Captain Underpants series, later developed the Ricky Ricotta and the Mighty Robot books, a similar series written at a lower readability level (see Tables 6.2 and 6.3 for titles at a range of difficulty levels).

Similarly, Joanna Cole created the Liz books for students reading on the first- or second-grade level to capitalize on the interest generated by the more difficult Magic School Bus series (see Tables 6.4 and 6.5 for a sample of titles at different difficulty levels). For the uninitiated, Liz is a lizard and the class pet in Mrs. Frizzle's class. Like all lizards, Liz can live in many diverse environments—a recurring

TABLE 6.1
The New York Times Bestseller Series Book List

Title, Author, Synopsis, and Interest Level	Number of Weeks on Top Ten Children's Book List	Rank for Week of 11/09/08
The Twilight Saga by Stephenie Meyer Vampires and werewolves in high school (Ages 12 & up)	64 weeks	#1
Magic Tree House by Mary Pope Osborne Children travel in time (Ages 6–9)	198 weeks	#6
Redwall by Brian Jacques A battle of good and evil among mice, rats, and other woodland animals (Ages 8 & up)	49 weeks	#9
Junie B. Jones by Barbara Park Antics in the classroom (Ages 4–8)	180 weeks	#10

Note. Adapted from the *Children's Book List*, found online at www.nytimes.com/2008/11/09/books/bestseller/bestchildren.html

TABLE 6.2
Captain Underpants Series by Dav Pilkey (Interest Level: Grades 3–5)

Title	Reading Level
The Adventures of Captain Underpants	3.5
Captain Underpants and the Big, Bad Battle of the Bionic Booger Boy, Part 1: The Night of the Nasty Nostril Nuggets	3.9
Captain Underpants and the Attack of the Talking Toilets	4.2
Captain Underpants and the Preposterous Plight of the Purple Potty People	5.2

TABLE 6.3
Ricky Ricotta Series by Dav Pilkey (Interest Level: Grades K–5)

Title	Reading Level
Ricky Ricotta's Mighty Robot	1.8
Ricky Ricotta's Mighty Robot vs. the Mutant Mosquitoes From Mercury	2.2
Ricky Ricotta's Mighty Robot vs. the Jurassic Jackrabbits From Jupiter	2.4
Ricky Ricotta's Mighty Robot vs. the Uranium Unicorns	2.8

TABLE 6.4
Magic School Bus Series by Joanna Cole (Interest Level: Grades K–3)

Title	Reading Level
The Magic School Bus in the Rain Forest	2.6
The Magic School Bus Sees Stars	2.9
The Magic School Bus on the Ocean Floor	3.5
The Magic School Bus Inside a Bee Hive	3.7

TABLE 6.5
Magic School Bus Liz Books by Joanna Cole and Others
(Interest Level: Pre-K to Grade 2)

Title	Reading Level
Lightning Liz	1.5
Liz On the Move	1.7
Liz Finds a Friend	1.9
Liz Sorts It Out	2.1

theme of the Magic School Bus series. Given the range of readability now available for many popular series, at least one or two books in a series should be accessible to most readers within a particular grade level, making author or series studies a realistic option for teachers.

Indeed, the adult committed readers in Ross's (1995) ethnography spoke of moving from one set of series books to another as they matured both in interest and reading skill. The early pleasure they experienced in reading series books sustained and motivated them to dip into less familiar and more complex literature, leading them ultimately to read "classic" literature. What was comforting and appealing to young, relatively novice readers may seem trite, redundant, and formulaic to more proficient readers. However, the very redundancy and formulaic patterns of series books provides support to novice readers at every stage of literacy development—those readers who are developing automaticity in word recognition, those who are building a robust vocabulary, and those who are developing understanding and interpretation of text.

Developing Fluency and Automatic Word Recognition From Language Redundancy

A surprising finding of the comprehensive fluency studies initiated at the University of Georgia (Kuhn et al., 2006) was that wide reading of a number of different books was as effective in developing fluency among second graders as repeated readings of exactly the same text. With the repetition of names (characters' names, the names of places, and so on) and other potentially troublesome vocabulary typical of series books, it is easy to see that reading all the Ricky Ricotta and the Mighty Robot books, for example, or Magic Tree House books, would provide ample support for fluent reading. For example, Chapter 2 of *Ricky Ricotta's Mighty Robot* (Pilkey, 2000) is entitled "The Bullies." There are only 85 words in that chapter but every 12th word or so is *bullies*, as in the following passage: "This is because Ricky was very small and the bullies picked on him. "Where do you think you are going?" asked one of the bullies. Ricky did not answer. He turned and started to run. The bullies chased him..." (pp. 9–12).

Experiencing Complex Language and Challenging Vocabulary in Context

One of the most accepted ideas in educational research is that reading supports language development. Several decades ago Carol Chomsky (1972) demonstrated that experience with children's literature was the most powerful correlate of advanced language development in children from 7 to 10 years old—even more so than age, IQ, family income, or parents' education. Chomsky was speaking of children's understanding of complex syntax—embedded ideas in sentences—and many studies since then have demonstrated the contribution of wide reading to vocabulary development as well. Although much recently has been made of the importance of oral language development and children's interactions with parents (see for example, Hart & Risley, 1995), it is through reading that children and adolescents are exposed to challenging vocabulary.

Rare words, that is, words with more specialized meanings that are not likely to be used frequently, appear *as often* in preschool books as in conversations among college graduates (Hayes & Ahrens, 1988). Rare words appear slightly *more often* in children's books than in transcripts of expert witness testimony, and comic books include more than *twice as many* rare words as expert testimony. Clearly, reading a lot will give children and adolescents many more opportunities to experience vocabulary in context and many more exposures to nuanced meanings of words.

As Stahl (2003) pointed out in *American Educator,* it is through repeated encounters with a word that readers develop an idea of its meaning. He noted that prior studies found that 4 encounters with a word were not enough to learn it but 12 encounters were. Each time readers see a word in context they learn a bit more about it—Stahl explained that "words are learned incrementally over multiple exposures" (p. 18). Students who engage in wide reading will have many more exposures to challenging words and therefore many more opportunities to add to their knowledge of vocabulary.

Even though series books have a reputation for being easy, there are innumerable challenging vocabulary words presented in very rich contexts. Take, for example, this description of an interaction between Mrs. Ribble, a cranky old teacher, and the hapless principal, Mr. Krupp, taken from *Captain Underpants and the Wrath of the Wicked Wedgie Woman* (Pilkey, 2001):

> Mrs. Ribble opened the card and read inside: *"Will you marry me?" Signed Mr. Krupp.* "Eeeeeeeeeeeeeewww," cried the children. The teachers <u>gasped</u>.
> Then the room grew silent. Mrs. Ribble <u>glared</u> over at Mr. Krupp, who had turned bright red and began sweating <u>profusely.</u> (p. 46)

Noticing the Conventions of Reading for Understanding and Interpretation

Literary critic Peter Rabinowitz (1998) described the "rules of notice and signification" that are automatic for proficient readers but must be learned by the novice. Examples of some of the elements of narrative texts that proficient readers notice are the titles of chapters in a book, phrases or words that are repeated, the dialogue or dialect that a character speaks, and typographical features like italics or capital letters that signify flashbacks, change in point of view, or speaker's tone. Although automatic and invisible, these rules enable understanding and interpretation of narratives. Because series books are formulaic and inherently highly patterned, many of the conventions of reading are made explicit to the novice, thereby easing the transition into longer and longer stretches of text.

Chapter Titles

Chapter titles need to be noticed and they support understanding, often serving as mini summaries. For example, in *Ricky Ricotta's Mighty Robot* (Pilkey, 2000), Chapter 11 is titled "The Big Battle," Chapter 13 is "Justice Prevails," and Chapter 14 is "Back Home," providing a succinct summary of the plot. The names of characters, not subtle at all in most series books, often provide clues about what to expect from them. In the same Pilkey book cited above, one of the characters is Dr. Stinky McNasty—clearly a villain.

Repetitions

Repetitions bear noticing as well. Ricky Ricotta is a lonely mouse, pining for a friend. His father tells him, "Someday something BIG will happen and you will find a friend" (Pilkey, 2000, p. 8). Later, at the end of Chapter 2 (beginning and final sentences in chapters are important, too) this idea is repeated: "And everyday Ricky wished that something BIG would happen" (p. 14). Again, at the beginning of Chapter 4: "Ricky did not know that something BIG was about to happen, but it was!" (p. 16). The big event was the arrival of the robot on earth, a turning point in the story.

Typographical Features

Typographical features, such as italics, or in the previous examples, capitalization, are also flags to pay attention. Sometimes italics signal a flashback or a change in point of view. In the Ricky Ricotta example above, the word *BIG* in all capital letters is a play on words—something big, meaning important, was going to happen, but the new character, Mighty Robot, was literally monstrously huge.

Character Dialogue and Narration

Occasionally, one of the characters in the series will come right out and tell the reader exactly what is significant to know to understand the story. Such is the case in the following excerpt from *Ramona the Pest* (Cleary, 1982), which Rabinowitz (1998) uses to illustrate a rule of significance—the writer does not need to tell the reader every detail about a particular character, only what is relevant to the story:

> Miss Binney stood in front of her class and began to read aloud from *Mike Mulligan and His Steam Shovel*...[Ramona] listened quietly with the rest of the kindergarten class to the story of Mike Mulligan's old-fashioned steam shovel, which proved its worth by digging the basement for the new town hall of Poppersville in a single day.... 'Miss Binney, how did Mike Mulligan go to the bathroom when he was digging the basement of the town hall?' Miss Binney's smile seemed to last longer than smiles usually last. Ramona glanced uneasily around and saw that others were waiting with interest for the answer.... 'Well,' said Miss Binney at last. 'I don't really know, Ramona. The book doesn't tell us.... The reason the book does not tell us is that it is not an important part of the story. The story is about digging the basement of the town

hall, and that is what the book tells us.'" (Cleary, 1982; pp. 22–24, emphasis added)

As these examples suggest, the patterned structure of series books offers the novice explicit guidance, scaffolding the reader's comprehension of increasingly longer and more complex texts.

Reading a Lot Makes People Smarter

In studies of out-of-school reading by fifth graders, researchers at the Center for Reading (Anderson, Wilson, & Fielding, 1988) found great variability in the time these upper elementary students spent reading (see Table 6.6). Those who read the most read on average for an hour and a half each day, whereas those who read the least read for less than two minutes a day! Students who read a lot—that is, those who fell at the 90th percentile—read as many minutes in a few days as students at the 10th

TABLE 6.6
Minutes Spent Reading Each Day

Readers at Different Percentiles	Minutes Reading
98	90.7
90	40.4
80	31.1
70	21.7
60	18.1
50	12.9
40	8.6
30	5.8
20	3.1
10	1.6
2	0.2

From Anderson, Wilson, & Fielding, 1988.

percentile read in a whole year. The authors of *Becoming a Nation of Readers* (Anderson, Hiebert, Scott, & Wilkinson, 1985) extrapolated stunning implications from these studies—namely, that increasing out-of-school reading time by just a few minutes each day would increase standardized test scores by up to 10 percentile points.

Other compelling evidence that wide reading supports achievement comes from students of summer reading loss. Close examination of achievement test scores before and after summer break led researchers to notice that students from middle class homes appeared to gain a month in improvement and achievement or so each summer but children from low-income families appeared to lose two or more months each summer. Digging deeper into the data, researchers discovered that the summer activity that made the difference was reading, an activity available to advantaged youth, but unfortunately, not to those without easy access to books or libraries.

As these studies demonstrate, differences in time spent reading likely will translate into significant disparities in reading achievement over the course of a school year—or many school years. Clearly, teachers and parents must do everything in their power to make books accessible, encourage reading, develop engagement, nurture reading for pleasure, and most important, to honor children's and adolescents' preferences for books. Through the ages—or at least the past 100 years—series books have made readers and kept them reading.

REFERENCES

Anderson, R.C., Wilson, P.T., & Fielding, L. (1988). Growth in reading and how children spend their time outside of school. *Reading Research Quarterly, 23*(3), 285–303. doi:10.1598/RRQ.23.3.2

Anderson, R.C., Hiebert, E.H., Scott, J.A., & Wilkinson, I.A.G. (1985). *Becoming a nation of readers: The report of the Commission on Reading.* Washington, DC: National Institute of Education.

Chomsky, C. (1972). Stages in language development and reading exposure. *Harvard Educational Review, 42*(1), 1–33.

Hart, B., & Risley, T.R. (1995). *Meaningful differences in the everyday experiences of young American children.* New York: Paul H. Brookes.

Hayes, D.P., & Ahrens, M.G. (1988). Vocabulary simplification in children: A special case of 'motherese'? *Journal of Child Language, 15*(2), 395–410. doi:10.1017/S0305000900012411

Kuhn, M.R., Schwanenflugel, P.J., Morris, R.D., Morrow, L.M., Woo, D.G., Meisinger, E.B., et al. (2006). Teaching children to become fluent and automatic readers. *Journal of Literacy Research, 38*(4), 357–387. doi:10.1207/s15548430jlr3804_1

The New York Times. (2008, November 9). *Children's books.* Retrieved May 5, 2009, from www.nytimes.com/2008/11/09/books/bestseller/bestchildren.html

Rabinowitz, P. (1998). *Before reading: Narrative conventions and the politics of interpretation.* Columbus: Ohio University Press.

Ross, C.S. (1995). "If they read Nancy Drew, so what?" Series book readers talk back. *Library & Information Science Research, 17*(3), 201–236. doi:10.1016/0740-8188(95)90046-2

Ross, C.S., McKechnie, L., & Rothbauer, P. (2005). *Reading matters: What the research reveals about reading, libraries, and community.* Westport, CT: Libraries Unlimited.

Stahl, S.A. (2003). How words are learned incrementally over multiple exposures. *American Educator, 27*(1), 18–19, 44.

Stelter, B. (2008, March 25). 'Goosebumps' rises from the literary grave. *The New York Times.* Retrieved May 5, 2009, from www.nytimes.com/2008/03/25/books/25stin.html

CHILDREN'S LITERATURE CITED

Cleary, B. (1982). *Ramona the pest*. New York: Dell.

Pilkey, D. (2000). *Ricky Ricotta's mighty robot*. New York: Scholastic.

Pilkey, D. (2001). *Captain Underpants and the wrath of the wicked wedgie woman*. New York: Scholastic.

Riordan, R. (2008). *The maze of bones*. New York: Scholastic.

SUGGESTED SERIES BOOKS

Cam Jansen by David A. Adler
Clifford by Norman Bridwell
Arthur by Marc Brown
Biscuit by Alyssa Satin Capucilli
The Magic School Bus by Joanna Cole
The Magic School Bus Liz by Joanna Cole
A Is for Amber by Paula Danziger
Amber Brown by Paula Danziger

Diary of a Wimpy Kid by Jeff Kinney
The Twilight Saga by Stephenie Meyer
Magic Tree House by Mary Pope Osborne
Junie B., First Grader by Barbara Park
Junie B. Jones by Barbara Park
Captain Underpants by Dav Pilkey
Ricky Ricotta's Mighty Robot by Dav Pilkey
Bone by Jeff Smith

Learning Through Literature That Offers Diverse Perspectives: Multicultural and International Literature

Junko Yokota

As a country, the United States is becoming increasingly diverse and will be continuing on this path in the foreseeable future. In addition, we live in a world that is increasingly global, as technology advances have closed the gaps when it comes to our relationship with world neighbors. Thus, in the 21st century, we can no longer afford to merely look inward, reading and learning only from literature that reflects who we are and our own corner of the world. Instead, as our students grow up in a world that allows them more direct contact with diversity than ever before, we—and they—are challenged to consider a wide range of perspectives and to take a global perspective on a variety of social, economic, scientific, political, and intellectual issues. In this chapter, we will consider the roles that multicultural literature (literature reflecting the diversity in the United States) and international literature (literature originating outside the United States) can play in helping students gain diverse perspectives of the world.

The Role of Books in Students' Lives

Books can hold an important place in the lives of young people. They can provide important information and offer insights into everything from interpersonal relations to social conditions, and how to live one's life. Books impact readers on many levels. They facilitate thinking processes well beyond a literal level of understanding the book. Books that are engaging and well written offer readers depth so they can return to the book again and again, finding insights and connections as they better understand themselves and their world. Multicultural literature has a particularly important role to play in such impacts (Harris, 1997). Reading about the diversity within the United States and the diversity of the world provides readers with settings and perspectives that allow them to imagine and consider a wider world beyond their own.

In this first decade of the 21st century, when computerized multiple-choice quizzes

Children's Literature in the Reading Program: An Invitation to Read (third edition), edited by Deborah A. Wooten and Bernice E. Cullinan. © 2009 by the International Reading Association.

are often used to determine the levels by which students choose their reading material and provide points for remembering a constellation of literal-level facts about a book, it is especially important to engage readers at a deeper level of thinking and understanding, and to choose books that can be meaningful to them as readers. It is also important to ensure that students have access to a wide range of reading materials, across many genres and spanning different reading levels. This ensures that readers have the opportunity to engage with text that is most appropriate for them, but also acknowledges that an individual child's interests and background experiences often enable that child to engage with and comprehend quite well a particular book that would ordinarily (and by the computer placement test) be considered beyond the child's reading level. Thus, a number of factors should enter into a thoughtful process of evaluating and selecting books for students.

Evaluating and Selecting the Best Multicultural and International Literature

When evaluating and selecting culturally diverse literature, a focal guiding point to keep in mind is to be diligent in the search for high quality literature that reflects authentic portrayals of diverse populations (Yokota, 1993). Culturally authentic books portray a culture in a way that seems plausible: The people seem real, the setting is believable, and the big picture of the theme as well as the details described all ring true (Cai, 2002; Fox & Short, 2003). These portrayals can range from ones that are culturally neutral and incidentally depict people of diversity, to those that are culturally specific where the story takes place *because* of the cultural context (Bishop, 1992).

To be avoided, however, are books that perpetuate erroneous information or have hurtful images.

In addition to generally accepted criteria for evaluating and selecting literature, the following are points to keep in mind specific to ensuring high quality multicultural and international literature is available to students:

- Do the author and illustrator present authentic perspectives?
- Is the culture portrayed multidimensionally?
- Are cultural details naturally integrated?
- Are details accurate and is the interpretation current?
- Is language used authentically?
- Is the collection balanced?

Details on each of these selection criteria and examples of specific multicultural and international titles that fit them can be found in Temple, Martinez, and Yokota (2006).

Getting Beyond Inclusiveness: What Are the Issues Today?

We are now well beyond the days of calling for multicultural literature to be included in the curriculum and in the school and classroom libraries for children to read independently. Curricula, commercially published reading materials such as basal series, classrooms, and libraries now routinely include multicultural and international literature in their work. Although the overall quality and range of multicultural literature that is available has been greatly enhanced in the past two decades especially, a number of issues are currently at the cutting edge of the inclusion of multicultural and international literature for today's students:

- Dealing with books, activities, and discussions that lead to problematic understandings
- Scaffolding student thinking about diverse perspectives
- Cultural "blindness" that is silently endorsed in an effort not to emphasize differences
- Understanding and incorporating international literature
- Growing in our adult understanding about diverse perspectives

Dealing With Books, Activities, and Discussions That Lead to Problematic Understandings

While the need for including culturally diverse literature in classrooms continues, that is clearly only a first step. In fact, we are now seeing that when teachers consider only inclusiveness, unintended problems can result. In some stances, for example, a well-intentioned book that centers on issues of cultural diversity may present a slice-of-life story with representations of a culture that lack multidimensionality to the point of being stereotyping. There are other instances of books, that in trying to sensitively address differences, end up being condescending or patronizing to the point where readers ultimately respond, "I'm glad not to be like those others." Whereas such attitudes were more overtly stated in books of generations ago, they continue to be published today, but with much more subtle—yet still present—attitudes that call for people who are different to blend in.

We need to go beyond merely being inclusive. A key to doing so is adopting a specific intentionality in what we do when we consciously seek to expand our awareness and understanding of a diverse world and its many different perspectives. This intentionality calls for educators to be diligent in not merely being inclusive, but in considering the why, what, and how of including literature that reflects diverse perspectives. Educators can model this thinking process by scaffolding their students' thinking about what matters.

Scaffolding Student Thinking About Diverse Perspectives

Our own personal background experiences in interacting with people of diverse backgrounds affects how comfortable we feel in discussing issues related to diverse perspectives. When students have had limited experiences, they may need scaffolding to consider perspectives they had not thought of before. Sometimes, students bring a set of understandings and attitudes that are biased or limited. In most cases, students benefit from teachers and librarians who are able to expand their understanding by asking questions, offering interpretations, and giving additional information as needed.

One specific example can be found in Gloria Ladson-Billings's (2003) study of middle school students discussing Spinelli's (1990) *Maniac Magee.* Ladson-Billings found that students adopted one mindset, and then used details from the book itself to support their case. What her research also revealed was that when teachers asked questions at the end of reading a multicultural book, some never asked questions that dealt with race relations at all, even if it was an overtly important aspect of the book.

Another example of offering additional information to scaffold student understanding is with An Na's (2008) book, *The Fold.* In the story, young teens are contemplating a surgery that would change the shape of their eyelids to include a crease. While this is the most frequently done cosmetic procedure in the world, it is almost exclusive to Asian women. It is likely that non-Asian readers would benefit from additional information that can readily be found on websites or in books to help readers understand the scope of this surgery's popularity, thus taking the situation in the story and putting it in a context that makes more sense to all readers, regardless of their prior knowledge.

Cultural Blindness That Is Silently Endorsed in an Effort Not to Emphasize Differences

Again, in an effort to embrace the notion of not singling out anyone and pointing out differences, some teachers take a color-blind position, maintaining that they do not "see" color—implying that they do not notice a person's race. Such a position, however, ignores some of the most culturally and ethnically distinct physical features and pretends that we are all similar. This denies the distinctions, silences the stories of diversity, and empowers the idea of cultural homogeneity, or the melting pot theory of eras past.

Understanding and Incorporating International Literature

The realization of the need for international understandings has become much more prevalent in recent years than in the past. What international literature offers that is not present in multicultural literature from the United States is perspectives that arise from societies and cultures from various places around the world. How, exactly, do international books differ from multicultural books? The technical answer is this: international books originate from outside the United States, are translated into English if the original is in a different lan-guage, are sometimes modified for the American market, and are made available by a publisher in the United States. What can be confusing is that many international books do not appear overtly international in theme, whereas a number of multicultural books written and published in the United States are clearly set in countries outside the United States and tell about a life that seems foreign to U.S. readers. However, the key distinction is the country of original publication. What international books allow us to enjoy and celebrate are the best of children's literature that is being enjoyed by children around the world, made available to children in the United States, as well. It also allows U.S. readers to see how other countries view themselves and see the world through their lens (rather than seeing those countries and cultures through American eyes). In addition, it allows us to share the stories and illustrations of the best authors and illustrators from around the world (Yokota, 2008).

In the past, the number of such books available in the United States was limited, and access to the books was even more limited. These days, there has been an increase in the publication of books that originate outside the United States and are made available here, and access through interlibrary loans has expanded the possibility of having materials even more widely available. Awards such as the American Library Association/Association of Library Services for Children's Mildred Batchelder Award for the best translated book from the previous year are now augmented with newer awards such as the annual list of the United States Board on Books for Young People's Outstanding International Books for Children. There are many stories that have become so familiar to U.S. audiences that they are considered classics in the United States as well as in their country of origin, such as

Pinocchio, Winnie-the-Pooh, The Little Mermaid, and in more recent times, the Harry Potter series.

Growing in Our Adult Understanding About Diverse Perspectives

The first step in making multicultural and international literature a vibrant and appropriate part of our students' lives is recognizing and monitoring our attitudes toward diversity. Consider what dispositions are necessary to think about the "other" in a way that gives consideration of other perspectives. *Tolerance* is a favored term frequently heard among those whose work looks at how to deal with diversity. In fact, tolerance is often paired with issues such as social justice and tolerance. Yet tolerance actually means that we will not fight against diversity and that we will put up with differences; in other words, *tolerate* has a negative connotation to it. It can be useful to think of tolerance as a first step in overcoming negative attitudes, if they exist. But such an attitude is only a first step toward acceptance.

It should also be recognized that for some people, a negative attitude is not the root of problems. Rather, it can be a lack of understanding—or, even harder to overcome, not even being aware of that lack of understanding. Not being aware of what one doesn't know can lead to a patronizing or condescending attitude, even when the intent is to be supportive and inclusive on matters of diversity. Therefore, an important basis for having a positive disposition toward diversity is to begin by recognizing and acknowledging what one doesn't know and developing an attitude of desire to learn about others, and then continuously monitoring how our attitudes come across. In the name of diversity, books are still being published that exhibit these kinds of patronizing or condescending attitudes, all with a desire to be inclusive. As educators, we can develop sensitivity to this issue with the result that we would not select such books for inclusion in our schools. Yet, owing to lack of awareness on the part of teachers, some books that reinforce racist attitudes toward a desire for melting pots of culture not only continue to be published, they get starred reviews and featured attention for recognizing an underrepresented culture.

How can we go about increasing our adult understanding? This can happen in many ways, with personal experience being at the top of the most influential ways of learning about diversity. True, it would be nice to travel and live among people different from ourselves and to learn from those experiences. But limited time and resources may not allow much of that. However, through books and other media, we, too, can continuously grow in our own understandings. Joining book clubs can give us opportunities to engage in adult-level discussions on these issues that challenge us. Technology has made it possible for us to engage in book discussion in virtual space as well as in real time. These virtual space discussions can take place any time if we have a computer with Internet access. Engaging with other educators can be particularly beneficial as we discuss new and innovative ways to engage students in learning about their world. Examples of virtual book discussions can be found by joining Goodreads.com or through public libraries, bookstores, or professional organizations and other social networking sites.

Next Steps

We have come a long way in providing our students with access to diverse perspectives, as represented in literature. The growth in the sheer number of books currently available is largely due to the educators and students who have found that such literature matters to them as important reading material. But the field is changing, and one change that will greatly benefit our search for quality books reflecting cultural diversity is better technology. Although still available from years past, we no longer rely much on such print resources as *Kaleidoscope* (e.g., Bishop & The Multicultural Booklist Committee, 1995) and related book-search tools (Schon, 2004, Seale & Slapin, 2004, Smith, 2004). New Web-based tools such as NoveList enhance the speed by which new materials are added, making timely updates, new connections, and so on. This technology also means access to things like online databases, International Children's Digital Library, digital formats of literature and other related technology-enhanced resources. In terms of multicultural literature, it means that we can access larger databases like the Children's Literature Database that are more comprehensive and allow small presses that represent culturally diverse literature to have more visibility and marketing. It also means access to publisher sites for small presses and bloggers who are focused on multicultural literature, or professional organizations related to international children's literature who are hosting interesting options beyond traditional membership materials.

In international literature, it means that we can be introduced to virtual exhibitions such as "Books From Africa, Books for Africa," from the International Board on Books for Young People. At this site, users can find books that are written in Africa, or written for Africa, available with information about the title, author, illustrator, language, and a synopsis. There are a few sample pages and the cover image shown as well. We can read entire books from countries around the world, cover to cover, on the International Children's Digital Library website at en.childrenslibrary.org. Although this site depends on the generosity of copyright holders donating their books to be scanned and included in the library, more than a million users from 166 countries participate in reading 3,887 books in 53 languages. Also, an Internet search will reveal other countries' websites related to children's literature, some offering complete books freely available online.

When shaping and supporting curriculum, it is critical to keep multicultural and international literature central to the book selection and also to the discussions and learning that follow. In Chapter 14 of this book, Gail Bush describes the process we used in the "Libraries, Literacy, and Learning" grant, working with teachers and librarians for them to "partner" as they worked together to support a mutually created curriculum where multicultural books were core materials for student learning. Partnering with public libraries, community organizations, parent groups, and others also created a situation of many people collaborating to support student learning. Some recommendations for partnering and planning for curriculum include the following:

- Recognize that books reflecting diversity are central and not to be set aside for featured recognition times only (i.e., African American Heritage Month).
- Consciously include books reflecting diversity in all areas of learning.
- Scaffold student thinking about diversity by framing discussion with important questions.

It is clear that culturally diverse literature can be and should be central to student learning, and well-selected, high-quality literature can have an impact on students' sense of self and sense of others (Bishop, 1992, 2007; Harris, 1997). We hope that multicultural literature will become increasingly inclusive so that more diversity will be seen in future works (Yokota & Frost, 2003). We can hope that as this generation of readers of multicultural literature grows up, they will have gained a sense of their world through their books.

REFERENCES

Bishop, R.S. (1992). Multicultural literature for children: Making informed choices. In V.J. Harris (Ed.), *Teaching multicultural literature in grades K–8* (pp. 37–54). Norwood, MA: Christopher-Gordon.

Bishop, R.S. (2007). *Free within ourselves: The development of African American children's literature.* Westport, CT: Greenwood.

Bishop, R.S., & The Multicultural Booklist Committee. (Ed.). (1995). *Kaleidoscope.* Urbana, IL: National Council of Teachers of English.

Cai, M. (2002). *Multicultural literature for children and young adults: Reflections on critical issues.* Westport, CT: Greenwood.

Fox, D.L., & Short, K.G. (2003). *Stories matter: The complexities of cultural authenticity in children's literature.* Urbana, IL: National Council of Teachers of English.

Harris, V.J. (1997). Children's literature depicting blacks. In V.J. Harris (Ed.), *Using multiethnic literature in the K–8 classroom* (pp. 21–54). Norwood, MA: Christopher-Gordon.

Ladson-Billings, G. (2003). *Still playing in the dark: Whiteness in the literary imagination of children's and young adult literature teaching.* Paper presented at the Assembly for Research Midwinter Conference, National Council of Teachers of English, Minneapolis, MN.

Schon, I. (2004). *Recommended books in Spanish for children and young adults: 2000–2004.* Lanham, MD: Scarecrow.

Seale, D., & Slapin, B. (2004). *A broken flute: The native experience in books for children.* Walnut Creek, CA: AltaMira.

Smith, H.M. (Ed.). (2004). *The Coretta Scott King Awards: 1970–2004* (3rd ed.). Chicago, IL: American Library Association.

Temple, C., Martinez, M., & Yokota, J. (2006). *Children's books in children's hands: An introduction to their literature* (3rd ed.). Needham Heights, MA: Allyn & Bacon.

Yokota, J. (1993). Issues in selecting multicultural children's literature. *Language Arts, 70*(3), 156–167.

Yokota, J. (2008). International literature: Inviting students into the global community. In S. Lehr (Ed.), *Shattering the looking glass: Challenge, risk and controversy in children's literature* (pp. 241–251). Norwood, MA: Christopher-Gordon.

Yokota, J., & Frost, S. (2003). Multiracial characters in children's literature. *Book Links, 12*(3), 51–57.

CHILDREN'S LITERATURE CITED

Na, A. (2008). *The fold.* New York: Penguin.

Spinelli, J. (1990). *Maniac Magee.* New York: Little, Brown.

SUGGESTED MULTICULTURAL AND INTERNATIONAL BOOKS

Multicultural

Nelson, K. (2008). *We are the ship: The story of Negro league baseball.* New York: Hyperion.

Nye, N.S. (2002). *19 varieties of gazelle: Poems of the Middle East.* New York: HarperCollins.

Say, A. (2005). *Kamishibai man.* Boston: Houghton Mifflin.

Tingle, T. (2006). *Crossing Bok Chitto: A Choctaw tale of friendship and freedom.* El Paso, TX: Cinco Puntos Press.

Woodson, J. (2000). *The other side.* New York: Putnam.

International

Beake, L. (2007). *Home now*. Watertown, MA: Charlesbridge.

Graham, B. (2001). *How to heal a broken wing*. Cambridge, MA: Candlewick.

Heylauff, L. (2005). *Going to school in India*. Watertown, MA: Charlesbridge.

Prats, J.D. (2005). *Sebastian's roller skates*. La Jolla, CA: Kane/Miller.

Tan, S. (2008). *The arrival*. New York: Scholastic.

The Role of Children's Literature in the Classroom

This section familiarizes the reader with a number of children's books and provides methods and strategies for implementing these books in your reading, writing, language, social studies, and math programs. In these chapters you will visit classrooms in which teachers are successfully incorporating children's literature into their curricular program.

In Chapter 8 we visit the classroom of Michelle Horsey, who has successfully integrated her mandated literacy program with a literature-based workshop model. Chapter 9 presents three strategies for upper and lower grades designed to help transform students into writers as learners and persons. Students in the showcased classrooms listened to and read culturally charged literature that served as mentor texts. As a result, student writings reflected strong voices that produced a better understanding of those different from themselves.

Chapter 10 describes reading responsive activities and comprehension strategies that function cohesively so that they enrich students' responses to text and improve students' awareness of their own personal strategic reading process. Chapter 11 addresses the growing need for content area literature that will enlighten students and deepen their understanding about language arts, science, math, and social studies.

Chapter 12 explains a methodology that helps students master listening, reading, writing, and speaking skills. After the teacher reads a selection of content area literature aloud, students reflect on it by writing a connection to the piece, sharing it aloud, and categorizing it with the help of classmates. Chapter 13 merges the International Reading Association's Children's Choices winners with Teachers' Choices winners in order to produce a list of books that both children and teachers have voted as their favorites. These books are then compared with the books that won several popular awards—and the similarities and differences make for interesting study.

CHAPTER 8

The Surreptitious Role of Children's Literature in Classrooms That Aim to Be "Exemplary"

Nancy Roser, Audra K. Roach, and Michelle D. Horsey

In America in the 1960s, a time of change in U.S. history when many citizens expressed a distrust of authority, when young people were sitting down in protest, and when citizens were standing up for social justice, Neil Postman and Charles Weingartner (1969) wrote *Teaching As a Subversive Activity*. In it, they argued that a drastically changing society required a drastically different system of education (and teachers willing to subvert the status quo). Human survival, said the authors, depended upon teachers offering students the intellectual strategies of "relativity, probability, contingency, uncertainty,...process, multiple causality, nonsymmetrical relationships, degrees of difference, and incongruity" (p. 218). An uncertain future, they wrote, calls for citizens who are active inquirers—curious, creative, tolerant, planful, skillful, and adaptive.

These are words that teachers continue to resonate with: We surely intend *all* learners to be active, skillful, creative, appreciative, and more. We not only salute these goals, but also believe they undergird the more perfunctory language we enter in our daily lesson plan books. And toward advancing these very ends, we who teach voice our beliefs in the power of children's literature (Walmsley, 1992). This chapter, like all the others in this text, is based on the proposition that good books are essential to effective teaching and learning.

Yet, when confronting the select scientific evidence for effective reading instruction, in the face of favored reports, policies, and mandates intended to ensure success for each low-performing child, children's literature may seem to become an easily forgotten aspect of the curriculum—banished to the corner to lap the leftovers of curricular time that has been judged to "count." But *has* children's literature really yielded its place? Perhaps more teachers than we suspect read deeply into contemporary reports and bodies of evidence to discover that wherever there is claim for long-term effectiveness, there is also the presence of quality books for kids.

We begin with a backward glance to gain perspective on the presence of literature in classrooms across time. Then we peek into a classroom of high-needs learners (and their teacher under the pressure of labels) who rely

Children's Literature in the Reading Program: An Invitation to Read (third edition), edited by Deborah A. Wooten and Bernice E. Cullinan. © 2009 by the International Reading Association.

on books across their day for learning, study, and pleasure. Finally, we follow this with some evidence that when we peel back the layers of multifaceted studies of best practices (especially those focused on children of poverty), literature is always implicated. That is, surreptitiously or not, good books strategically and purposefully placed are still central to literacy instruction—and perhaps still serving literary purposes as well.

In Place of Literature?

When America was young, young Americans were offered the New England primer, the scriptures, and moralistic treatises as reading material (Monaghan, 2005). Even the most innovative of secular primers, such as the *Instructions for Right Spelling* (1702, as cited in Rosenbach, 1966) offered little in the way of good stories well told:

> Ask the Carpenter for his Ax;
> If he leave not Coughing, he will soon be put in a Coffin;
> He has 3 Sutes (sic) of Apparel and 3 Suits in Law
> (pp. xxxviii-xxxix).

Children spelled and eventually sounded their way to literacy.

One hundred years ago, in his now classic *Psychology and Pedagogy of Reading*, Edmund Huey (1908) recommended that literature serve a central role in learning to read. Even so, across the early decades of the 20th century, the methods texts teachers studied aimed more toward *how* to make children literate than toward the *type* of literature that should surround them in their classrooms and what teachers might do with it (Martinez & Roser, 1982). And little wonder: The burgeoning world of children's literature hadn't yet burgeoned, so books for young children were comparatively few and not always more well-written than the school "readers" designed specifically to serve literacy learning. That is, for much of our history, literature that was simplified, didactic, cloying, plot-thin, or unsurprising outnumbered terrific reads, fresh language, and glorious illustrations.

By the time children's book publishing gained secure footing, market, and audience, the 20th century was nearly half complete (Bader, 1976; Marcus, 2008). Midcentury, libraries serving baby boomers would have supplied books by Margaret Wise Brown, Ludwig Bemelmans, Virginia Lee Burton, H.A. Rey, and Dr. Seuss. At home, children may have read Little Golden Books or comic books (Lester, 2007). It was indeed possible for avid midcentury readers like little Phyllis Fogelman to completely "read up" the children's room of her public library—and she did (Marcus, 1999). School libraries (especially in rural areas) were even more limited—more likely to be book closets, cupboards, or a visiting book mobile than the well-lit, book-lined spaces of many contemporary school libraries (Martinez & McGee, 2000). There was no threat of literature assuming a place of prominence in most literacy or content curricula in most of the 20th century, so teachers bringing books to children could hardly have viewed their role as subversive.

The proliferation of children's trade books published in the late 1970s and 1980s occurred alongside theories and practice providing evidence for sharing the best and most natural of language in classrooms—and the best of language, as Bernice Cullinan, coeditor of this book, always says, is to be found in the best of children's books. So, as the 20th century grayed toward its senior years, literature began to claim classroom shelves, cubbies, and curricular time. Teachers spoke and wrote about their literature-based programs. Yet almost as soon as trade book production and the valuing of fine texts began to produce a promising synergy, policymakers noted falling reading test scores. The converging forces of depressed standardized scores (too closely following the installation of "real books" in classrooms to have been the culprit), dissatisfaction with the products of schooling, as well as the systematic collection and dissemination of scientific evidence (quantitative and comparison-based studies) seemed to speak to a need for more direct instruction, more systematic practice, and more of everything measurable and sure.

So, with this 21st century have come more prescriptive teaching manuals, as well as installed practices focusing on the *how* and *when* and *what words* kids should read, along with abundant assessments to discern the skills and strategies they lack. Especially targeted are children slipping below the cut-lines of mandated assessments. Those children need (some authorities contended) texts specifically designed for practice of their accruing set of understandings. And yet, through it all, fine children's literature, like all contraband, seems to have retained a marketshare, a value, and an underground life of its own in classrooms.

On and Between the Lines

I (Michelle D. Horsey, coauthor of this chapter), am a third-grade teacher whose children could be labeled. They could be labeled "at-risk," or "of poverty." They could be labeled as receivers of "free- or reduced-cost lunch," and from "immigrant families." They could be labeled "second-language learners" and from an "urban school" that is "failing" (i.e., historically, the school has not mapped to average yearly progress on state assessments). In short, my school has not yet beaten the odds. But I have labels for my students, too. I label them as "treasures," as "learners," as "readers and

writers," as "experts," and as "fact checkers." Inside my classroom, my 16 children read voraciously, talk vociferously, and write prolifically. All these adverbs are to signal that my students are up for the odds that come their way. To use the parlance of the day, my children are "exemplary," as measured by external and internal standards. There are two important spaces for children's books in my classroom: everywhere and all day. But before the "how" of this classroom is explained, notice how many decisions have been made before I start to teach each day.

The Mandates

In this era of renewed interest in accountability, proven programs, and scientific evidence about what works in reading instruction, teachers (particularly those in high-poverty schools) are faced with mandated scripts, prescriptive reading materials, and strictly enforced pacing schedules for literacy instruction. One-size-fits-all solutions are often proffered to schools labeled as failing. Further, there is pressure on teachers to relinquish the time, space, and place for literature in their classrooms. However, some teachers choose to teach against the grain.

My students are 80% Latino, 20% African American, and of those two groups 25% are English-language learners. Mine is a classroom like many others across the United States that has been challenged to close the achievement gap. We are designated a Reading First school. This well-intentioned and "research-based" federal program provides me with a script and a slew of published materials to guide my students' literacy. For 90 minutes each day, I am to conduct my class following a prescribed regimen. The prescription is intended as a kind of teacher-proofing attempt to ensure that my students receive the essentials of reading instruction. Further, each of the teachers at my grade level is required to pace the children through the same instructional sequence. We all post the prescribed skills of the week on the board. We all open our teachers' guides to the appropriate page and place them on our tables, ready for monitors who might drop by to check that the materials are being used and that curriculum is being implemented.

All of us unwrap the same cellophaned readers, copy the same worksheets, and are urged to recite the same boldfaced words. Sometimes we compare our curriculum to prepackaged food: At its best, it may have nutrients and stave off starving, but at its worst, it can be soggy, colorless, predictable, and stale. To extend that metaphor further, I often find myself wondering just how many teachers hide spices in their cupboards to titillate children's tastes—so that developing readers and writers have something more satisfying to chew and digest. Good meals are about good ingredients, good company, and good talk. Should we expect anything less from good literacy instruction?

Richard Allington (2002) says that exemplary teachers reject scripted programs that constrain the quality and variety of texts in their classrooms, even if it means spending their own money to get the kinds of texts they know children need. Among my colleagues, the rejection of the scripted program hasn't been blatant. We are not radical reformers. We dutifully open our teacher guides to the appropriate five-day planner, indicating our awareness of the skills and strategies for the week. We dutifully post the central skills. For example, a comprehension focus may be identifying character traits, while skills goals might include learning to recognize and define homophones and to decode verbs with inflectional endings (*–ed* and *–ing*). However, I also incorporate one of my own long-term goals for

the curriculum: helping children decide what makes for heroism across texts and life. So, come into my classroom and let me show you what happens next.

The Morning Meeting

Juan, Jasmine, Ramon (all names are pseudonyms), and their classmates gather on the rug by my rocker. My state, my district, and the children's parents hold expectations that I offer necessary instruction in phonemic awareness, phonics, fluency, vocabulary, and comprehension. But my students come to the rug each morning with expectations for story and talk. I hold up a book—the first of many in this morning's meeting. The class will soon be drawn into a discussion of character, and while caught up in characters' dilemmas will trace the qualities that begin to define a hero. Students will indeed be identifying character traits but also discussing the significance of traits, and letting characters guide them through plot. However, we typically begin our day with poetry—expansive enough to include everyone. Poems that beckon toward a purpose-filled literary journey announce that we are gathering around good texts as one way of understanding ourselves and others.

This day, our class begins with the poem "I Can" by Mari Evans from *Pass It On: African American Poetry for Children* (Hudson, 1993, p. 19). I read the poem aloud more than once and then distribute copies for reading together. The copies will become part of each child's poetry folder and be revisited and reread in many ways. After the read-alouds, I ask my students to think about what this poem says to them personally. They turn to talk with a partner; within a few minutes, partners share their ideas with the group. As they talk, the notion that actions are results of choices comes from the children—seeding the idea that heroes are persons who make and act on heroic decisions (no matter how small). I reach for *Up From Slavery: Autobiography of Booker T. Washington* (2008), choosing to read an excerpt describing his deep desire to learn to read. While the students are caught up in our discussion of the obstacles to be overcome and the big, important accomplishments that lie ahead for this hero, we wonder together if a person becomes a hero because of hard work or great deeds. We wonder, too, about the quiet roles others play in a hero's life—a dad who reads aloud, a teacher who teaches, a librarian who helps find the right book, or a friend who shows how reading works—small acts that help to shape an extraordinary life.

The discussion this day is fulsome; there is plenty to lead the class into consideration of when a character becomes a hero. The class builds a list together of the traits, qualities, and attributes that are associated with extraordinary heroes in our books (see Figure 8.1). Building from these ideas, the students turn to talk and then record together the ways that each of them undertakes small heroic acts in their own lives. As we construct these lists, I use the opportunity to point out some ways in which language works. That is, by charting the list as "Actions of Heroes in the Past" (e.g., sav*ed* people; invent*ed* a vaccine; start*ed* schools for African Americans) and "Our Own Heroic Acts" (e.g., help*ing* smaller children; runn*ing* errands for older people), we are able to use and note how past tense and present progressive verbs (containing –*ed* and –*ing*) are used to record meaning.

Dispersing to Write and Read

Following the whole-class discussion, children take a few minutes to add thoughts to their journals, and then it becomes a readers' workshop, with children selecting independent

FIGURE 8.1
Studying Character Features of Heroes

reading from individual book boxes or from tabletop baskets filled with books on heroes, such as *Casey Back at Bat* (Gutman, 2007), *Lucky Jake* (Addy, 2007), *Sugar Cane: A Caribbean Rapunzel* (Storace, 2007), and *Ghost-Eye Tree* (Martin & Archambault, 1988), and with biographies, such as *Moses: When Harriet Tubman Led Her People to Freedom* (Weatherford, 2006), *Sundiata: Lion King of Mali* (Wisniewski, 1992), and *I, Matthew Henson: Polar Explorer* (Weatherford, 2007), and more in which heroic characters make critical choices. Students may also select from countertop book displays, from the class library (in Figure 8.2), from their growing collection of student-authored works, from news periodicals, or children's magazines. Some of the students' just-right choices will be from the books provided by the program (but not all). The goal is to lose little time in finding a place to read, with sticky notes and pencils at the ready to mark characters' heroic decisions or actions (and be ready to talk about them). Students scatter to find their own book nook (as illustrated in the diagram in Figure 8.3), snagging a pillow or beanbag to settle into their favorite time of the day. I check my list to see where I will start individual and small-

FIGURE 8.2
Michelle Horsey's Classroom Library

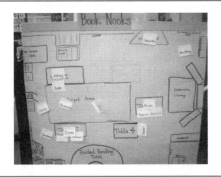

FIGURE 8.3
Planning Places to Read

group conferences. I could turn the page in my Guide; we are doing well.

Circles and Teaching and Talk

The second half of our workshop supports small-group instruction with guided reading groups and literature circles, as well as time within differentiated literacy centers. I believe that literature circles (book clubs) are a place to let children explore genres, the works of focus authors, and the content units of science and social studies. I order sets of chapter books and nonfiction texts from the district lending library to supplement my own collection as well as collections from the school library. In small groups, students are working toward more thoughtful book discussions, with time to observe, conjecture, and connect. The talk is authentic and natural. Because they are used to small groups by now (the 21st week of school), there are no roles assigned to participants. The expectation instead is to come to the book club with thoughtful jottings of their "reader voice."

A group that is meeting with me has just finished Roald Dahl's (1998) *The Magic Finger*, and (besides laughing) we have some choice dilemmas to sort out: Can a character with magical powers be a true heroine? And, if so, was Dahl's unnamed major character a heroine in this book (or a troublemaker)? The group's discussion focuses on the decisions that lead characters into conflict. The group members giggle as they revisit a favorite episode, but they seriously debate their stances on hunting, a central issue of the story.

While this group meets, others have moved to literacy centers. Students clamor for headphones in the listening center, where the autobiography of Booker T. Washington (2008) from the adopted basal anthology is cued up and ready for them, just as they are now ready for it. Modifying according to individual needs, I plan for partners in the word study center to try their hand at word sorts and building words with the inflectional endings we've just studied. Other students play homophone memory games and make homophone puzzles. We chant our word wall words as we line up and play some spelling games in the hallway. Again, acknowledging our Guide but choosing our own route to the goals.

Right after lunch, before anything else interferes, we meet again on the rug to read *The Rag Coat* (Mills, 1991). The students list the heroes in that story, and we add to and change our list to reflect our thinking. Students work with partners to scour the room for other titles with favorite heroes. They work for nearly an hour reading and recording the traits that make for heroic characters (real and fictional). Too hard to narrow to one trait, our class sets up organizers that capture and give order to their thinking (see the trait chart in Figure 8.4).

All through the day, I will continue to slip books into hands (and minds and ears). I am not abandoning the published program materials—rather, I think of them as the supporting cast, the extras who wait in the wings, while quality books for children star in the show.

Inspecting the Evidence

In Michelle's classroom, children's books do not have to live underground or work their magic behind closed doors. And for good reason: Inspect the scientific evidence closely and you will discover that research supports children's literature in the open air of effective teaching. Studies of effective classrooms provide inventories of best practices that are either correlated or causally connected with student achievement. When the studies are designed with control groups and quantitative analyses of treatment measures, they become potential candidates for a canon of scientific evidence as cited in the No Child Left Behind Act of 2001. We gathered and looked closely at frequently cited collections of research that made a difference, such as the report of the National Reading Panel (NRP; National Institute of Child Health and Human Development [NICHD], 2000). We read compilations of literacy studies that attempted to uncover "what works" or "best practices" (e.g., Pressley, 1998), as well as research that examines schools that "beat the odds" (e.g., Taylor, Pearson, Clark, & Walpole, 2000).

FIGURE 8.4
Trait Chart

Often the studies are broad in scope and take wide-angle portraits of the participants. But look closer and the studies contain evidence that often doesn't make it to the official findings sections. We claim a significant finding across these studies: Good books are an integral part of effective classrooms. The following section outlines three ready claims teachers can use to support their work with children's literature that need not stay under wraps.

Out-in-the-Open Claim #1: It Is Important for Effective Teachers to Understand How Instruction Generalizes Across Text Genres.

When you're introducing genre studies or literature units, when you're up to your ears in helping children discover the features of well-selected texts, when you're learning how different texts affect readers, or when you're helping young writers draw from fine published works, you can announce to potential critics, "We're at work here on the study of children's knowledge of genre, as the NRP recommends." You can explain to possible nay-sayers and monitors that after the compilers of the NRP examined 203 studies, they drew some recommendations for the teaching of comprehension and identified additional areas where more study was needed. Among the promising areas was this:

> It will be important to know whether successful instruction generalizes across different text genres…and texts from different subject content areas. The NRP review of the research indicated that little or no attention was given to the kinds of text that were used. (NICHD, 2000, p. IV-7)

So there you have it. As the NRP recommends, you and your children are immersed in discoveries about how the distinctions, features, and challenges of a variety of fine texts inform reading and writing. When your children are surrounded by literature, you are giving close attention to the "kinds of text" children read, and helping both your children and your field develop necessary understandings.

Out-in-the-Open Claim #2: When Effective Teachers Are Asked What Makes a Difference in Their Classrooms, They Say They Rely on Children's Literature.

When Michael Pressley and his colleagues (Pressley, Rankin, & Yokoi, 1996) asked 83 kindergarten-, first-, and second-grade teachers (who were nominated by their supervisors as effective in promoting literacy) about their practices, they predictably named modeling, teaching all the children, and monitoring progress. But they also pointed to the extensive and diverse types of reading they offered children. In their data tables, the researchers display practices that claimed effective teachers' instructional time. Tracing the cells, readers can notice that teachers cited the use of trade books and poetry more frequently than basal stories, claiming that 73% of the materials they employed represented fine trade literature (and higher when they counted information texts). So, if you are asked why stories, picture books, poetry, and trade literature are claiming instructional time in your classroom, you can openly say, "Reputationally effective teachers (for example, those in Pressley et al., 1996) implicated reliance on children's literature across grades."

Out-in-the-Open Claim #3: The Students of the Most Accomplished Teachers in the Most Effective Schools Talk and Write About Books.

When Taylor and her colleagues (Taylor et al., 2000) studied 14 schools with high to moderate percentages of students from low-income homes, they found an interplay of school and teacher factors associated with effectiveness. The most effective teachers in the most effective schools, though, were more likely to engage students in book discussion and written responses. The NRP, too, pointed toward the promising nature of teachers' facilitating student discussions in which "students collaborate to form joint interpretations of text" (NICHD, 2000, p. 16). So when your students meet on the rug to think and talk about a great story, you can nod wisely and explain to observers, "Both the NRP and effective teacher studies (such as Taylor and colleagues) associate literature discussion and writing with effective classrooms."

Literature in Place

Perhaps the state-sanctioned books we hand children represent collective values (cultural, ethical, spiritual) that good folks argued should be there. Perhaps the trade books that wiggle through publication have survived a different kind of vetting (through editorial and marketing department considerations). But perhaps it is we who teach, we who are closest to the readers, who have the most responsibility to hang on to the presence and ensure the quality of books in classrooms.

When Lee Galda, Gwynne Ash, and Bernice Cullinan (2000) produced a review of research on children's literature for the *Handbook of Reading Research*, they indicated that the third volume of the handbook marked the first time a chapter on children's literature was included. They concluded that although literature is present in many studies of literature-based classrooms or of reading comprehension, it is not necessarily attended to. We must make it our charge to gather and make sense of the shards until the preponderance of evidence is arrayed.

For example, we know that successful teachers in high-poverty classrooms and schools hold on to literature for good reasons. In the hands of knowledgeable and strategic teachers, books serve a variety of purposes for literacy instruction. They invite rich discussions in which students engage in active meaning-making and response (Taylor, Pearson, Peterson, & Rodriguez, 2003); and they develop greater understanding of written language (Purcell-Gates, McIntyre, & Freppon, 1995). Successful teachers are known to draw upon well-chosen literature to provide authentic purposes and contexts for the application of reading skills (Wharton-McDonald, Pressley, & Hampton, 1998). Literature-rich classrooms seem to support growth in composition, comprehension, vocabulary, and attitudes toward reading, and are tied to increased motivation to read at home and at school (Morrow, 1992). Thriving urban schools also realize the potential for literature to help create a dialogue that connects school-based learning to students' cultural and linguistic experiences outside of school, "weaving a web of interconnected experiences" (Langer, 2001, p. 876) among the content of school, literature, and students' lives.

Just look closely at stories of schools that defy the odds (e.g., Teale & Gambrell, 2007) and you'll find that good books are integral to their success. Amid prescriptions for *how* and *when* and *what words* kids should read, exemplary teachers think more about qualities of texts and the purposes for which people read. Children's literature continues to support intensive curricula and deep thinking in the classrooms of inquiring children and resourceful teachers who hold fast. The evidence is not undercover, but just awaiting voicing.

REFERENCES

Allington, R.L. (2002). What I've learned about effective reading instruction from a decade of studying exemplary elementary classroom teachers. *Phi Delta Kappan, 83*(10), 740–747.

Bader, B. (1976). *American picturebooks from Noah's ark to the beast within*. New York: Macmillan.

Galda, L., Ash, G.E., & Cullinan, B.E. (2000). Children's literature. In M.L. Kamil, P. Mosenthal, P.D. Pearson, & R. Barr (Eds.), *Handbook of reading research* (Vol. 3, pp. 361–379). Mahwah, NJ: Erlbaum.

Huey, E. (1908). *The psychology and pedagogy of reading*. Cambridge, MA: MIT Press.

Langer, J.A. (2001). Beating the odds: Teaching middle and high school students to read and write well. *American Educational Research Journal, 38*(4), 837–880. doi:10.3102/0002831203 8004837

Lester, J. (2007, October 13). The place of books in our lives. In *Olio*. Retrieved April 18, 2008, from acommonplacejblolio.blogspot.com/

Marcus, L.S. (1999). An interview with Phyllis J. Fogelman. *The Horn Book, 75*(2), 148–164.

Marcus, L.S. (2008). *Minders of make-believe: Idealists, entrepreneurs, and the shaping of American children's literature*. Boston: Houghton Mifflin.

Martinez, M.G., & McGee, L.M. (2000). Children's literature and reading instruction: Past, present and future. *Reading Research Quarterly, 35*(1), 154–169. doi:10.1598/RRQ.35.1.11

Martinez, M.G., & Roser, N. (1982). Literature in the reading program: Tracing roots. *Reading Professor, 8*, 23–30.

Monaghan, E.J. (2005). *Learning to read and write in colonial America*. Boston: MIT Press.

Morrow, L.M. (1992). The impact of a literature-based program on literacy achievement, use of literature, and attitudes of children from minority backgrounds. *Reading Research Quarterly, 27*(3), 250–275. doi:10.2307/747794

National Institute of Child Health and Human Development. (2000). *Report of the National Reading Panel. Teaching children to read: An evidence-based assessment of the scientific research literature on reading and its implications for reading instruction: Reports of the subgroups* (NIH Publication No. 00-4754). Washington, DC: U.S. Government Printing Office.

Postman, N., & Weingartner, C. (1969). *Teaching as a subversive activity*. New York: Delacorte.

Pressley, M. (1998). *Elementary reading instruction that works: Why balanced literacy instruction makes more sense than whole language or phonics and skills*. New York: Guilford.

Pressley, M., Rankin, J., & Yokoi, L. (1996). A survey of instructional practices of primary teachers nominated as effective in promoting literacy. *The Elementary School Journal, 96*(4), 363–384. doi:10.1086/461834

Purcell-Gates, V., McIntyre, E., & Freppon, P.A. (1995). Learning written storybook language in school: A comparison of low-SES children in skills-based and whole language classrooms. *American Educational Research Journal, 32*(3), 659–685.

Rosenbach, A.S.W. (1966). *Early American children's books*. New York: Kraus Reprint.

Taylor, B.M., Pearson, P.D., Clark, K., & Walpole, S. (2000). Effective schools and accomplished teachers: Lessons about primary grade reading instruction in low-income schools. *The Elementary School Journal, 101*(2), 121–166. doi:10.1086/499662

Taylor, B.M., Pearson, P.D., Peterson, D.P., & Rodriguez, M.C. (2003). Reading growth in high-poverty classrooms: The influence of teacher practices that encourage cognitive engagement in literacy learning. *The Elementary School Journal, 104*(1), 3–28. doi:10.1086/499740

Teale, W., & Gambrell, L.B. (2007). Raising urban students' literacy achievement by engaging in authentic, challenging work. *The Reading Teacher, 60*(8), 728–739. doi:10.1598/RT.60.8.3

Walmsley, S.A. (1992). Reflections on the state of elementary literature instruction. *Language Arts, 69*(7), 508–514.

Wharton-McDonald, R., Pressley, M., & Hampton, J.M. (1998). Literacy instruction in nine first-grade classrooms: Teacher characteristics and student achievement. *The Elementary School Journal, 99*(2), 101–128.

CHILDREN'S LITERATURE CITED

Addy, S. (2007). *Lucky Jake*. New York: Houghton.

Dahl, R. (1998). *The magic finger*. New York: Puffin.

Evans, M. (1993). I can. In W. Hudson (Ed.), *Pass it on: African American poetry for children* (p. 19). New York: Scholastic.

Gutman, D. (2007). *Casey back at bat*. New York: HarperCollins.

Martin, B., Jr., & Archambault, J. (1988). *Ghost-eye tree*. New York: Henry Holt.

Mills, L.A. (1991). *The rag coat*. Boston: Little, Brown.

Storace, P. (2007). *Sugar Cane: A Caribbean Rapunzel*. New York: Hyperion.

Washington, B.T. (2008). *Up from slavery: Autobiography of Booker T. Washington*. Radford, VA: Wilder. (Original work published 1901)

Weatherford, C.B. (2006). *Moses: When Harriet Tubman led her people to freedom*. New York: Hyperion.

Weatherford, C.B. (2007). *I, Matthew Henson: Polar explorer*. New York: Walker.

Wisniewski, D. (1992). *Sundiata: Lion king of Mali*. New York: Clarion.

SUGGESTED PICTURE BOOKS ABOUT HEROES

Fictional Heroes

Ada, A.F. (1991). *The gold coin*. New York: Atheneum.

Anzaldúa, G. (1997). *Friends from the other side/ Amigos del otro lado*. San Francisco: Children's Book Press.

Cooney, B. (1982). *Miss Rumphius*. New York: Viking.

Coville, B. (2007). *Hans Brinker*. New York: Dial.

dePaola, T. (2006). *Now one foot, now the other*. New York: Puffin.

Fox, M. (1985). *Wilfrid Gordon McDonald Partridge*. La Jolla, CA: Kane/Miller.

Hesse, K. (2004). *The cats in Krasinski Square*. New York: Scholastic.

Isaacs, A. (1994). *Swamp angel*. New York: Dutton.

Kellogg, S. (1992). *Pecos Bill*. New York: Mulberry.

Lester, J. (1994). *John Henry*. New York: Dial.

McKissack, P., & Moss, O. (2005). *Precious and the Boo Hag*. New York: Atheneum.

Mitchell, M.K. (1993). *Uncle Jed's barbershop*. New York: Simon & Schuster.

Peet, B. (1983). *How Droofus the dragon lost his head*. Boston: Houghton Mifflin.

Polacco, P. (1992). *Chicken Sunday*. New York: Philomel.

Rathman, P. (1995). *Officer Buckle and Gloria*. New York: Putnam.

Rylant, C. (1996). *An angel for Solomon Singer*. New York: Scholastic.

Seuss, Dr. (1940). *Horton hatches the egg*. New York: Random House.

Stanley, D. (1996). *Saving Sweetness*. New York: Putnam.

Steig, W. (1986). *Brave Irene*. New York: Farrar, Straus and Giroux.

Steig, W. (1992). *Amos and Boris*. New York: Farrar, Straus and Giroux.

Woodson, J. (2001). *The other side*. New York: Putnam.

Real-Life Heroes

Bridges, R. (1999). *Through my eyes*. New York: Scholastic.

Brown, D. (2007). *Dolley Madison saves George Washington*. New York: Houghton Mifflin.

Brown, M. (2007). *My name is Gabito/Me llamo Gabito: The life of Gabriel García Márquez*. Flagstaff, AZ: Rising Moon.

Burleigh, R. (1998). *Home run: The story of Babe Ruth*. Orlando, FL: Harcourt.

Edwards, P.D. (2003). *The Wright brothers*. New York: Hyperion.

Giovanni, N. (2005). *Rosa*. New York: Henry Holt.

Golenbock, P. (1990). *Teammates*. New York: Gulliver.

Goodall, J. (1996). *My life with the chimpanzees*. New York: Aladdin.

Jordan, D. (2000). *Salt in his shoes: Michael Jordan in pursuit of a dream*. New York: Simon & Schuster.

Krull, K. (2000). *Lives of extraordinary women: Rulers, rebels (and what the neighbors thought)*. Orlando, FL: Harcourt.

Krull, K. (2003). *Harvesting hope: The story of Cesar Chavez*. San Diego, CA: Harcourt.

Lindbergh, R. (1993). *Johnny Appleseed*. New York: Little, Brown.

Rappaport, D. (2001). *Martin's big words: The life of Dr. Martin Luther King, Jr*. New York: Hyperion.

Ryan, P.M. (1999). *Amelia and Eleanor go for a ride*. New York: Scholastic.

Ryan, P.M. (2002). *When Marian sang*. New York: Scholastic.

St. George, J. (2008). *Stand tall, Abe Lincoln*. New York: Philomel.

Stanley, D. (1996). *Leonardo da Vinci*. New York: HarperCollins.

Vaughan, M. (1999). *Abbie against the storm: The true story of a young heroine and a lighthouse*. Hillsboro, OR: Beyond Words.

Winter, J. (2005). *The librarian of Basra: A true story from Iraq*. San Diego, CA: Harcourt.

CHAPTER 9

Young Writers Use Mentor Texts

Jane Hansen

When children and young adolescents read and talk about books, what they read and talk about are pieces of writing. Therefore, when children and young adolescents create their own pieces of writing, they do so under the influence of the books they have read, talked about, and appreciate. When these children write, they mentally and physically refer to the books they know—they use them as mentor texts.

In this chapter, students use mentor texts to inform them when they create their own texts. They were not told by their teacher to write *about* books they had read. Instead, these young writers participated in classrooms where they created their own books, poetry, and essays by using ideas from mentor texts when they chose their formats, point-of-view, and topics. These children produced their texts as part of their science, English, and social studies classes.

In the first section you will see a first-semester, first-grade writer whose class is studying the classes of animals, and he decides to write a book about them using the format—and information—of the texts they have studied. The format he uses shows the impact of information and format in mentor texts on young scientists and learners who write. Next, I present a seventh-grade writer in an urban

school whose class is reading *Witness* (Hesse, 2001). Adapting the format that author Karen Hesse uses in this book, the students write new vignettes for *Witness* in which they show the ways it enables them to reflect on the racism in their own lives. The compelling poem written by the student in this section shows the impact a powerful mentor text can have on the complicated lives of adolescent writers.

In my final section I focus on immigration in two different situations. One involves a group of students in grades 6 through 9 who read Amy Lee-Tai's (2006) book, *A Place Where Sunflowers Grow* and then study and write about the internment of Japanese Americans by the U.S. government during World War II. The other involves third-grade students who read various texts, including Francisco Jiménez's (1997) memoir, *The Circuit: Stories From the Life of a Migrant Child*, as they study and write about immigration in the United States presently. Together, the journeys of these students show us how the new ideas in mentor texts can influence the insights of writers.

Support for the Use of Mentor Texts by Young Writers

The idea of mentor texts is not new but started to receive renewed attention when writers

---

Children's Literature in the Reading Program: An Invitation to Read (third edition), edited by Deborah A. Wooten and Bernice E. Cullinan. © 2009 by the International Reading Association.

began to realize that the kinds of writing valued for tests frequently determined the kinds of writing teachers ask students to write. Typically, test texts differ from the literature the children read, hear, and love. Before long, writers of books about the teaching of writing stepped onto the stage to change that.

One of the earliest books of its kind was Katie Wood Ray's (1999) *Wondrous Words: Writers and Writing in the Elementary Classroom*. In it, she shows how immersion in the wondrous words of authors brings professional writers' unpredictable, nonformulaic ways with words to young writers, a very different approach from the oft-prescribed paragraph formats suggested by texts. Later, Ray (Ray & Cleaveland, 2004) showed the specific ways in which very young writers use mentor texts when they write their own books.

Lynne Dorfman and Rose Cappelli (2007) and Lester Laminack and Reba Wadsworth (2006) attend to features of a wide array of children's literature that young writers can incorporate into their texts, some of which are writing in the persona of another, using ellipses to create a pause, and using a one-word sentence for emphasis. As they study the moves writers make, the children try similar ones. Overall, teachers and children alike may borrow from professional writers in a multitude of ways as they intentionally try to grow as writers.

Stephanie Jones (2004) reinforces the findings of Laminack and Wadsworth (2006) when she writes about the significance of the talk that surrounds read-alouds. Important for children as writers, the talk that literature begets often provides the bridge between it and students' lives. Plus, the overall context of an inviting read-aloud brings young writers into the lives of authors.

Taking the talk about read-alouds a step further, the act of storytelling itself is important. Children's cultures provide the foundation upon which they stand as speakers, learners—and writers. Mari Riojas-Cortez, Belinda Flores, Howard Smith, and Ellen Clark (2003) show us what to recognize in young children's oral stories so that we can use them as mentor texts when we support our students as writers of stories. Often their dialogue is rich with cultural terminology, and young writers need encouragement so they know these words will be valued in their in-school writing.

Quite recently, graphic texts and other forms of popular culture have been recognized as mentor tests that teachers need to bring into classrooms for students to study as pieces of writing (Newkirk, 2007). When students write in these cherished forms, their growth as writers not only can become pronounced, but also they start to see themselves as writers—as different from seeing themselves as students who write. For example, the middle school students of Donna Mahar (Chandler-Olcott & Mahar, 2003) write anime-inspired "fanfictions" as they explore the notion of multiliteracies, and the fifth-grade students of Laurie Swistak (Allen & Swistak, 2004) study mentor texts in many genres, from epitaphs to sonnets, when they decide which ones to use for their multigenre research papers.

Even podcasts can serve as a form of mentor text for students to study and create. Tony Vincent and Mark van't Hofft (2007) show third-grade students who produce and publish podcasts for their city as their audience. Young writers can also present their writing on the Internet—for a worldwide audience. The vision mentor texts can provide is only beginning to show its influence on us and on our young writers.

Young Writers' Uses of Mentor Texts

This section explores the experiences of young writers who use different kinds of mentor texts in a variety of ways. You will read about a first-grade boy who challenges himself to replicate the format of informational texts, and a seventh-grade girl who mimics Karen Hesse's vignettes to create one about her own life. Finally, you will read about various students who find information about immigration to be troubling and create their own formats to explore this topic—as the writers of mentor texts tend to do. Overall, the impact of the information in mentor texts drives these young writers to try formats that bring their own thinking to new heights.

Young Writers Present Scientific Information in Professional Formats

Ms. Meaney's first-grade students started to write daily in their writing workshop on the first day of school. Most of them dived in, wrote willingly, and shared with care. A few, however, hesitated. Such was the case of Bernard (student names are pseudonyms)—he didn't excitedly raise his hand, "Call on me! Call on me!" as the others did when it was time to share their writing. He didn't walk directly to a table to write when the children left her focus lesson.

In October, however, Bernard changed. The class was studying the animal kingdom as a science unit and, at the same time, they were studying nonfiction books. Ms. Meaney read to the students and they excitedly browsed through the children's literature, intent on gaining as much information as possible from the text and illustrations. Along with Ms. Meaney, students learned about the classifications of animals and the conventions authors

often used in informational literature. Bernard was intrigued by all the new information they talked about. The books fascinated him, the illustrations intrigued him, and the format of the books caught his writer's eye.

At the beginning of one science lesson, Ms. Meaney asked the children, "What have you noticed that authors do when they write information books?" The class generated the following list, which Ms. Meaney wrote on a chart:

- They have indexes
- Some have a table of contents
- The pictures have labels
- Important words are in bold
- There are a lot of pictures
- Some pictures have captions underneath
- They ask questions and then answer them
- They use real photographs

Ms. Meaney invited her students to write about the animals they were studying in any format they wanted. Surprisingly, Bernard was the first child to get started! For several days he worked on five pages, one on each group of animals: insects, fish, birds, reptiles and amphibians, and mammals.

Bernard's page on mammals can be found in Figure 9.1. Each of the five pages is identical in format. Notice his title, his bold headings, his main body of text on the right, his smaller piece of text on the left, his little feature in the upper left—with a caption, his two labeled drawings, his use of color, and his page number. All of these features were in the informational books the children had studied as mentor texts.

After Bernard had created his pages, he came to Ms. Meaney and asked, "Now what's the difference between a table of contents and an index again?" She told him how they are organized differently and suggested he look at a book to see what she meant. He spent the rest of that writers' workshop and the next working on getting the table of contents and index exactly right. To alphabetize the index led to much erasing; Bernard diligently pursued his work. He *wanted* this to be correct.

When Bernard finished, he was a proud author of his first book. It showed what he learned about the animal kingdom—and about informational texts. It also demonstrates that Bernard has become a writer—and it was informational text that intrigued him enough to make him want to become a writer. For some children, the personal narratives that were at one time the hallmark of writers' workshops are not their way into the world of writing. Therefore, it is clear that we must, as teachers of writing, be sure to include writing across the curriculum in our writers' workshops. Informational texts served as the perfect mentor texts for this first-grade writer.

Young Writers Wrestle With Their Personal Struggles in Poetic Format

A seventh-grade class in an urban middle school is reading *Witness* (Hesse, 2001). They have just finished reading *The Giver* (Lowry, 1993) in English class and, concurrently, in U.S. history, they studied the personal qualities of our nation's leaders (Hansen, 2008). As part of those endeavors, the students discussed the ideal leaders for utopian communities, created their own communities, and developed brochures in which they described characteristics of their leaders.

Within this context, the class of mostly African American students talks extensively about the racism and violence in *Witness*, and they analyze the power of the words of the characters, as advocated by Petit (2003). The

FIGURE 9.1
Bernard's Book, Mammals Page

events in the book occurred in the 1920s when the Ku Klux Klan invaded a small town in Vermont, and the students analyze the book at both literary and personal levels.

Witness is a collection of poetic vignettes, each written from the point of view of one of the characters; together the vignettes create the novel. An assignment during their readings of *Witness*—students read it twice—is to write three additional poetic vignettes for it. As with any excellent novel, there is much room for readers to think beyond the text, and these students easily find spaces for additional vignettes.

Kanicia writes the following vignette from the point of view of Fitzgerald Flitt, the town doctor and a reasonable man. You will see no capital letters, as there are none in Hesse's book.

fitzgerald flitt
it's a shame what the world's coming to today.
people killing themselves, others getting shot.
i feel sorry for that little girl ester,

that poor girl probably can't sleep at night.
they shot her daddy
and now they're trying to separate her from
sara chickering.
what is this world coming to?

When I stop beside Kanicia she says, "It was the KKK, you know, who shot her," and she goes on to tell about the violence in her own life: "I'm afraid of the dark...My brother was shot. He was walking down the street in our city, and someone drove by in a car and shot him in the arm. He's all right...." Several weeks after that conversation, Kanicia was absent for a few days. When she returned, I asked if she had been sick, but she replied, "No, my sister was stabbed in a bar and was in the University hospital. She's going to be OK."

Then, a few weeks later, a classmate accidentally shot and killed his sister. The students attended the funeral, and when I went to the school the following week, I asked Kanicia about it. "The church was full and people were standing outside. It was so sad. Her grandma fainted." We visited, and then I continued to circulate. The students were supposed to be working but some weren't. I stopped beside Portia and Ellen. Their work was spread before them, but they were talking about their classmate. Ellen said, "He feels like it's his fault, but it's everybody's fault."

I'd heard more than one student express that concern. Whose fault is it that these teens happened to find a gun in a friend's apartment—a loaded one? Whose fault is it that it is legally correct to keep a loaded gun in a place that is accessible to teens? Someone intentionally created the community they live in as one in which a young boy can accidentally kill his sister. These students know about the prevalence of social injustices (George, 2002), which they address in their vignettes and dream of changing in their utopian communities.

Students' concerns, interactions, and writings show their intense need and willingness to transform their lives (Quintero, 2004). Importantly, they realize how difficult this task is. The violence of *Witness* in the 1920s arises in their current lives, but they see a better world and, at the same time, they worry. "What is this world coming to?" asks Kanicia in her vignette about the killing. The incidents she related from her own life—with people being shot and not able to sleep at night—appear in her vignette. The mentor text helps her realize that her own tumultuous life is valid material for her writing. Writer Karen Hesse can write about cruel topics in elegant prose, and so can writer Kanicia.

The students' writing enables them to consider possibilities, to craft their selves (Romano, 2004). Their thoughts connect them to what they read and to one another—and inspire them to keep going (Key, 2001). Students think about the ways their selves and their classmates can lead them into and support their futures. The novels they read serve as their mentor texts. They influence the students' ways with words, their ways of thinking—toward hope.

Young Writers' Texts Show the Impact of Controversial Public Policies on Their Social Consciences

To my Teaching of Writing Across the Curriculum class, I read Amy Lee-Tai's (2006) book, *A Place Where Sunflowers Grow*, about her grandmother's experiences in a Japanese internment camp during World War II. It had just received the Jane Addams Children's Book Award for Peace and Tolerance, and I believed it to be tremendously important. My class caught my conviction. Soon, they created practicum experiences for themselves, and preservice teacher Ms. Sanderson decided to use that book as the centerpiece for a unit of study. Because she did not have access to a classroom, she created a community group of multiage (11–14) youth and studied their engagement in this topic.

Before she read the book to them, Ms. Sanderson and her students talked. Living near Washington, DC, all of them had visited the Holocaust Museum, and most were shocked to hear President Franklin D. Roosevelt refer to the World War II Japanese internment camps in the United States as "concentration camps." They had equated this term with the camps created in Europe at this time.

After listening to *A Place Where Sunflowers Grow*, the group read letters written by youth in the internment camps to a librarian in San Diego, California, in the 1940s. After discussing these letters, Ms. Sanderson told the students to write letters from the perspective of someone their age in a camp—to a person of their choice back home. The students complied, and some of them became emotionally engaged in the project. Others, however, appeared to view this as an assignment they were required to dutifully fulfill; their letters were dry. Somehow, these students had not become engaged enough with the letters written by youth in the internment camps for those letters to serve as compelling mentor texts for their own writing.

The group revisited the book and then read newspaper articles and editorials from 1942—other forms of mentor texts. In them, the students encountered blatant racism and one student asked if the articles were real; their emotional connections to this topic intensified. They viewed part of the Oscar-nominated documentary *Unfinished Business–The Japanese-American Internment Cases* (Okazaki, 1985)—another form of mentor text—that shows the experiences of three Japanese American families. They en-

gaged in a heated discussion of it and everyone, including Ms. Sanderson, wrote a reflection. Nash, a ninth-grader, wrote:

> America has a talent at hiding its mistakes. Any injustice it commits, only minute details must be taught to future generations of boys and girls. In school, when we learn about Pearl Harbor and World War II, we learn about the "evil" Japanese, and the American heroism in Germany. Other than battles like Iwo Jima and Midway, and the dropping of the atom bombs at Hiroshima and Nagasaki, the Japanese get completely forgotten in the Americanization of WWII. In that time frame, however, something sinister and poisonous was happening at our western coast.
>
> "Concentration camps." In America, when someone says that phrase, we think of Hitler and Nazi Germany enslaving and murdering millions of Jews and other "Aryan outcasts." However, during World War II, Franklin Delano Roosevelt, beloved American president, forcefully imprisoned all people of Japanese descent and expelled them from the west coast community. He called these prisons, "Concentration Camps." Today, however, we do not compare FDR with Hitler, we call the prisons "Internment Camps." As much as white Americans yearn to be blameless and perfect and racially tolerant, merely by forgetting and avoiding this dark past, we are equally as racist as we have ever been.

In this reflection piece, we hear his passion, outrage, and connections to today, which led to another discussion. At this point Ms. Sanderson introduced poetry written by children and adults living in the internment camps—and this spoke to the heart of Caroline, a sixth-grader who had not yet appeared to personally identify with the pain of the interned youth. She wrote the poem seen in Figure 9.2 in the form of a Japanese flag.

Through these experiences, Ms. Sanderson learned of the importance of many mentor texts, used in succession. Eventually, the impact of the harsh treatment of the interned Japanese Americans touched the conscience of every child in the group. By studying at

FIGURE 9.2
Student's Poem About Japanese Internment Camps

least four kinds of mentor texts, all of the students eventually found one that spoke to them so that they, as writers, could each create a text that showed their strong feelings.

In another classroom, students use mentor texts to learn about current issues surrounding immigration and the power that discriminatory words continue to exert on others. We enter the third-grade classroom of Ms. Buchholz, who teaches in a rural school, the population of which is gradually changing as developers build for middle and upper-middle socioeconomic status families who are new to the area. A few children in the class are immigrants from various countries, but they have, as yet, said little about their lives. Ms. Buchholz wants to break their silence.

In November, Ms. Buchholz reads to the class *The Memory Coat* by Elvira Woodruff (1999), a book about a Jewish family that comes to the United States from Russia. It is relevant to the children because one of the immigrants in the class is from Russia, and the

book opens the door to his life. As they learn about him before he arrived and currently, Ms. Buchholz decides to engage the class. Their interest in this book leads Ms. Buchholz to consider an ongoing, critical study of immigrants.

She chooses *The Circuit: Stories From the Life of a Migrant Child*, by Francisco Jiménez (1997), as her next read-aloud, and begins by reading the first story. The boy in the class whose first language is Spanish—and whose English is still new—beams when he can properly pronounce the Spanish phrases. The class learns about Francisco's family's dangerous trip when they sneak across the border from Mexico into the United States. Very few of Ms. Buchholz's students knew that there are rules about who can and cannot enter the United States, and most didn't even realize that the United States shares a border with Mexico and that the United States is actually building a wall along it.

Over the next few days the class learns about the lives of families in Mexico and why they will risk so much to make their dangerous journeys. As part of their research they watch a short documentary, and the students' questions and opinions increase in number. They are becoming engaged.

Ms. Buchholz poses this question to the class: "Should anyone who wants to be able to come to the United States and become a citizen?" To begin their exploration, the students write their opinion, with one reason to support it, on sticky notes. The graph of their notes shows a split, with a few more sticky notes in the column for those who believe that everyone who wants to come to the United States should not be able to come.

Then the class divides into pairs, and the partners return to their tables to engage in written conversations, a type of writing they have used on previous occasions. The children pair with someone whose opinion differs from theirs and write back and forth. The following is part of what Ms. Buchholz read as she walked among the students and stopped to observe one pair of students:

> I think we should not let them come because what if there are people like terrorists with big machine guns and start killing people in the U.S.
>
> > There will be guards but no gates.
>
> Yeah, but what if somebody kills the guards from far away?
>
> > Yeah, but there will be vehicles.
>
> What do you mean vehicles? So what if there's vehicles? People could get killed in the U.S.
>
> > MMM... I agree!! But Not a Lot.
>
> Yes. I knew I could convince you to believe me. Now, do you agree with me on this? Bad people could come to the U.S. right?
>
> > But, also, poor people can come, right?
>
> Well, yeah... but what if those people come and start to have secrets and start killing all of the people in CA?
>
> > NOW I agree a Lot.

The child on the right is an immigrant. He tries to convince his classmate that immigrants should be able to come, especially poor ones. His classmate, however, harbors fears, and uses strong arguments to try to influence his friend's thinking.

Overall, only a few of Ms. Buchholz's students sound sympathetic to the difficulties faced by immigrants. She feels a clear disconnection between their lives and the lives of immigrant families like Francisco's in *The Circuit*. The students hold strong stereotypes about immigrants, and their opinions do not seem to be influenced by the fact that they are in a classroom with immigrants who are

friends—children with whom they play and learn without tension. There seems to be a divide between the overall issues that surround immigrants and the respect they hold for the immigrants they interact with every day. Not one student mentions the immigrants in their classroom or others they know.

Over the next six weeks Ms. Buchholz continues to read *The Circuit* aloud, and the children read books about immigrants on their own and engage in other kinds of writing. As their study draws to a close, Ms. Buchholz invites the students to create something in a format of their choice that shows what is significant to them about the experiences of immigrants. Some re-create memorable scenes from *The Circuit*, others write poetry, and a few create posters to increase social awareness around ideas raised in *The Circuit*.

One student creates a poster for a local grocery store as seen in Figure 9.3 and the following piece of writing:

> I was very shocked when I heard the pickers (in the true story, *The Circuit*) only got 1 cent a

FIGURE 9.3
Student's Poster on Immigration Based on *The Circuit*

pound. My collage is called: Where your pro-duce comes from.

In *The Circuit*, Francisco (the author) and Roberto picked cotton for money, but they earned less than a nickel! Cotton is prickly but all they needed was money. They'd do anything for it. But they seemed to manage.

The student draws a strawberry picker who earns very little. Importantly, this young author–illustrator gives voice to the often silent stories of immigrants. She wants to use her poster to teach people buying fruit how the food got to the shelves. She says, "It helps people understand the story of Francisco's family and how we all need to think about where our food comes from." This young writer is experimenting with the power her words can have on others. Similar to how the book brought powerful ideas to her, she now, for the first time in her life as a writer, uses her written words to provide a strong message to others.

Their written conversations—and the books they heard and read—served as mentor texts. These young citizens felt the words of others written in strong voices. Those emphatic words, in turn, help them show with their own creations the possible power of effective expression.

Conclusions

The young voices in this chapter benefited from diverse uses of mentor texts. Always,

these pieces of writing serve as sources of ideas and content. That is the primary purpose of writing—writers have something to say. The first-grade boy learned about the animal kingdom from mentor texts, and the format of the informational books fascinated him, so he tried to emulate that writing style.

The seventh-grade students studied fairness and justice in the books they read and wrote about applications to their own lives. When they created brochures, they used brochures of many types to determine their layouts, and for their poetry they used the vignettes in Hesse's (2001) book as frameworks for their own.

Finally, the students in two settings studied immigrants and prejudice. In doing so, they met unfair policies and mistreated persons presented in mentor texts that ranged from film to children's literature to original documents in the form of letters. As the children became engaged with the topics and texts, they wrote about these important, controversial issues in various genres, and in powerful words.

Overall, the teachers of these young writers strive to find ways to invite their students into the worlds of professional writers who know a great deal about content and how to relay content in a captivating manner. In turn, the children admire the mentors they continually acquire—and strive to emulate them as they bring their own writing to new heights.

REFERENCES

Allen, C.A., & Swistak, L. (2004). Multigenre research: The power of choice and interpretation. *Language Arts*, 81(3), 223–232.

Chandler-Olcott, K., & Mahar, D. (2003). Adolescents' anime-inspired "fanfictions": An exploration of multiliteracies. *Journal of Adolescent & Adult Literacy*, 46(7), 556–566.

Dorfman, L.R., & Cappelli, R. (2007). *Mentor texts: Teaching writing through children's literature, K–6.* Portland, ME: Stenhouse.

George, M.A. (2002). Living on the edge: Confronting social injustices. *Voices From the Middle*, 9(4), 39–44.

Hansen, J. (2008). "The way they act around a bunch of people": Seventh-grade writers learn about themselves in the midst of others. *Voices From the Middle*, 16(1), 9–14.

Jones, S. (2004). Living poverty and literacy learning: Sanctioning topics of students' lives. *Language Arts*, 81(6), 461–469.

Key, D. (2001). "Knots on a counting rope": Teaching stories. *English Journal, 90*(4), 90–95. doi:10.2307/821908

Laminack, L.L., & Wadsworth, R.M. (2006). *Learning under the influence of language and literature: Making the most of read-alouds across the day.* Portsmouth, NH: Heinemann.

Newkirk, T. (2007). Popular culture and writing development. *Language Arts, 84*(6), 539–548.

Okazaki, S. (Producer/Director). (1985). *Unfinished business–The Japanese-American internment cases* [Motion picture]. United States: Docurama.

Petit, A. (2003). "Words so strong": Maxine Hong Kingston's "No name woman" introduces students to the power of words. *Journal of Adolescent & Adult Literacy, 46*(6), 482–490.

Quintero, E. (2004). Can literacy be taught successfully in urban schools? In S.R. Steinberg & J.L. Kincheloe (Eds.), *19 urban questions: Teaching in the city* (pp. 157–172). New York: Peter Lang.

Ray, K.W. (1999). *Wondrous words: Writers and writing in the elementary classroom.* Urbana, IL: National Council of Teachers of English.

Ray, K.W., & Cleaveland, L.B. (2004). *About the authors: Writing workshop with our youngest writers.* Portsmouth, NH: Heinemann.

Riojas-Cortez, M., Flores, B.B., Smith, H.L., & Clark, E.R. (2003). Cuéntame un cuento [Tell me a story]: Bridging family literacy traditions with school literacy. *Language Arts, 81*(1), 62–71.

Romano, T. (2004). *Crafting authentic voice.* Portsmouth, NH: Heinemann.

Vincent, T., & van't Hofft, M. (2007). For kids, by kids: Our city podcast. *Social Education, 71*(3), 125–128.

CHILDREN'S LITERATURE CITED

Hesse, K. (2001). *Witness.* New York: Scholastic.

Jiménez, F. (1997). *The circuit: Stories from the life of a migrant child.* Albuquerque: New Mexico Press.

Lee-Tai, A. (2006). *A place where sunflowers grow.* San Francisco: Children's Book Press.

Lowry, L. (1993). *The giver.* Boston: Houghton Mifflin.

Woodruff, E. (1999). *The memory coat.* New York: Scholastic.

SUGGESTED CHILDREN'S BOOKS FOR TEACHING THE ART OF WRITING THROUGH LITERATURE

Cooper, F. (2004). *Jump! From the Life of Michael Jordan.* New York: Philomel.

> A biography of Michael Jordan's early years, a story of determination, and a tale of two brothers. It can invite young writers to write about any of these themes, and the fold-up page of Jordan's famous jump is a feature young writers like to incorporate into their work.

dePaola, T. (1989). *The Art Lesson.* New York: Putnam.

> Probably my all-time favorite piece of children's literature—for writers and teachers of writing. It shows this central characteristic of writers in striking fashion: Writers are the ones who make the decisions about what they will write.

Elvgren, J.R. (2006). *Josias, Hold the Book.* Honesdale, PA: Boyds Mills.

> Realistic fiction, winner of the 2007 Americas Award, this Haitian boy's story invites young writers to tell their tales of struggle and determination. The use of dialogue, a challenge young writers usually enjoy, is the crux of the story.

Feelings, D., & Dawes, K. (2005). *I Saw Your Face.* New York: Dial.

> A beautiful, poetic book. It started with art from the estate of Feelings, and then Dawes created the text—a geography of black cultures across the globe. A multidimensional book, it includes a map to locate all the countries and inserts on it to locate the cities. Many ideas for young writers as they design their creations.

Goodall, J. (2004). *Rickie & Henri: A True Story.* New York: Penguin.

> A gripping story of a young chimpanzee—and love. It helps young writers realize that true accounts can be passionate, compelling texts.

Hesse, K. (2004). *The Cats in Krasinski Square*. New York: Scholastic.

> Historical fiction created from a true incident, this story shows the inside of the Warsaw ghetto during WWII. Written in poetic format, it shows young writers what they can create from historical information.

Jenkins, P.B. (1995). *A Nest Full of Eggs*. New York: HarperCollins.

> This is one of the many nonfiction books Ms. Meaney (in this chapter) and her first graders appreciated when they studied conventions of texts within their study of animal groups.

Johnson, A. (2004). *Just Like Josh Gibson*. New York: Simon & Schuster.

> Based on true stories of African American female baseball players and written as if it's the story of the author's grandmother, this tale shows the importance of honoring what you can do well. Young writers can use various aspects of its structure when they decide how to structure their own texts.

Lock, D. (2004). *Feathers, Flippers, and Feet*. New York: Dorling Kindersley.

> This is one of the books Ms. Meaney's first-grade students used, and enjoyed a great deal, when they studied the conventions of nonfiction within their study of animal groups.

Morales, Y. (2003). *Just a Minute: A Trickster Tale and Counting Book*. San Francisco: Chronicle.

> Written in Spanish and English, this counting book gives young, bilingual writers ideas for their own texts.

Rappaport, D. (2008). *Lady Liberty: A Biography*. Cambridge, MA: Candlewick.

> Beautiful, nonfiction, poetic text and layout. This account of the construction of the Statue of Liberty is told in biographical snippets of the various persons involved. It shows young writers that genres are yet to be invented, to be tried, to use when you have an account to tell that begs its own look.

Sís, P. (2007). *The Wall: Growing Up Behind the Iron Curtain*. New York: Frances Foster.

> This autobiographical book has no bounds. It is an excellent example of multigenre literature. It invites young writers to experiment and explore the unlimited boundaries of the texts they create.

Winter, J. (2004). *The Librarian of Basra: A True Story From Iraq*. Orlando, FL: Harcourt.

> A current, clear story of bravery. The format, with changes of colors to show changes in time, invites young writers to consider alternative ways to indicate sequence. And it may invite them to tell other Iraq stories, other librarian stories, stories of bravery, or stories of other elderly women.

CHAPTER 10

Responding and Comprehending: Reading With Delight and Understanding

Lauren Aimonette Liang and Lee Galda

In the last decade, teachers have become increasingly aware of the need to provide comprehension strategy instruction for their students. Pivotal publications such as the National Reading Panel report (National Institute of Child Health and Human Development [NICHD], 2000) and the RAND report (RAND Reading Study Group, 2002) gradually have affected teacher professional development, school district policies, and basal reading programs to the extent that most teachers are aware of the importance of comprehension strategy instruction, although research has indicated that, in most classrooms, not enough time is given to this type of instruction (Pressley, 2006).

In attempting to include this needed instruction in the classroom day along with all the other facets of language arts and reading, many teachers are forced to sacrifice time spent encouraging response to literature. Worse, many decide the solution is to tack response activities onto a comprehension strategy lesson using authentic literature. The latter decision typically results in frustration for both teacher and students. The literature selection often becomes "basalized" as students adopt a more pragmatic approach to the literature selection to complete the comprehension strategy lesson correctly. The students' work with the response activity is thus hampered as it becomes difficult for them to adopt the needed aesthetic approach, or stance, to the literature. Rosenblatt (1978) explains the aesthetic stance as having a nearly virtual experience while reading—identifying with characters, taking on a participatory role in the story, and especially being aware of the sound of the text and the personal feelings it evokes.

Teachers used to the type of work students are able to do on response activities when they take this aesthetic stance are disappointed with the responses students make when the literature is used for too many purposes (Galda & Liang, 2003). Students, too, frequently are not able to engage with the literature in the same way they would if given a chance to experience the text through an aesthetic stance, which can result in a decreased motivation to read more literature. When asked to read for other purposes such as answering questions or remembering specific

Children's Literature in the Reading Program: An Invitation to Read (third edition), edited by Deborah A. Wooten and Bernice E. Cullinan. © 2009 by the International Reading Association.

information, students may miss out on the potential of stories and poems and thus on the possibility of spending time under the spell of a good book.

So is the case of comprehension strategy lessons and response activities one where "never the twain shall meet"? Clearly, when one considers the goals of comprehension strategy instruction and the goals of reader-response instruction, this does not have to be the case. Both types of instruction actually have very similar purposes. Effective strategy instruction focuses on helping students to use strategies to actively make meaning of text and to engage with it more thoroughly. Strategic reading relies on students being metacognitive and using appropriate strategies flexibly. Classroom activities that teach students about strategic reading lead to students interacting more deeply with the text and, in a collaborative classroom, with one another, and they ultimately lead to a deep consideration of the text and its ideas.

Instruction from a response perspective encourages students to adopt an aesthetic stance when reading stories and poems—to read for the experience the text offers. It also focuses on student engagement and asks students to create meaning with the text. Sharing responses with others leads to students working together to create both a deeper understanding of the text and of one another.

We suggest in this chapter that response activities and comprehension strategy lessons can be combined, and, furthermore, that when done with careful consideration of the goals of each, can actually enhance student engagement and understanding of a text, enrich student response to a text, and improve students' awareness of their own personal strategic reading. Indeed, key comprehension strategies such as predicting, interpreting, connecting, evaluating, visualizing, confirm-

ing, questioning, summarizing, and generalizing are also important components of aesthetic reading and responding. The key to the combination of the two, we feel, lies largely in the particular stage of the comprehension strategy lesson.

Research on comprehension strategy instruction has indicated that one of the most effective ways to teach strategies is through a direct explanation method (Duffy, 2002; Duke & Pearson, 2002; NICHD, 2000). This method begins with teacher modeling and explanation of the strategy, then turns to guided practice and ultimately individual student practice. Responding and comprehension strategy instruction can be combined when the strategies in question have already been well explained and modeled, guided practice has occurred, and the students are now working on more independent practice with feedback from teachers and peers. When students are at this point in their understanding and use of a comprehension strategy, teachers can create lessons that combine both response to the literature and practice of the particular strategy. The combined lesson can help students understand how they can use the strategies they know as part of an aesthetic approach to reading literature to deepen their understanding of and engagement with the text. Additionally, students can see how their response to the text might be affected by their use of the strategy as well as how the strategies they select need to match the possibilities in the text they are reading.

A compelling description of responsive aesthetic reading (Benton, 1979, 1983) resonates with research in the field of reading comprehension. Aesthetic reading involves anticipation and retrospection, picturing or imaging, interacting with text, and evaluating. In this model, anticipation is much like prediction, retrospection much like confirmation, picturing is visualization, interacting involves connecting with the story or poem, and evaluation also involves generalization. Further, as in strategic reading, readers purposefully select "an intended path" (Afflerbach, Pearson, & Paris, 2008, p. 368) that will allow them to achieve their goal. In the case of stories and poems, that intended path is an aesthetic stance and teachers and readers select specific strategies to enhance the aesthetic experience of a particular text.

In this chapter we offer some examples of activities that combine the goals of both strategic reading and responsive, aesthetic reading. The lessons we suggest are intended for encouraging students' aesthetic response to fiction and poetry through the processes of anticipation/retrospection and picturing, and their use of two similar comprehension strategies—predicting and visualizing, both of which are widely taught and are effective. These activities are designed for students who have already been taught about the purpose of the comprehension strategy and how to use it through both teacher modeling and guided practice. The students should be at the point of determining on their own when using the strategy will offer them the possibility for greater engagement in a particular story or poem.

Responding and Practicing Predicting

One of the most commonly taught comprehension strategies is generating predictions about the text to be read. Elementary teachers frequently encourage the practice of making predictions through activities like picture walks, where students explore the illustrations in a text to predict what the book may be about. Predicting is easy to teach and is an easy strategy for students to learn. It is also a strategy that research shows to be quite pow-

erful in helping students better understand a text (Dewitz, Carr, & Patberg, 1987; Hansen, 1981; Hansen & Pearson, 1983). This research focused on students both making predictions and evaluating them, or anticipation and retrospection. Unfortunately, however, many teachers teach students to make predictions but not how to evaluate their predictions and think about why they did or did not come true (Gersten, Diminio, & Jayanthi, 2008).

The link between predicting and responding is heavily dependent on this evaluation piece, or retrospection. Because responses are dependent on one's background knowledge and experiences, the initial response to the literature guides what the student predicts or anticipates. Additionally, the retrospective evaluation of the prediction often affects the response of the reader to the text. This flow between anticipation and retrospection is a part of aesthetic reading as skilled readers practice it.

After students have made their predictions, read a bit to see what really happens in the text. Stopped to evaluate their predictions, students will also find themselves responding to the text and the predictions, saying, for example, "I thought X would happen, but Y happened instead and that made me feel..." or "I predicted that the main character would do X because that is what most characters do in these sorts of books, but he didn't and that really made me think about how the author took me by surprise."

The following two activities help students see how predicting is an integral part of responding. Both are also designed to remind students to use their predicting strategy and responding techniques when reading outside of class on their own. Both activities use contemporary realistic fiction as it is a genre particularly suited to predicting and responding with its easy connections to students' own experiences and background knowledge.

Activity #1: Predicting and Responding Using Because of Winn-Dixie (Upper Elementary and Middle School Grades)

Newbery Medal–winning author Kate DiCamillo published her first book, *Because of Winn-Dixie*, in 2000. A 2001 Newbery Honor book, the novel was quickly popular with adults and children because of its rich and memorable cast of characters and well-described turn of events. It currently remains a widely used text in upper elementary classrooms across the United States. The following activity would work well with other contemporary realistic fiction novels, books where students can easily relate to the situations and events characters face.

Procedure. The activity will occur over several days. Begin the first day by telling students they are going to be reading a book titled *Because of Winn-Dixie* over the next few weeks. Explain that the book is about a girl their age who moves to a new town and begins to make friends and becomes part of her new community. Ask students to raise their hands if they have ever moved to a new town, or transferred to a new school with very few people they knew, or gone to a summer camp or other experience away from home, or if they have made friends with people who were newcomers. Then tell them you want them to think about their experience of being or befriending the newcomer. Explain that most people at one point or another have experienced what it is like to be new to a place, and that perhaps the biggest challenge of being the newcomer is making friends. Ask students to close their eyes and think quietly about a time when they were the new person or first met the new person. How did it feel to not know anyone? Did they try to start conversations with others? Did they watch people closely? Can they remember what it felt like when they first met someone who might be a friend? Next have students open their eyes and share their thoughts with a partner.

Use this discussion as a springboard to help students make predictions about the book. Remind them of the predicting strategy they have learned to use to better understand what they read. Tell them that they have now activated their background knowledge about things that might be part of this story, something they should try to do as they read all texts. As a class, have the students contribute predictions of what might happen in this story based on what they personally have experienced as newcomers. Make a big list of these predictions on chart paper and hang it in a place where students will be able to reference it throughout the coming class periods.

Next, have students read the first chapter of *Because of Winn-Dixie* silently or listen to you read it aloud. At the end of the chapter, refer students to the class prediction chart they just made. Read aloud each prediction and see if any have occurred or if something opposite has occurred that demonstrates a prediction will not come true. When you reach one that has occurred or one where another text event indicates the prediction is not going to happen, stop and ask the students to write the prediction down. Then they should write if the prediction came true and why or why not. Remind students that this is the process of evaluating predictions. Now ask students how they feel about the story now that this prediction has or has not come true. What sort of reaction (response) do they have to the text now? Let students explore this question by writing or thinking on their own first. Then move them to small groups to talk about their responses and feelings for a few minutes. After students have done this, ask them if their responses changed even more after discussing them with their peers. Finally, have students record any new predictions they have now based on this evaluation of the prediction, their personal responses to the text, and their sharing with others.

As students continue to read the novel, have them stop and go through this procedure at the end of each chapter. To remind them of the process, write the steps on a chart or on the board, as in Table 10.1, for them to reference as needed. This will help when students begin to record their predictions and responses without your prompt. When reaching the final third of the book, have students stop and evaluate predictions and respond at points where they feel they would like to do so. This will help students begin to use the strategy and to respond more flexibly and use their own metacognitive skills to predict, evaluate, and respond when it

would be a natural aid. At the completion of the novel, ask students to reflect on how using this process while reading affected their understanding and enjoyment of the book. Explain that although they used the process as a group while reading *Because of Winn-Dixie*, and thus were able to listen to others' responses and perhaps change their own based on what they heard, the process is one they can use when reading a book individually, too.

Activity #2: Predicting and Responding Using The Snowy Day (Preschool and Primary Grades)

Preschool and primary-grade students can and should be taught to begin using comprehension strategies (Pearson & Duke, 2002). At this age, the teaching of strategies may happen

---

TABLE 10.1
Predicting and Responding Chart for Activity #1

When you first pick up a book...	Think about what you know about the general topic of the text. Look at the title, back and front flaps, and pictures to help you. Then make **predictions** about what you think might happen in the book based on your own background knowledge about the topic.
Step 1	**Read** the chapter or section of the text.
Step 2	Look over your list of predictions. **Evaluate each prediction** to see if it has occurred or if something has happened to indicate the prediction will not happen.
Step 3	How do you feel about the story now that this prediction has or has not come true? What sort of response do you have to the text now? **Write your response.**
Step 4	Now **talk about your response** with a partner or your small group.
Step 5	**Has your response changed** even more after discussing it with your peers? Write if your response has or has not changed, and in what ways.
Step 6	Finally, **record any new predictions** you have now based on your evaluation of the prediction and you responses to the text. Then start over with Step 1.

more during read-alouds, but introduction to strategies now will help students make the transition to using them for their own reading in the future. It also helps build the expectation for young students that they can engage with and understand every text they read (Pearson & Duke, 2002). The following activity has similarities to the previous one for upper elementary students but takes place in one class lesson. The text used, Ezra Jack Keats's (1962) well-known Caldecott Medal–winning *The Snowy Day*, is a contemporary realistic fiction picture book that students from northern climates, in particular, will find easy to relate to. The activity suggests a short script that could be easily used with many contemporary realistic fiction picture books.

Procedure. This activity is designed for a small group of students. While sitting in a circle with the students, begin by telling them that today they are going to practice the predicting strategy they have learned to use earlier in the year. Remind students that the strategy involves making good guesses, or predictions, about what might happen in a story and checking to see if the guesses come true or do not come true as they read. Tell students they will also discuss what they like and don't like about the story and the characters and how the story makes them feel.

Hold up the book *The Snowy Day* and read aloud the title to the students. Ask students if they like snowy days and why or why not. Encourage them to discuss what sorts of things they do on snowy days. Ask students what the little boy on the cover is doing and if they have ever done that. Use the following general script to begin reading and discussing the book.

Read aloud the first page: "One winter morning Peter woke up and looked out the window. Snow had fallen during the night. It covered everything as far as he could see." Ask students, "How does that page make you feel?" and allow for some student answers. Add, "Does it remind you of any of your experiences?" and encourage student answers. If needed, you may want to prompt with specifics, such as asking students, "Have you ever woken up in the morning and seen snow that wasn't there the night before? What did it look like in your yard or on your street? What did you do?" Then say, "Think about the things you just said. Now let's make some predictions about what might happen next." As students offer predictions, record them on chart paper.

Continue reading aloud: "After breakfast he put on his snowsuit and ran outside. The snow was piled up very high along the street to make a path for walking. Crunch, crunch, crunch, his feet sank into the snow." Stop and ask students, "Have any of your predictions happened?" Lead the students in evaluating their predictions, reading down the list and checking each one. After evaluating all the predictions, ask students, "What do you think about the story so far?" As students answer, use other questions to encourage responses such as "What do you like?" "What do you think about Peter?" "Does the story remind you of anything you do on snowy days?" Again, specific prompts can be used if students are not responding initially, such as "Do you like walking in the snow? Do you walk in the snow differently from how you normally walk? Why?" When students are finished responding say, "Think about the things you just said and what we just read. Do you have any more predictions to make about what might happen in the story?"

Continue in this pattern of reading a few pages and stopping and asking students to evaluate predictions, respond, and make new predictions. When you are finished reading the story and evaluating the predictions, ask each student to draw and write (with your help) about their favorite part of the story and why they liked it. Have students share their drawing and writing with the small group. Then use what they said to emphasize the responses they made to the story and how this helped them make predictions about the story and better understand and enjoy it. For example,

> José liked when Peter made angels in the snow because he also likes to do that when it snows. Often when we read we find ourselves remembering things that we do or say or think that are similar to what the main character does. This is a type of response to a story. Thinking about things we do or say that are similar to what happens in a story can also help us make predictions about what might happen next in the story. Making predictions and responding to a story are both things you can do to better understand a story and enjoy it more.

Responding and Practicing Visualizing

For mature, skilled readers, visualizing, or imaging as it is sometimes called, seems out of place in a list of comprehension strategies. "That's just what you *do* when you read!" the skilled reader might think, and indeed, that is what skilled readers do. Visualizing is an important and highly effective strategy for improving student understanding of both expository and narrative text (Gambrell & Bales, 1986). For expository text the emphasis is frequently on visualizing and then representing the content in the text in some way, such as a chart or graph, that demonstrates relationships between ideas. During aesthetic reading of stories or poems, visualizing is the primary means by which readers experience the secondary world of story (Benton, 1979, 1983). However, creating images in one's mind of the characters, setting, and events of a story is not so natural for all readers, as becomes obvious when they are asked to reproduce these images on paper or in another format.

With all of the visual stimuli available to students in the form of television, video, films, computer games, and picture books, it might seem that students do not need to visualize. They can simply look at and use the images of, for example, the illustrator, to help them engage in aesthetic reading. Indeed, many are so used to doing this that they lament the loss of illustrations when they move on to chapter books (Galda, Rayburn, & Stanzi, 2000). Storytelling requires students to visualize, as does reading chapter books. So, too, does reading poetry, especially because many poems are found in collections that are not true picture books and where the words are dominant. It is easier to ask students to create their own images when they know that the image has not already been created for them! Further, the sometimes complicated use of language in poetry can create student confusion and using the visualizing strategy can be quite helpful in aiding understanding. Additionally, many poets make use of the technique of imagery, and understanding how imagery works helps students understand how poetry works as well. Responding to the images created in the poem helps to engage readers with the work and further increase their understanding.

The following two activities help students see the importance of visualizing to responding, particularly when reading poetry. Both are also designed to remind students to use their visualizing strategy and responding techniques when reading outside of class on their own.

Activity #1: Visualizing Using All the Small Poems and Fourteen More (Preschool and Primary Grades)

Many poets make use of sensory imagery to present ideas and emotions in poetry. Poets such as Valerie Worth (1987) in her book *All the Small Poems and Fourteen More* or Kristine O'Connell George (2001) in her book *Toasting Marshmallows: Camping Poems* bring the sights, sounds, tastes, smells, and feel of their subject to readers through their use of vivid images. Learning to "see" what poets have written helps students both understand and engage aesthetically with poetic texts. While imagery encompasses all of the senses, visualizing is a basic strategy to begin with.

Procedure. Valerie Worth's (1987) collection, *All the Small Poems and Fourteen More* is a small book containing all of her brief poems, with small pencil sketches by Natalie Babbitt that accompany each poem. The size of the book itself is also small, so it is not a book that lends itself for sharing pictures with a large or even small group; however, it is perfect for sharing with young readers when you want them to supply their own ideas as they interpret the words with which the poet presents them.

Begin by reading a few poems each day, until you have read several and students are comfortable with the shape and sound of the poems in the collection. As you read, ask students, "What do you notice?" and "What do you see?" and accept their answers. If you are fortunate enough to have different ideas offered, discuss those different visions as individual interpretations. After a few days of this, remind students that they have already learned how to visualize as they read, and that it is important to visualize while reading poems because it makes them easier to understand.

When you notice that most students are able to describe the "pictures in their heads" after you share a poem with them, you can ask them to draw or paint what they see. It's important to use media that allow them to select color, because the images in many poems bring to mind particular colors. One such

poem, "dandelion," calls forth images of this ubiquitous flower with words such as "green space," "sun," "bright," "burning," "husk," "cratered moon," and "starry smithereens." Color, in this case, supports the idea of the way dandelions change from bright yellow flowers to puffs to nothingness in just a few days. Asking children to paint what they visualize will help them understand that the poem goes beyond the image of the cheerful yellow flower. Other poems, such as "rags," might inspire collage or other artistic constructions. The entire collection asks readers to notice small things and to think about them in new, interesting ways. Visual presentation of the images and ideas in the poems will help young readers do that. A collection of art inspired by Worth's poems also makes a wonderful display when mounted alongside of the poem that inspired it.

Introducing students to visual imagery through Worth's poems is only the beginning. Once students have experienced creating their own images for the words offered by an author, they will continue to do so if you provide them with opportunities to respond using a variety of media. And don't be surprised if students begin experimenting with imagery in their own writing.

Activity #2: Creating Images Using Words With Wrinkled Knees (Upper Elementary and Middle School Grades)

Upper elementary and middle school readers can develop a sophisticated understanding of how poets use imagery to present and enhance their ideas. The students for whom this activity is best suited would be well practiced in visualizing as they read. They would also have had experience with reading and discussing poetry that uses imagery to convey layers of meaning. Books such as Paul Janeczko's

(2000) *Stone Bench in an Empty Park*, Paul Fleischman's (1988) *Joyful Noise: Poems for Two Voices*, and Joyce Sidman's (2003) *The World According to Dog: Poems and Teen Voices* are full of poems that haunt the senses. Barbara Juster Esbensen's (1997) *Words With Wrinkled Knees* goes one step beyond the skillful use of imagery and offers students a glimpse at what the writer thought words themselves looked like, not just the animals they represented. In a remembrance of his wife in a commemorative edition of *Words With Wrinkled Knees*, Esbensen's husband quotes the poet as saying,

> I began from a different point of view. It seemed to me that some words are so perfect for what they are that it is almost as though they invented themselves.... For example, I could see the long word *xylophone* with an arm at each end, tapping out its name. (Esbensen, 1997, n.p.)

After becoming skilled at visualizing images while reading poems, studying poets' use of imagery, and experimenting with imagery in their own writing, students will be ready for the challenge Esbensen (1997) poses.

Procedure. Read aloud the poems, projecting them on an overhead so that all students can see the words, but without sharing the pencil sketches that accompany them. Discuss each poem, asking students questions such as "What did this poem make you see?" "What did you notice about the poem?" "What is the poet doing here?" and "What is different about these poems from what you have read before?" After spending a few days reading, viewing, and discussing the words that Esbensen uses, look at each poem again. Discuss what students notice and feel is important in poems such as the title poem, "Elephant." In this poem students might notice words such as "cumbersome," "lumbering," "gray," with "ears"

that are "huge and flap," with "wrinkled knees" and "toes like boxing gloves," a "wide name."

After writing these words on chart paper or an overhead, project the black-and-white image that accompanies the poem. Ask students to describe what the illustrator has done, what he or she chose to represent for the poem. In this case, the illustrator has drawn a picture of an angry elephant, with its trunk and one of its feet breaking the plane of the illustration and projecting onto the page that contains the words. After discussing the image in relation to the ideas that Esbensen presents, ask students if there is something else that could represent the ideas and images that they noticed in each poem. Challenge students to create new illustrations for their favorite poems, using the word itself as the central motif. For example, how would they make the word *elephant* "cumbersome," "lumbering," and "gray."

After working with these poems students can go on to create responses to other poems that contain a variety of sensory imagery. For example, they could translate taste, touch, or smell imagery into visual, verbal, or auditory representation. The goal is to find ways to represent the feelings and ideas that the use of imagery in a particular poem evokes in an individual reader.

Engaging in the Reading Experience: Comprehending and Responding

Skillful readers read and respond to stories and poems by using an array of strategies that are directed at the goal of engaging aesthetically with a text, whether it is entering the secondary world of story or experiencing a vision of life as seen through a poet's eye. In this chapter, we have focused on two commonly taught comprehension strategies that are also effective aesthetic responses to literary texts: predicting (or anticipation/retrospection) and visualizing (or picturing). In both cases, use of these particular strategies can enhance a reader's aesthetic encounter with a specific text, and the activities we suggest were created for that specific text. Other comprehension strat-

egies might work as well but might not; it all depends on their relevance to the specific text as well as the skill and experience of the readers. Once taught, comprehension strategies can become part of how readers read, tools for creating meaning with text that allow readers to engage in the aesthetic experiences that story and poetry offers us.

REFERENCES

Afflerbach, P., Pearson, P.D., & Paris, S.G. (2008). Clarifying differences between reading skills and reading strategies. *The Reading Teacher, 61*(5), 364–373. doi:10.1598/RT.61.5.1

Benton, M. (1979). Children's responses to stories. *Children's Literature in Education, 10*(2), 68–85. doi:10.1007/BF01145701

Benton, M. (1983). Secondary worlds. *Journal of Research and Development in Education, 16*(3), 68–75.

Dewitz, P., Carr, E.M., & Patberg, J.P. (1987). Effects of inference training on comprehension and comprehension monitoring. *Reading Research Quarterly, 22*(1), 99–121. doi:10.2307/747723

Duffy, G.G. (2002). The case for direct explanation of strategies. In C.C. Block & M. Pressley (Eds.), *Comprehension instruction: Research-based best practices* (pp. 28–41). New York: Guilford.

Duke, N.K., & Pearson, P.D. (2002). Effective practices for developing reading comprehension. In A.E. Farstrup & S.J. Samuels (Eds.), *What research has to say about reading instruction* (3rd ed., pp. 205–242). Newark, DE: International Reading Association.

Galda, L., & Liang, L.A. (2003). Reading as experience or getting the facts? Stance and literature in classrooms. *Reading Research Quarterly, 38*(2), 268–275. doi:10.1598/RRQ.38.2.6

Galda, L., Rayburn, S., & Stanzi, L.C. (2000). *Looking through the faraway end: Creating a literature-based reading curriculum with second graders.* Newark, DE: International Reading Association.

Gambrell, L.B., & Bales, R.J. (1986). Mental imagery and the comprehension-monitoring performance of fourth- and fifth-grade poor readers. *Reading Research Quarterly, 21*(4), 454–464. doi:10.2307/747616

Gersten, R., Diminio, J., & Jayanthi, M. (2008). Toward the development of a nuanced classroom observational system for studying comprehension and vocabulary instruction. In B.M. Taylor & J. Ysseldyke (Eds.), *Effective instruction for struggling readers, K–6* (pp. 196–215). New York: Teachers College Press.

Hansen, J. (1981). The effects of inference training and practice on young children's reading comprehension. *Reading Research Quarterly, 16*(3), 391–417. doi:10.2307/747409

Hansen, J., & Pearson, P.D. (1983). An instructional study: Improving the inferential comprehension of good and poor fourth-grade readers. *Journal of Educational Psychology, 75*(6), 821–829. doi:10.1037/0022-0663.75.6.821

National Institute of Child Health and Human Development. (2000). *Report of the National Reading Panel. Teaching children to read: An evidence-based assessment of the scientific research literature on reading and its implications for reading instruction* (NIH Publication No. 00-4769). Washington, DC: U.S. Government Printing Office.

Pearson, P.D., & Duke, N.K. (2002). Comprehension instruction in the primary grades. In C.C. Block & M. Pressley (Eds.), *Comprehension instruction: Research-based best practices* (pp. 247–258). New York: Guilford.

Pressley, M. (2006). *Reading instruction that works: The case for balanced teaching* (3rd ed.). New York: Guilford.

RAND Reading Study Group. (2002). *Reading for understanding: Toward an R&D program in reading comprehension.* Santa Monica, CA: RAND.

Rosenblatt, L.M. (1978). *The reader, the text, the poem: The transactional theory of the literary work.* Carbondale: Southern Illinois University Press.

CHILDREN'S LITERATURE CITED

DiCamillo, K. (2000). *Because of Winn-Dixie*. New York: Candlewick.

Esbensen, B.J. (1997). *Words with wrinkled knees*. Honesdale, PA: Boyds Mills.

Fleischman, P. (1988). *Joyful noise: Poems for two voices*. New York: Harper & Row.

George, K.O. (2001). *Toasting marshmallows: Camping poems*. New York: Clarion.

Janeczko, P. (Ed.). (2000). *Stone bench in an empty park*. New York: Orchard.

Keats, E.J. (1962). *The snowy day*. New York: Viking.

Sidman, J. (2003). *The world according to dog: Poems and teen voices*. New York: Houghton Mifflin.

Worth, V. (1987). *All the small poems and fourteen more*. New York: Farrar, Straus and Giroux.

SUGGESTED CHILDREN'S BOOKS TO USE FOR PREDICTING AND RESPONDING

Preschool and Primary Grades

Bang-Campbell, M. (2002). *Little rat sets sail*. New York: Harcourt.

Graham, B. (2003). *"Let's get a pup!" said Kate*. New York: Candlewick.

Grey, M. (2005). *Traction man is here!* London: Jonathan Cape.

Hills, T. (2006). *Duck & goose*. New York: Schwartz & Wade.

Willems, M. (2007). *Knuffle Bunny too: A case of mistaken identity*. New York: Hyperion.

Upper Elementary Grades

Birdsall, J. (2008). *The Penderwicks on Gardam Street*. New York: Knopf.

Gantos, J. (2000). *Joey Pigza loses control*. New York: Farrar, Straus and Giroux.

Horvath, P. (2001). *Everything on a waffle*. New York: Farrar, Straus and Giroux.

Kadohata, C. (2004). *Kira-Kira*. New York: Atheneum.

Park, L.S. (2002). *When my name was Keoko*. New York: Clarion.

SUGGESTED CHILDREN'S BOOKS TO USE FOR VISUALIZING AND RESPONDING

Preschool and Primary Grades

Elliott, D. (2008). *On the farm*. New York: Candlewick.

Hopkins, L.B. (Ed.). (2002). *Home to me: Poems across America*. New York: Scholastic.

Issa, K. (2007). *Today and today*. New York: Scholastic.

Janeczko, P. (2007). *Hey, you!: Poems to skyscrapers, mosquitoes, and other fun things*. New York: HarperCollins.

Larios, J.H. (2008). *Imaginary menagerie: A book of curious creatures*. New York: Harcourt.

Upper Elementary Grades

Carroll, L., (2007). *Jabberwocky*. New York: Hyperion.

Grandits, J. (2007). *Blue lipstick: Concrete poems*. New York: Clarion.

Hughes, T. (2007). *Collected poems for children*. New York: Farrar, Straus and Giroux.

Lewis, J.P. (1995). *Black swan white crow: Haiku*. New York: Simon & Schuster.

Park, L.S. (2007). *Tap dancing on the roof: Sijo (poems)*. New York: Clarion.

CHAPTER 11

Enhancing Learning: Implementing Content Area Children's and Young Adult Literature

Carole S. Rhodes and Janice Smith

To be successful in school and in life, students must develop strong literacy skills and background knowledge in the content areas. In order to effectively learn content area material, students must have requisite background knowledge and the ability to read and understand such content. According to the National Center for Education Statistics there are more than 8 million students in grades 4–12 who are struggling readers and who cannot master middle and high school level content material. The New York State Education Department (2008) points out:

> Although content area teachers might like to assume that all students can comprehend texts, identify the words in the texts, understand the meaning of these words, use information from texts to construct knowledge, and demonstrate their understanding, this is not always the case. (p. 2)

If students cannot read, then they will not be able to develop content area knowledge.

Therefore, content area teachers need to implement literacy practices as a regular part of their teaching and learning to ensure that all students can develop the skills they need to meet challenging content area standards. Literacy is a critical factor that affects the ability of students to grasp concepts in math, science, social studies, and English language arts, and to articulate their understanding of those concepts. When a teacher teaches literacy and content together, the teacher expands students' chances to learn both. In an increasingly competitive global playing field, all students need to improve academically and stand to benefit from literacy instruction across the curriculum.

Teachers of all the content areas in all grades have their own special nuances and teaching techniques that they use to help their students comprehend the material. However, we argue that an integral part of their techniques should include the use of trade books and picture books in particular. Although some content area teachers are often skeptical about including trade books in their classes or may feel that they must rely only on textbooks or that teaching reading is the job of the English teacher, the reality is that all of these concepts can be better understood within the

Children's Literature in the Reading Program: An Invitation to Read (third edition), edited by Deborah A. Wooten and Bernice E. Cullinan. © 2009 by the International Reading Association.

context of a book—whether students are reading and writing poetry, reading or solving mathematical word problems, reading or generating lab experiments, or following a historical timeline.

Content area teachers are becoming increasingly more comfortable and familiar with using novels, historical fiction, or nonfiction books in their classrooms. For instance, history and social studies teachers have to teach decades, centuries, and millennia of history, and in New York City classrooms, teachers have to teach the 160 years of American history from Reconstruction to the present. One way to facilitate this process would be to use Walter Dean Myers's (2008) historical fiction book *The Glory Field*. It tells the story of the generations of one family from slavery, beginning in the 18th century, right up to the 1990s. Within other eras and events—women's rights, the 1920s, the Second World War, the Vietnam War—students can read a variety of fiction or nonfiction books that bring to life and deepen understanding of life in the past.

Likewise, science teachers can use trade books to replace or supplement textbooks. For example, a picture book called *The Big Bang* (Fleisher, 2005) can be introduced at the beginning of the year to teach the theory of the universe's origins. They can use *The Perfect Storm* (Junger, 2007) to supplement instruction on weather and *Within Reach: My Everest Story* (Pfetzer & Galvin, 2000) and *Into Thin Air* (Krakauer, 1999), both trade nonfiction books about mountains, geology, and weather to teach those concepts.

Even math teachers can get in on the game. Last summer I read a book called *The Curious Incident of the Dog in the Night-Time* by Mark Haddon (2004). It's a wonderful story about an autistic boy who enjoys science and math. If I were to create my dream school, the math, science, and social studies teachers

and I would get together and create lessons around this book in January—when the rest of the kids in the state are taking tests!

Although content area teachers are being pressured to teach more and more material, textbooks, complete with their pages and pages of information, cover this content adequately. However, these same content area teachers can turn to picture books—young adult fiction and nonfiction—to invigorate, enlighten, and deepen students' learning in subject areas. Textbooks generally provide only one way of looking at something and that often is rather opinion neutral and uninspiring whereas trade books often espouse a point of view and can spark good discussions such as "What is the author's point of view? Why do you think he or she feels that way? What facts support that point of view?"

Using Picture Books to Enhance Learning in the Content Areas

Picture books have the "potential to act as a magnifying glass that enlarges and enhances the reader's personal interactions with a subject" (Vacca & Vacca, 2005, p. 161). Today's students are immersed in and used to technology and visual media. Using picture books in content area classrooms is one way to bring the vitality of visual media into our classrooms, meet the educational needs of visual learners, and differentiate instruction. Picture books provide rich and rewarding reading and learning experiences and increase students' comprehension of subject material. They can bring foreign worlds closer; they can provide contexts for historical events or scientific information; they can help students see the purpose for learning mathematical, historical, or scientific information; and they can spark students' curiosity about subjects in general or specific topics.

Picture books should be an important component of content area classes for many reasons. Picture books can present provocative topics and stimulate thinking, expose students to varied literary genres, or introduce extended thematic studies. Despite being shorter than chapter books, picture books are complex, deep, and rich in information, and they often explore controversial topics or themes. The illustrations facilitate students' comprehension and understanding of the material. Readers faced with a difficult text often look for pictures to help them understand the writing and are relieved when they arrive at one. The use of picture books can provide the same sense of relief for students with learning challenges. This also helps English-language learners by illustrating vocabulary and concepts that may be new to them. The shorter text combined with illustrations enable all students to easily access content information quickly and with ease.

By contrast, skillful readers may ignore the pictures in favor of the text in a picture book. They can be encouraged to use their skills in visual literacy as well as verbal literacy to more deeply understand what the text is saying. By noticing the details of the illustrations that are absent in the words, skillful readers will have a better sense of context. They will think less literally about the context and develop a better appreciation of the subtlety and complexity of the stories (Falk, 2005). Characters' decisions and reactions are often more fully revealed in the illustrations. The pictures allow the readers to form specific mental representations of the content presented. Powerful illustrations are deeply and strongly embedded in memory and can be recalled long after the corresponding words have been forgotten.

In selecting picture books consider the reader, the text, and the context. Today's students are complex beings and, as such, they need to have books that appeal to their maturity and cognitive level. They need to find ways to make the content area material relevant. Consequently, one important use of picture books for every school-age student can be to introduce controversial or provocative issues and to stimulate critical thinking and discussion about these issues. As noted by Costello and Kolodziej (2006), "Contemporary picture books explore issues such as homelessness, war, drugs, death, violence, racism, and divorce." Marybeth Lorbiecki's (1996) *Just One Flick of a Finger* for example, contends with the topic of guns in school. *Smoky Night* by Eve Bunting (1994) grapples with issues surrounding the Los Angeles riots. Books like these can then become a basis for thoughtful reflection and even social action. This can only occur if the students can relate the picture book in some way to their lives. Questions such as the following can assist with that process:

- What is the message or important issue of this book? Is it relevant to life today?
- What did you already know about this topic before you read the book?
- How do the language, pictures, and characters in this book help you understand the author's point of view on the topic? Are other points of view represented?
- What is your opinion on this topic? Did your opinion change after reading the book?
- Where could you go for more information that could be trusted as accurate?

Look for books that are aesthetically pleasing and have interesting design elements and illustrations. The design and illustrations should extend or enhance the story, not interfere with the text. They should establish the mood of the story and reveal details not stated in the text. The pictures should have a sense of flow and lead the reader from one page to the next. The more visually appealing books often make use of an unusual medium or combination of media to enhance the story. Are the illustrations skillfully done and visually intriguing? Is the text skillfully placed on the page so that it fits with the illustration rather than competing with it for the reader's attention?

The text should have rich vocabulary and be well written with strong character development, a point of view, and a worthwhile message. It should be readable by the students and contain information that is accurate, authentic, engaging, free of bias, and free of stereotypes. The goal is also to foster a love of reading for personal enjoyment. Students should become hooked on picture books as another desirable genre for personal entertainment. Because of this, your first criteria for choosing a book must be your own reaction to it. If you cannot enthusiastically recommend it to other teachers—let alone your students—do not use it in your classroom. You must be excited about the book in order for your students to be able to become exacted about it.

Picture Books and Language Arts

One of the most obvious ways to use picture books is to teach the use of literary devices. Excellent suggestions for using picture books in this manner can be found in *Using Picture Story Books to Teach Literary Devices: Recommended Books for Children and Young Adults* by Susan Hall (2007). One of a series that ranges in publication dates from 1990–2007, the book offers a wealth of annotated bibliographies and suggestions for using picture books to teach many aspects of literature. Some of the topics included in the series are analogy, simile, metaphor, puns, alliteration, parody, irony, and flashback.

However, picture books can often be used for more than one content area. The context of the book should be one that matches your intended purpose and curriculum areas of study. Although you may select a book for a particular instructional objective, think broadly about what else the book could offer your students. For instance, if you are using a book for science or history that makes use of literary devices such as symbolism, be sure to point that out. When teaching *Fences* by August Wilson (1986), first have students read *The Other Side* by Jacqueline Woodson (2001). This picture book is about a young black girl and a young white girl who live next door to each other. The only thing separating the two girls from playing together is a long fence (see Figure 11.1). Symbolically, the fence is meant to represent the racial boundary that separates their families. Use this book to get students to think about obstacles and boundaries. It also gets them to think about how images contribute to an author's intent in writing a story.

Similarly, there are many ways to use picture books to teach writing. In *Teaching Writing With Picture Books as Models* by Jurstedt and Koutras (2000) there are suggestions for using picture books to teach writing for mood, voice, point of view, pacing, dialogue, and many other techniques. Each topic includes suggested picture books and teaching strategies.

Picture Books and Science

As an example of using a wide range of reading materials in the classroom, students enjoy reading David Macaulay's (1988) book *The New Way Things Work* as a visual guide to understanding concepts of science they were studying at the time (see Figure 11.2). The images help the students comprehend complicated scientific concepts. This should be true for all science-related picture books—they

FIGURE 11.1
Cover From *The Other Side*

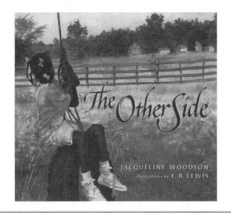

Cover from Woodson, J. (2001). *The Other Side*. Illustrated by E.B. Lewis. New York: Putnam. Reprinted with permission.

FIGURE 11.2
Cover From *The New Way Things Work*

Cover from THE NEW WAY THINGS WORK by David Macaulay. Compilation copyright © 1988, 1998 Dorling Kindersley Ltd., London. Illustrations copyright © 1988, 1998 David Macaulay. Reprinted by permission of Houghton Mifflin Company. All rights reserved.

should use pictures to help the students accurately understand the content.

Macaulay's other works can enhance understanding of eras in European history. His books *Castle* (Macaulay, 1977), *Cathedral: The Story of its Construction* (Macaulay, 1973), *City: A Story of Roman Planning and Construction* (Macaulay, 1974) provide information not only about the construction and building but also about the lives of the people involved in their creation. On a more modern level, *Underground* (Macaulay, 1976) explains the layers at work beneath a 20th-century city that allowed for transportation and waste removal. This can lead to discussions of how a 21st-century city might best accomplish those tasks and to student-designed books to illustrate their ideas. It is wise to keep in mind that not all students best reveal their knowledge orally or in writing. Some students have greater strengths in visual expression and need occasional opportunities to display what they know in their most comfortable mode of presentation.

Scientific controversy can also be sparked by picture books. *A River Ran Wild: An Environmental History* by Lynne Cherry (1992) raises issues surrounding industrial development and the goals of conservationists by tracing the history of the Nashua River in New Hampshire. The book includes a timeline and maps. Alternating pages are framed with illustrations of artifacts from the time period under discussion. This book would make an excellent copycat project for students. They could create a similar book for a river or other geographic feature for their geographic area. Groups could be assigned specific eras or epochs and the class's work could be assembled to create the book.

Similarly, two books by Denise Fleming could be used as models for copycat projects on ecosystems. *In the Small, Small Pond* (Fleming, 1993) and *In the Tall, Tall Grass* (Fleming, 1995) are brightly colored rhyming books that are interesting in their own right but which can also provide models for classroom projects.

Biographies are another type of picture book that can be related to many curricula areas. *Starry Messenger* by Peter Sís (1996) can greatly enhance three curriculum areas: astronomy, geography, and European history. The title comes from a treatise Galileo wrote in 1610 about discovering the moons of Jupiter, and the book is illustrated with cartographic drawings that imitate Renaissance artistry.

Another science biography we particularly enjoy is a biography of John Harrison, *The Man Who Made Time Travel* by Kathryn Lasky (2003). This book is a great way to introduce concepts of longitude and latitude and the difficulties of navigation. Harrison's inspiring story of perseverance is told with a rich, descriptive vocabulary. Like David Macaulay, Lasky has written books on many nonfiction topics. In addition to several other biographies, her works include *Surtsey: The Newest Place on Earth* (Lasky, 1992) about an evolving volcanic island, *Monarchs* (Lasky, 1993) about the butterflies, *The Most Beautiful Roof in the World: Exploring the Rainforest Canopy* (Lasky, 1997), and *Interrupted Journey: Saving Endangered Sea Turtles* (Lasky, 2001).

Picture Books and Math

Another Lasky (1994) biography that deserves special mention is *The Librarian Who Measured the Earth*, which is about Eratosthenes and his geometric contributions on angles and circumference. It also has interesting information about schooling and life in general in ancient Greece.

In a more humorous vein, we love *Math Curse* by Jon Scieszka (1995) and its sequel *Science Verse* (Scieszka, 2004; see Figure 11.3). In the first book, a girl is caught by a teacher's casual remark that many things can be viewed as mathematics problems. The next day she sees her whole world as a series of math prob-lems to be solved, often in a hilarious way. Similarly, but in comical rhymes, the sequel sees almost everything as a science experiment. While both books are built on ridiculous premises, the concepts they present are solid content from mathematics and science.

Another entertaining book that broadens students' ideas of math by using creative problem solving of riddles is *The Grapes of Math: Mind-Stretching Math Riddles* by Greg Tang (2001). These riddles focus on the mathematical concepts of grouping, subtracting to add, using patterns, and symmetry. An example from the realm of fantasy is the book *The Number Devil: A Mathematical Adventure* (Enzensberger, Berner, & Heim, 1998), in which a boy learns mathematics from a number devil. It includes principles about multiplication, division, prime numbers, and square roots, among others.

An author whose works often have a mathematical basis is Mitsumasa Anno, often abbreviated to simply Anno. Although many

FIGURE 11.3
Cover From *Science Verse*

Cover from Scieszka, J. (2004). *Science Verse*. Illustrated by Lane Smith. New York: Viking. Reprinted with permission.

of this author's works might be used to advantage in mathematics classes, we especially like *Anno's Mysterious Multiplying Jar* (Anno, 1983) as a creative way to introduce factorials. Another interesting book is *Anno's Math Games* (Anno, 1987). Creative mathematics teachers may also want to take a look at other books by this Japanese author.

Picture Books and Social Studies

There are many high-quality picture books available that relate to aspects of the social studies curriculum. Several high-quality historical biographies have already been mentioned, and there are many more available about all types of human endeavor. Mathematicians, scientists, inventors, writers, artists, musicians, dancers, and many others can be found in picture books. We will leave it to the reader to explore the lists of suggested books cited at the end of this chapter. Indeed, we can discuss only a few of the wonderful works available in any of these areas, and so teachers should pursue these pleasures on their own.

Costello and Kolodziej (2006) suggest that it is realistic characters that help students relate to other cultures and historical periods because lifelike characters help students draw connections between the books and themselves and between the social concepts being studied and the society in which students live. Costello and Kolodziej also suggest that the best picture books are the ones that have allegorical or hidden meanings that teach ethics or social values. Often these books convey ideas from a perspective that is different from that of the students.

To begin an exploration of African American history, there are several exceptional biographies that must be mentioned. *Rosa* by Nikki Giovanni (2005) is an excellent version of the story of Rosa Parks and the Montgomery bus boycott. It includes many of the background details as well as the basic facts of the story. *Henry's Freedom Box: A True Story From the Underground Railroad* by Ellen Levine (2007) is a touching story about what it meant to be a slave in America and one man's bold way of making it to freedom. In addition, there are many books about Harriet Tubman, but *Moses: When Harriet Tubman Led Her People to Freedom* by Carole Boston Weatherford (2006) is among the best. The beautiful illustrations and clear text tell the story of this heroine.

Two noteworthy books describe the forced immigration of the Africans who became slaves. The first, *Bound for America: The Forced Migration of Africans to the New World* by James Haskins and Kathleen Benson (1999) features pictures by Floyd Cooper tell the story even better than the words. A second book, perhaps best reserved for older students, is Tom Feelings's (1995) *The Middle Passage: White Ships/Black Cargo*, a wordless art book of incredibly powerful charcoal drawings. Part of the power comes from the ghostly way the white participants in the slave trade are rendered. Many of the scenes include realistic, graphic portrayals of the violence inflicted on the Africans and are perhaps inappropriate for some classes and students. Nonetheless, we feel that there is no better depiction of this aspect of American history, and we believe this book should be required reading for older secondary school students.

Similarly, we feel that all students should be exposed to the power and beauty of James Wheldon Johnson's (1995) *Lift Every Voice and Sing*, illustrated by Jan Spivey Gilchrist. These illustrations are not literal depictions of the lyrics but artistic paintings of the meaning and ethos behind Johnson's words. The people on these pages are imaginary and yet inspirational. They are paintings "full of the faith that the dark past has taught us" and "full of the hope that the present has brought us" (n.p.).

Discussion of the meaning of the lyrics and their interpretation in the illustrations can occur in classrooms at a wide variety of ages and cognitive levels.

Two books with similar titles evoke the atmosphere of the middle to late 20th century. *The Wall* by Eve Bunting (1990) tells the story of a little boy and his father searching for the grandfather's name on the Vietnam War Memorial in Washington, DC. This can easily lead to a discussion on the merits of that conflict and of war in a more general sense. Similarly, *The Wall: Growing Up Behind the Iron Curtain* by Peter Sís (2007) is a powerful book about the Cold War. It is written on many levels simultaneously from the very simple to a more complex description for older readers. Each page is like a vocabulary lesson from the Cold War era. Most readers would come to better understand the impact of the Communist era on the people of that time by reading this book.

Skillfully used by socially aware teachers, picture books portraying aspects of various cultures can help students accept different ethnic and racial groups. They can also develop and refine concepts of social justice and equity. There is a wealth of books depicting the lives of immigrants to the United States and the ensuing clash of cultures. Three beautifully crafted books about Japanese immigrants by Allen Say are particularly noteworthy: *Grandfather's Journey* (Say, 1993), *Music for Alice* (Say, 2004) and *Kamishibai Man* (Say, 2005). However, similar collections exist in picture book format for many cultures, and they often address similar issues. Teachers simply need to be sure that the books they choose to represent cultures that are not their own are accurate depictions of life and events within those cultural contexts (see Chapter 7 for further exploration on multicultural and international literature that presents accurate depictions of life and events within cultural contexts). *Grandfather's Journey* (Say, 1993) is a tribute to Say's grandfather, but it transcends this simple pretext by evoking the underlying problems of assimilation. It explores what it means to be from more than one place and to rarely be comfortable in any of them for very long. *Music for Alice* (Say, 2004) is about World War II and the displacement of Japanese Americans, but it is also based on a true story of one woman's long and courageous life and her love of dancing. In many ways this is a very subtle book that would be much less effective without the illustrations. In the last book of these three, the Foreword explains the importance of the *Kamishibai Man* (Say, 2005) in Say's early life, and the Afterword tells more about Kamishibai as an art form. However, the story itself causes readers to think about progress and what is lost when traditional ways of entertainment are replaced by electronic ones. Similar issues arise today with the use of individual music players, cell phones, and computers. Will there be picture books in the future? Will there be other artistic forms of learning?

Moving on to history and politics, a more lighthearted topic is addressed in the book *So You Want to Be President?* by Judith St. George (2004) and illustrated by David Small. It contains lots of trivia about the American presidents; the sketches are not labeled, and so an interesting activity would be to try to name all those depicted (there is a key in the back of the book). A short biographical comment on each president is included. Students could be challenged to write a similarly succinct biography for the current president.

Picture Books in Action

No matter what the curriculum area, it is important for teachers in all grades to read aloud to their students as a way to enhance their literary knowledge, their language, and their knowledge of content. This chapter discussed a small sample of the books that are available for use in the content areas. For further information, readers might want to look at the International Reading Association's Teachers' Choices lists, *The Horn Book*, the National Council of Teachers of English's Orbis Pictus Awards, or publications from the American Library Association. As a final thought, let's look inside an inner-city classroom to see how one teacher very effectively used picture books with her students.

Amy Graffeo, a social studies teacher, was teaching about citizenship and the naturalization process to her class. She decided to use the picture book *The Journey to Ellis Island: How My Father Came to America* by Carol Bierman (1999) as an introduction to the lesson. After the unit, the students were going to go on a virtual tour of the Tenement Museum in New York. She decided to turn this virtual experience into a project. She says, "Even though it was a picture book the students loved it and got to use their imagination. At some point in school we stop making the students use their imagination, which is a vital part of learning."

After the book was envisioned, described, and discussed, she had another task for the students to master. She evaluated the students by having them make interactive trifold boards based on the picture book. The task did not end there. She told them to keep in mind the sixth graders, because they would be presenting it to the sixth-grade class and teaching them about immigration. She modeled what an interactive trifold board should look like, but her intervention stopped there. She did not have a written format that she wanted them to follow; she wanted them to be as creative as possible.

One of the classes designed golden doors for the outside of the board (see Figure 11.4). These golden doors signify the doors on Ellis Island separating families as they enter into America. The inside of this particular trifold board consists of games using a continuity tester (see Figure 11.5), crossword puzzle (see Figure 11.6), and a matching column (see Figure 11.7). If the facts were matched up cor-

---

FIGURE 11.4
Class Project, Golden Doors of Ellis Island

FIGURE 11.5
Continuity Tester

FIGURE 11.6 Crossword Puzzle	**FIGURE 11.7** Matching Column

rectly the continuity tester would light up, giving immediate satisfaction.

Amy's class project exemplifies how the use of a picture book can help inform students on a topic and act as a springboard to what teachers and students can do to enhance content learning. Although the content material was somewhat difficult for students to comprehend using their traditional textbook, the use of a picture book enhanced their learning as it gave them background knowledge and advanced information. An extra benefit of Amy's project is that the students created these games and activities for use with younger children in their school, thus their motivation level was increased. By seeing what this class did, others can easily replicate the process with other books and other content areas.

REFERENCES

Costello, B., & Kolodziej, N.J. (2006). A middle school teacher's guide for selecting picture books. *Middle School Journal, 38*(1), 27–33.

Falk, L. (2005). Paintings and stories: Making connections. *Arizona Reading Journal, 31*(2), 19–21.

Hall, S. (2007). *Using picture story books to teach literary devices: Recommended books for children and young adults* (Vol. 4). Phoenix, AZ: Oryx Press.

Jurstedt, R., & Koutras, M. (2000). *Teaching writing with picture books as models*. Albany, NY: Delmar Learning.

Vacca, R.T., & Vacca, J.L. (2005). *Content area reading: Literacy and learning across the curriculum* (8th ed.). Boston: Pearson Education.

CHILDREN'S LITERATURE CITED

Anno, M. (1983). *Anno's mysterious multiplying jar.* New York: Philomel.

Anno, M. (1987). *Anno's math games.* New York: Philomel.

Bierman, C. (1999). *Journey to Ellis Island: How my father came to America.* New York: Hyperion.

Bunting, E. (1990). *The wall.* New York: Clarion.

Bunting, E. (1994). *Smoky night*. San Diego, CA: Harcourt Brace.

Cherry, L. (1992). *A river ran wild: An environmental history*. San Diego, CA: Harcourt Brace Jovanovich.

Enzensberger, H.M., Berner, R.S., & Heim, M.H. (1998). *The number devil: A mathematical adventure*. New York: Henry Holt.

Feelings, T. (1995). *The middle passage: White ships/black cargo*. New York: Dial.

Fleisher, P. (2005). *The big bang*. Minneapolis, MN: Twenty-First Century Books.

Fleming, D. (1993). *In the small, small pond*. New York: Henry Holt.

Fleming, D. (1995). *In the tall, tall grass*. New York: Henry Holt.

Giovanni, N. (2005). *Rosa*. New York: Henry Holt.

Haddon, M. (2004). *The curious incident of the dog in the night-time*. London: Vintage.

Haskins, J., & Benson, K. (1999). *Bound for America: The forced migration of Africans to the new world*. New York: Lothrop, Lee & Shepard.

Johnson, J.W. (1995). *Lift every voice and sing*. New York: Scholastic.

Junger, S. (2007). *The perfect storm*. New York: HarperCollins.

Krakauer, J. (1999). *Into thin air*. New York: Anchor.

Lasky, K. (1992). *Surtsey: The newest place on earth*. New York: Hyperion.

Lasky, K. (1993). *Monarchs*. San Diego, CA: Harcourt Brace.

Lasky, K. (1994). *The librarian who measured the earth*. Boston: Little, Brown.

Lasky, K. (1997). *The most beautiful roof in the world: Exploring the rainforest canopy*. San Diego, CA: Harcourt Brace.

Lasky, K. (2001). *Interrupted journey: Saving endangered sea turtles*. Cambridge, MA: Candlewick.

Lasky, K. (2003). *The man who made time travel*. New York: Melanie Kroupas.

Levine, E. (2007). *Henry's freedom box: A true story from the underground railroad*. New York: Scholastic.

Lorbiecki, M. (1996). *Just one flick of a finger*. New York: Dial.

Macaulay, D. (1973). *Cathedral: The story of its construction*. Boston: Houghton Mifflin.

Macaulay, D. (1974). *City: A story of Roman planning and construction*. Boston: Houghton Mifflin.

Macaulay, D. (1976). *Underground*. Boston: Houghton Mifflin.

Macaulay, D. (1977). *Castle*. Boston: Houghton Mifflin.

Macaulay, D. (1988). *The way things work*. Boston: Houghton Mifflin.

Myers, W.D. (2008). *The glory field*. New York: Scholastic.

Pfetzer, M., & Galvin, J. (2000). *Within reach: My Everest story*. New York: Puffin.

Say, A. (1993). *Grandfather's journey*. Boston: Houghton Mifflin.

Say, A. (2004). *Music for Alice*. Boston: Houghton Mifflin.

Say, A. (2005). *Kamishibai man*. Boston: Houghton Mifflin.

Scieszka, J. (1995). *Math curse*. New York: Viking.

Scieszka, J. (2004). *Science verse*. New York: Viking.

Sís, P. (1996). *Starry messenger*. New York: Farrar, Straus and Giroux.

Sís, P. (2007). *The wall: Growing up behind the Iron Curtain*. New York: Farrar, Straus and Giroux.

St. George, J. (2004). *So you want to be president?* New York: Philomel.

Tang, G. (2001). *The grapes of math: Mind-stretching math riddles*. New York: Scholastic.

Weatherford, C.B. (2006). *Moses: When Harriet Tubman led her people to freedom*. New York: Hyperion.

Wilson, A. (1986). *Fences*. New York: Penguin.

Woodson, J. (2001). *The other side*. New York: Putnam.

SUGGESTED LISTS OF PICTURE BOOKS FOR USE WITH ADOLESCENTS AND OLDER READERS

Hurst, C. *Picture books for curriculum areas*. www.carolhurst.com/subjects/curriculum.html

Picture books: Enjoyable at any age. literacyconnections.com/PictureBooksforAdultReaders.html

Picture books for secondary students. www.uiowa.edu/~crl/bibliographies/pdf/picbooks_print.pdf

Schliesman, M. (2007). *Never too old: Picture books to share with older children and teens*. www.education.wisc.edu/ccbc/books/detailListBooks.asp?idBookLists=259

Inviting All Students Into the Literacy Arena Through Writing and Sharing Connections

Deborah A. Wooten and Patricia W. White

I n today's technological age, it is more important than ever for students to know how to read and write clearly, critically, and concisely. However, "serious reading problems exist among adolescent learners, as evidenced by declining national reading scores and increased dropout rates" (Boling & Evans, 2008, p. 59). Teachers in all content areas can help rectify this problem by guiding their students in acquiring good reading and writing skills. In this chapter, we describe the Writing and Sharing Connections method, a process that supports content area learning while addressing the mechanics of reading and writing. Writing and Sharing Connections intrinsically differentiates learning so that all students are actively engaged in the process (Wooten, 2000, 2008; Wooten & Cullinan, 2004). Relatively simple to install and conduct, Writing and Sharing Connections becomes an enjoyable interdisciplinary literature-based approach to teaching and learning.

Steps for Writing and Sharing Connections

Writing and Sharing Connections serves as a skeletal framework for listening, reading, writing, sharing, and reflecting about literature read aloud in the classroom. It is a means for holding students accountable for what you have read aloud to them. Because books read aloud during a Writing and Sharing Connections session are content related, schema is being cultivated (Anderson, 1984; Duke & Bennett-Armistead, 2003; Duke & Pearson, 2002; Grolnick & Ryan, 1987; Marzano, 2004). The books are used to build background knowledge and to demonstrate to students how to apply literacy strategies (Beck & McKeown, 2006; Robb, 2008; Wilhelm, 2001, 2005) during the Connections process. The following sections outline the steps of the Connections process.

Children's Literature in the Reading Program: An Invitation to Read (third edition), edited by Deborah A. Wooten and Bernice E. Cullinan. © 2009 by the International Reading Association.

Step 1: Read Aloud a Book, Excerpt From Text, or Short Story

A Writing and Sharing Connections session is perfect for the first day of school—and, in fact, any day—because it creates the foundation for constructing a healthy learning community, allowing teachers to learn about the students' abilities for writing and listening as well as to learn about them as individuals. An excellent book for the first day of school is *Wilma Unlimited: How Wilma Rudolph Became the World's Fastest Woman* (Krull, 2000), the story of a woman who overcomes polio to win three Olympic gold medals. This book is a good choice because it features the importance of overcoming obstacles in order to succeed.

A staple of the Connections process is selecting the right book for the right moment. Books read aloud should tie directly to and support the content being studied. This is most easily accomplished with books that connect to the science or social studies curriculum. Books should capture the imaginations of the students while cultivating background knowledge. Read picture books, excerpts from chapter books, informational text, and poetry, anything that you believe will pique students' interest. Look for books that have relatable emotional appeal, feature strong characters that overcome obstacles, and contain elements of shock, suspense, and surprise. A list of excellent books for use in conducting Writing and Sharing Connections in the elementary classroom is included at the end of this chapter.

Once a book is selected, move the students to a carpeted area of the classroom for a read-aloud session. Have students gather around the reader for a friendly, community ambiance. This environment needs to be one where students can take risks, make inferences, and check their conclusion against the text at hand (Zemelman, Daniels, & Hyde, 2005).

Introduce and market the book. Be genuinely excited about the selection, and students will sense your enthusiasm. Have students predict what they think the book is going to be about. Tell your students why you think they will enjoy it. And most important, have fun. Revealing a good story to a reluctant reader can motivate the desire to read. Whatever strikes the spark of personal relevance can create the conditions for leading the young reader into ever richer and more challenging literary experiences (Rosenblatt, 2005). Through the Writing and Sharing Connections process, students are exposed to many genres, increasing the likelihood of finding books that spur their growth (Ellis & Marsh, 2007).

Step 2: Students Write Their Connection on Sticky Notes

After the book has been read aloud, move students back to their desks. This movement serves as a signal that it is time to return to work and allows students to stretch their legs for a moment. Once seated, students are given a couple of minutes to discuss the book with their neighbors, allowing them to learn through socialization (Vygotsky, 1978) and helping them to clarify their thoughts.

Connections are written on sticky notes. Have pads of sticky notes available in various colors and allow students to choose the color(s) they desire. The element of choice with tasks is a motivator for the literacy experience (Robb, 2008). Provide students with an example of a connection. The usual format for the beginning Connections writer looks like this: "The book reminds me of (connection to the text) because (the reason why the connection is related to the story)." Citing reasons for opinions, claims, arguments, and ideas is a curriculum requirement with which many students struggle. Requiring the students to use the word *because* guides them to develop a habit of validating their claims with examples from the text.

Move among the students as they write, making note of those students who struggle to write and helping those who experience difficulty. The teacher and peer experts should serve as learning mediators, which also validates a case for differentiating reading instruction (Vygotsky, 1978). Some students will resist writing anything—this is OK. Have them draw a picture representing a part of the story they liked or of something of which they were reminded during the reading. Experience suggests that after these students observe the varied writings of others, they will eventually begin writing. Try letting students who are struggling leaf through the book for ideas. There is choice as to how students will respond to the book read aloud but the expectation is that all students will respond to the read-aloud experience (Ellis & Marsh, 2007).

Remember that connections are never graded. Writing connections remains a means for students to freely relate to literature on a personal level. One of the goals of writing a connection is to realize that there are writing opportunities all around them (Calkins, 1983). Focus on what the student is saying, not how it is being said. The following are some actual connections that fourth graders have written during the first Connections session of the school year while reading the book *Wilma Unlimited: How Wilma Rudolph Became the World's Fastest Woman* (Krull, 2000; all names are pseudonyms):

Matt: This book reminds me of the biathlon. I came in second place. My legs felt like jello when I finished the race.

Tiffany: It reminds me of when I tried to do a cartwheel and finally did it.

Matt and Tiffany clearly comprehended the message of the book and were able to connect themselves to the book with specific experiences.

Fast forward five months in the school year. The same students have written connections to *Molly Bannaky* (McGill, 1999). This story is about an indentured servant who purchases a slave and later falls in love and marries him. The closing page of this book features Molly teaching her grandson how to read. This grandson becomes the famous Benjamin Bannaker, author of the first almanac published by an African American. The following is Matt's Connection to the text:

> This book reminds me of Sacagawea because both proved Civil Rights. Sacagawea proved it for the Shoshone and Molly Bannaky for the African American. This book also reminds me of Balboa. Balboa got married to a Native American like how Molly Bannaky got married to an African American prince. Molly Bannaky is a hero without her where would Benjamin Bannaker be.

Students can only write about what they comprehend and know (Alvermann & Phelps, 2002; Robb, 2002, 2008) and Matt has provided us with a rich connection. The content revealed in this connection is information that has been taught throughout the school year. Matt connected to two historical figures, both of whom appear on the student-driven timeline that serves as a graphic organizer (Wooten, 2000, 2008; Wooten & Cullinan, 2004), constantly reminding students of what has been learned through the school year. The timeline will be discussed later in this chapter. His first connection was to Sacagawea (1788–1812) who was added to our timeline while we were studying the Lewis and Clark Expedition. Earlier in the year, as we studied explorers, Vasco Núñez de Balboa (1475–1519) was added to our timeline. It is clear that Matt comprehended the story about Molly Bannaky. He reviewed what had been taught and then connected his content-related background knowledge with his new knowledge. He took a risk with his opening statement in providing an understanding of the concept of civil rights and connecting this to the main character. Matt closes with the assured statement that Molly is a hero, supporting his claim by associating her with other famous people in history. In Matt's first connection, he relates to himself, whereas in his second connection, Matt has moved on to relate to the world. Moreover, each of his five sentences specifically includes the "how's" and "why's" that his connection relates to the book read aloud. Matt added the word *because* as well as his vernacular for because (*like how*) to his second connection. Students know why they write their connections because they create them. The source of the connection lies within, making the process a natural one.

Tiffany, in referencing Clara Barton, has also apparently referred to our student-driven timeline in her Connection, as follows:

> This book reminds me of Clara Barton because she was a nurse just like Molly. She helped people. It also reminds me of my mom because she was a nurse.

Clara Barton (1821–1912) was the founder of the American Red Cross. In the story, Molly Bannaky (McGill, 1999) served as a nurse to some of the people in Maryland for extra money. Tiffany seems to have comprehended the story and has added her insight to it by associating Molly Bannaky and Clara Barton through the nurse connection. Finally, Tiffany allows us one more bit of insight into her family by revealing that her mother is also a nurse. Tiffany, similarly to Matt, moved from connecting to herself to connecting with the content taught in the classroom. She also includes the personal information that her mother is a nurse. Both of Tiffany's connections give us a glimpse into her life outside of the classroom.

Writing and Sharing Connections provides a natural way for the students and the teacher to get to know about one another.

Step 3: Each Student Shares Their Connection With Classmates

Each student comes to the front of the room, stands next to the teacher, and reads his or her Connection aloud. Students should feel as comfortable as possible. After students read their Connection to the class, *always* find something positive to say about the Connection. It may be as simple as "Your comment is interesting because…," but each student should be rewarded for the sharing of a Connection with positive feedback.

It is vital that a class community be developed so that students feel secure while sharing aloud. Opening children's minds so they want to learn without fear of appearing less than perfect depends on a feeling of trust with teacher and classmates. Teachers and students must never have reason to fear reactions from others as they share their learning. Writing and Sharing Connections lays the groundwork for that safe haven, allowing all students, even the most timid, to participate, develop communication skills, and increase self-confidence.

With Writing and Sharing Connections, students learn from one another. Research provides evidence that students learn more effectively when they serve as the teacher (Glasser, 1986). Sharing a Connection is an opportunity for each student to serve as a teacher. One student commented about this in the following Connection:

> Before kid's opinions didn't really matter much. But here, it is different. Here everybody puts in a certain percentage of the info. If the teacher puts in 100% of her info, that's her info. There is really no whole there. But we have 16 kids, and if each kid brings 10% to the discussion you have 160% of the info. 160% is a lot more than just 100%.

Having the opportunity to listen to each student share his or her Connection provides the teacher with instant feedback about what they processed during the read-aloud experience. Comprehension of the text, gathering inferences, analyzing, synthesizing, and ability to summarize are some of the indications of learning that the teacher can detect from evaluating connections.

Step 4: Collect and Categorize Each Student's Connection on a Connection Chart

In the front of the classroom on the chalkboard, adhere a piece of 24" × 30" chart paper for collecting and categorizing the connections, as illustrated in Figure 12.1. Write the title of the book and the date at the top of the chart paper for all to see. Once the student has shared his or her Connection attach their sticky note to the chart paper with a piece of tape for reinforcement. Ask the student to help decide which category the Connection best represents. The categories need to be broad. The objective is to drill for the main idea or the "source" of the Connection. Examples of categories are self, family, media, favorite part, book, question, comment, history, science, famous person, experience, prediction, friend, point of view, and comparison. Once the category is determined, write the name of the category and the student's name next to the sticky note. One suggestion is to use the same colored marker for each category when a category is repeated. For example, a red marker is used for all connections that are categorized as family, while a purple marker is used for all connections categorized as media.

When everyone has responded you have a document that has the title of the book read aloud, date, and everyone's Connection categorized with their name next to their sticky

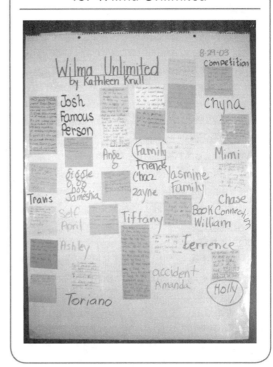

FIGURE 12.1
Connection Chart
for *Wilma Unlimited*

note. Laminate your charts and post them in your room for future review and evaluation. The chart becomes a convenient reference when evaluating student's learning developmentally and sharing students' work with parents or other interested observers.

Step 5: Students Take Notes During Sharing Sessions

Students write the title of the book read and the date on the top of the page. Under the title and date, they write the name of each student as he or she shares and the category of that student's Connection as presented to the class. Having the students record their classmates' names and category of Connection helps to teach them note-taking skills as well as to keep them focused during other students' presentations.

Step 6: Hang a Student-Driven Timeline

Constructing visuals is a form of strengthening the topic studied in which the learner creates some type of representation and, in doing so, engages in deeper processing of text which, in turn, leads to better memory for the information (Holley & Dansereau, 1984). Therefore, all Writing and Sharing Connections classrooms need a student-driven timeline. This three-dimensional classroom-wide graphic organizer allows students to "see" time relationships quickly and efficiently that are otherwise buried in a two-dimensional display found in a textbook (Larkin & Simon, 1987). Two dimensons are revealed in the horizontal display of events in time sequence. The other is in the vertical display of events that occurred in the same time frame. Entries for events that occurred or began in the same year are simply hung one beneath another with clear tape. As you can see in Figure 12.2, Michelangelo and Balboa were both born in 1475.

FIGURE 12.2
Student-Driven Timeline

The timeline is made from 1/8-inch nylon cord, stretched tightly between screw hooks along the full length of at least two adjacent walls in the classroom (Wooten, 2008). If any single length is longer than 25 feet, a third screw hook should be added to the middle for support. Extra cord is added as needed. Most classrooms have student-driven timelines surrounding the room on all four walls by year's end. As the timeline grows, slide entries left and right to make room for additional entries and to keep the chronology correct.

A student-driven timeline contains entries depicting what is studied in the classroom all through the year. What should appear on the timeline? Kings, queens, explorers, artists, inventors, inventions, discoveries, famous people, books, wars, every person or event presented in the classroom that can be associated with a date.

To create timeline entries, fold an 8½" × 11" piece of paper in half. Write the name and date of the person or event on one side in large print. Students decorate each timeline entry with colorful artwork that relates to the person or event. When finished, the entry is added to the timeline in its proper chronological position. Entries for people are placed by year of birth.

People and events from Writing and Sharing Connections literature are also added to the timeline. For example, if *Wilma Unlimited: How Wilma Rudolph Became the World's Fastest Woman* (Krull, 2000) was read aloud, a timeline entry for Wilma Rudolph (1940–1994) is created. A student personalizes the entry with artwork, and the entry is placed on the timeline at 1940 (see Figure 12.3).

Students are selected to personalize timeline entries on a rotating basis so that all students will eventually have artwork on display. Provide a timeline minicenter with crayons and markers available for artistic creation. Allow time for work on timeline pieces each day and aim for adding each timeline entry within two days of instruction while information is fresh. Personalizing each timeline entry is a form of embellishment in which learners create their artwork and, in doing so, engage in deeper relationship with text which, in turn, leads to better memory for the information (Holley & Dansereau, 1984). The teacher has the students applaud as each finished timeline entry is hung.

Development of a student-driven timeline allows students to take charge of constructing the graphic organizer (Barron & Stone, 1984; Bean, Singer, Sorter, & Frazee, 1986). This type of student-driven learning engages students to become active participants in their learning process while they assume ownership of their learning (Langer, 1992).

Making the Connection to Make Meaning

Reading, an active process of constructing meaning, is not just constructing meaning; it is also enjoying all the nuances of the meaning. Writing and Sharing Connections aids students to construct meaningful learning by helping them find joy in reading, connect to the text, and visualize the story. In order for students to develop a love of reading, "Students need to be helped to have unimpeded aesthetic [reading] experiences" (Rosenblatt, 2005, p. 29). During Writing and Sharing Connections, students listen to a text and pay attention to the qualities of the feelings, ideas, situations, scenes, and emotions in the words. Students experience a blend of aesthetic and efferent reading experiences. As their aesthetic reading develops, students find joy in reading and become more motivated to read. One student describes this development by stating, "This method helps me think more creatively and now I pay more attention to books"

FIGURE 12.3
Wilma Rudolph Timeline Entry

(Wooten, 2000, p. 87). Providing students with the opportunity to think creatively and to visualize text develop traits of good readers. By helping students to develop visualization, reading aloud strengthens comprehension skills (Bruce, 1983) as well as other higher order thinking skills.

Writing and Sharing Connections supports learning in all content areas by unifying thought and language, supporting schematic learning, and developing the ability to draw inferences. Vygotsky taught us that thought and language are interrelated in a dynamic process of development; it is only the union of the two that deepens our understanding of thought and increases our use of language to express even more complex thoughts (Wink & Putney, 2002). Writing and Sharing Connections unites language and thought by allowing students to share internal thoughts about connections with text verbally. Schema theory suggests that students will remember and file that new bit of information as learned knowledge more readily by associating it with information that is already accepted in their mental filing cabinet, or knowledge base (Anderson, Spiro, & Anderson, 1985).

Writing and Sharing Connections increases students' general knowledge base so that when they encounter new texts, they have knowledge from which to draw to comprehend the texts (Steffensen, Joag-Dev, & Anderson, 1979). The process of writing connections onto a sticky note as the text is read awakens the student's ability to connect themselves to books read aloud. Louise Rosenblatt sums up how this is done in her statements on the value of transacting with text during an interview in May of 1999:

> Meaning "happens" during the interplay between the text and a reader. Actually, as soon as we start to say what a text means, we are reporting and analyzing the transaction we have just engaged in. We return to the text to see how, drawing on a personal reservoir to transact with the text, we arrived at our particular interpretation. Comparison of our interpretations and the application of criteria such as I have suggested can lead to self-criticism and increased reading ability. (cited in Karolides, 1999, p. 166)

As students practice making connections to their life, other text, and media around them and categorizing those connections through Writing and Sharing Connections, they naturally not only comprehend text but also employ higher level thinking skills.

REFERENCES

Alvermann, D.E., & Phelps, S.E. (2002). *Content reading and literacy: Succeeding in today's diverse classrooms* (3rd ed.). Boston: Allyn & Bacon.

Anderson, R.C. (1984). Role of reader's schema in comprehension, learning, and memory. In R.C. Anderson, J. Osborn, & R.J. Tierney (Eds.), *Learning to read in American schools* (pp. 243–257). Hillsdale, NJ: Erlbaum.

Anderson, R.C., Spiro, R.J., & Anderson, M.C. (1985). *Schemata as scaffolding for the representation of meaning in connected discourse* (Tech. Rep. No. 24). Urbana, IL: University of Illinois, Center for the Study of Reading. (ERIC Document Reproduction Service No. ED136236)

Barron, R.F., & Stone, V.F. (1974). Effects of student-constructed traditional post organizers upon learning vocabulary relationships. In P.L. Nacke (Ed.), *Interaction: Research and practice for college-adult reading* (23rd Yearbook of the National Reading Conference, pp. 172–175). Clemson, SC: National Reading Conference.

Bean, T.W., Singer, H.K., Sorter, J., & Frazee, C. (1986). The effect of metacognitive instruction in outlining and graphic organizer construction on students' comprehension in a tenth-grade world history class. *Journal of Reading Behavior, 18*(2), 153–169.

Beck, I.L., & McKeown, M.G. (2006). *Improving comprehension with questioning the author.* New York: Scholastic.

Boling, C.J., & Evans, W.H. (2008). Reading success in the secondary classroom. *Preventing School Failure, 52*(2), 59–66. doi:10.3200/PSFL.52.2.59-66

Bruce, B.C. (1983). Action! Suspense! Culture! Insight! Reading stories in the classroom (Reading Ed. Rep. No. 45). Urbana, IL: University of Illinois, Center for the Study of Reading. (ERIC Document Reproduction Service No. ED237929)

Calkins, L.M. (1983). *Lessons from a child: On the teaching and learning of writing.* Portsmouth, NH: Heinemann.

Duke, N.K., & Bennett-Armistead, V.S. (2003). *Reading and writing informational text in the primary grades: Research-based practices.* New York: Scholastic.

Duke, N.K., & Pearson, P.D. (2002). Effective practices for developing reading comprehension. In A.E. Farstrup & S.J. Samuels (Eds.), *What research has to say about reading instruction* (3rd ed., pp. 205–242). Newark, DE: International Reading Association.

Ellis, L., & Marsh, J. (2007). *Getting started: The reading-writing workshop, grades 4–8.* Portsmouth, NH: Heinemann.

Glasser, W. (1986). *Control theory in the classroom.* New York: Harper & Row.

Grolnick, W.S., & Ryan, R.M. (1987). Autonomy in children's learning: An experimental and individual differences investigation. *Journal of Personality and Social Psychology, 52*(5), 890–898. doi:10.1037/0022-3514.52.5.890

Holley, C.D., & Dansereau, D.F. (1984). *Spatial learning strategies: Techniques, applications, and related issues.* New York: Academic.

Karolides, N.J. (1999). Theory and practice: an interview with Louise M. Rosenblatt. *Language Arts, 77*(2), 158–170.

Langer, J.A. (1992). *Literature instruction: A focus on student response.* Urbana, IL: National Council of Teachers of English.

Larkin, J.H., & Simon, H.A. (1987). Why a diagram is (sometimes) worth ten thousand words. *Cognitive Science, 11*(1), 65–99. doi:10.1016/S0364-0213(87)80026-5

Marzano, R.J. (2004). *Building background knowledge for academic achievement: Research on what works in schools.* Alexandria, VA: Association for Supervision and Curriculum Development.

Robb, L. (2002). Multiple text: Multiple opportunities for teaching and learning. *Voices From the Middle, 9*(4), 28–32.

Robb, L. (2008). *Teaching reading: A differentiated approach* (Rev. ed.). New York: Scholastic.

Rosenblatt, L.M. (2005). *Making meaning with texts: Selected essays.* Portsmouth, NH: Heinemann.

Steffensen, M.S., Joag-Dev, C., & Anderson, R.C. (1979). A cultural perspective on reading comprehension. *Reading Research Quarterly, 15*(1), 10–29. doi:10.2307/747429

Vygotsky, L.S. (1978). *Mind in society: The development of higher psychological processes* (M. Cole, V. John-Steiner, S. Scribner, & E. Souberman, Eds. & Trans.). Cambridge, MA: Harvard University Press.

Wilhelm, J. (2001). *Improving comprehension with think-aloud strategies.* New York: Scholastic.

Wilhelm, J. (2005). *Reading is seeing: Learning to visualize scenes, characters, ideas, and text worlds to improve comprehension and reflective reading.* New York: Scholastic.

Wink, J., & Putney, L.G. (2002). *A vision of Vygotsky.* Boston: Allyn & Bacon.

Wooten, D.A. (2000). *Valued voices: An interdisciplinary approach to teaching and learning.* Newark, DE: International Reading Association.

Wooten, D.A. (2008). Timeless timeline: Visualizing the past and future. In J. Flood, S.B. Heath, & D. Lapp (Eds.), *Handbook of research on teaching literacy through the communicative and visual arts* (Vol. 2; pp. 559–561). Newark, DE: International Reading Association.

Wooten, D.A., & Cullinan, B.E. (2004). Metacognition through writing and sharing connections. In D. Lapp, C.C. Block, E.J. Cooper, J. Flood, N. Roser, & J.W. Tinajero (Eds.), *Teaching all the children: Strategies for developing literacy in an urban setting* (pp. 294–304). New York: Guilford.

Zemelman, S., Daniels, H., & Hyde, A.A. (2005). *Best practice: Today's standards for teaching & learning in America's schools* (3rd ed.). Portsmouth, NH: Heinemann.

CHILDREN'S LITERATURE CITED

Krull, K. (2000). *Wilma unlimited: How Wilma Rudolph became the world's fastest woman.* San Diego, CA: Voyager.

McGill, A. (1999). *Molly Bannaky.* Boston: Houghton Mifflin.

SUGGESTED BOOKS FOR WRITING AND SHARING CONNECTIONS

Avi. (2003). *Silent movie.* New York: Simon & Schuster.

Chandra, D., & Comora, M. (2003). *George Washington's teeth.* New York: Farrar, Straus and Giroux.

Clinton, C. (2008). *Phillis's big test.* Boston: Houghton Mifflin.

Giovanni, N. (2005). *Rosa.* New York: Henry Holt.

Krull, K. (2004). *A women for President: The story of Victoria Woodhull.* New York: Walker.

Krull, K. (2005). *Houdini: World's greatest mystery man and escape king.* New York: Walker.

Moss, M. (2004). *Mighty Jackie: The strike out queen.* New York: Simon & Schuster.

Rumford, J. (2004). *Sequoya.* Boston: Houghton Mifflin.

Sís, P. (1996). *Starry messenger.* New York: Harper Collins.

Vander Zee, R. (2003). *Erika's story.* Mankato, MN: Creative Editions.

Yolen, J. (1992). *Encounter.* San Diego, CA: Harcourt Brace.

CHAPTER 13

So Many Books— How Do I Choose?

Colleen P. Gilrane

hildren's literature in the reading program—a fabulous idea! But how do you choose which books to include? The answer, of course, depends on your purposes at the time that you are deciding, and other chapters in this book contain many useful suggestions about books that are appropriate for particular instructional tasks in children's literacy development. In this chapter, however, the overwhelming purpose for book selection will be children's interest—and we will move on from there to books that not only engage children, but also are found to be useful by their teachers. We focus on children's interest in books because no matter how relevant to our curriculum a book's content is, if the kids won't read it, it's just not part of the reading program!

It can be overwhelming, in the face of so many books and (usually) not so many dollars, to try to decide which books to have available in the classroom for children's self-selection, or to use in teaching about literature, about writing, or about any unit of study. After using literature for many years, teachers will know the books well enough and know their children well enough to make sound choices (and this is the very best route to take). But

before that happens, what are reliable sources of information to inform our decisions? We want the books to appeal to the children and to us. We want to know that if we are using them in content areas, their information is sound. We want the books to be part of the literate environment that helps our classrooms and schools to be literate communities. This chapter will help you make those decisions.

Books That Appeal to Children: Children's Choices

For several years while I was in high school and college, I was fortunate to have a part-time job in a wonderful branch of the Orange County Public Library System in Orlando, Florida, USA. Our head librarian knew I was going to be a teacher, so she made it part of my job to work on the summer reading programs and storytelling sessions we held, and she arranged for me to attend the workshops held for librarians about the "Sharing Literature With Children" program. All of that interaction with children and with books was invaluable—I knew which books I wanted in my classroom because the kids loved them

Children's Literature in the Reading Program: An Invitation to Read (third edition), edited by Deborah A. Wooten and Bernice E. Cullinan. © 2009 by the International Reading Association.

so much we could not keep them on the shelves. I also knew which books lived forever on the shelves—being dusted, and rearranged, but never borrowed and read by children. A good number of those books were award winners, but clearly the criteria used by the adults giving the awards were different than the criteria of the children who were choosing *not* to read those books!

If you have ever selected a book from a list of award winners only to discover that children won't have anything to do with it, you will understand the frustration that can come from depending on outside experts to recommend books. When you do consult booklists, try to find out what the criteria were for the selecting the books on the list and who the judges were. The most important book list I am going to share with you is one for which children are the judges, and children determine the criteria for their selections: Children's Choices.

Children's Choices is a joint project of the International Reading Association (IRA) and the Children's Book Council (CBC) in which 10,000 schoolchildren from five different regions of the United States read newly published children's and young adult trade books each year and vote on their favorites. Since 1975, the final list of about 100 books per year has been published in *The Reading Teacher*. You can find the new list in the October issue or at www.reading.org/resources/booklists/childrenschoices.aspx where lists for the past several years are archived. This list is designed to help anyone who is interested in making available books that children will choose to read for pleasure and is ideal for use in outfitting classroom libraries or for choosing read-alouds that are intended to draw children into books (IRA/CBC, 2007).

In its current form, the Children's Choices list each year is divided into the categories Beginning Readers (ages 5–7), Young Readers (ages 8–10), and Advanced Readers (ages 11–13), indicating which age levels of children actually read and voted on the books in that category. But do look at levels other than the one(s) corresponding to your grade level, as many wonderful books blur these lines. The list also includes annotations written by teacher members of the five teams across the United States who organized that year's project, so there is a lot of good information for you to use in deciding on which books to look at more closely. Children's Choices is the very best resource I know for selecting books for your classroom that have a high probability of engaging students' interests and being read by them—thus being useful additions to your classroom library.

Books That Appeal to Children *and* to Their Teachers

Now we know which books the kids like the best (for the past 30 or so years, anyway), but we need to narrow the list a bit further, assuming that funds are not unlimited. So what if we knew which of those Children's Choices are also books that teachers like and have chosen for use in their classrooms? Good news—we know!

Teachers' Choices, begun in 1989 by IRA, is an annual project in which seven regional teams of teachers and librarians try out newly published books in their classrooms and libraries to determine which would be the best for use in the curriculum. Each book considered is read by a minimum of six teachers or librarians in each region, and rated according to the following criteria:

- Books that reflect high literary quality in style, content, structure, beauty of language, and presentation

- Books that might not be discovered or fully appreciated by children without introduction by a knowledgeable educator or other adult
- Books that have potential for use across the curriculum

Teachers incorporate such strategies as reading aloud, displays, group projects, and art/music/drama productions. All curriculum areas are covered in the selections (IRA, 2007, p. 261).

Each year's final list of Teachers' Choices appears in the November issue of *The Reading Teacher*, and by going to www.reading.org/resources/booklists/teacherschoices.aspx you can find the most recent lists archived. These lists also include annotations and grade-level information.

In the 18 years that both projects have been going on, 43 different books have appeared on both lists and are listed in Table 13.1. These would seem to be surefire winners—when each year's votes from more than 10,000 children and from dozens of teachers and librarians were counted, these books rose to the top. Certainly they are worth a closer look and can give you many good ideas for great books to add to your classroom collection. Most of them can be counted on to include good information while entertaining children at the same time. For example, *If You Made a Million* (Schwartz, 1989) brings many abstract ideas about money into humorous, child-friendly focus, while *Miss Alaineus: A Vocabulary Disaster* (Frasier, 2000) does the same for words. *Sacagawea* (Erdrich, 2003), by a Native American author and a Native American illustrator, includes an afterword, a helpful timeline of events, and a bibliography for further reading. *Gonna Sing My Head Off! American Folk Songs for Children* (Krull, 1992) will support integrating music and poetry into any social studies unit focused on the United States.

Notable Social Studies Trade Books for Young People

The CBC has worked collaboratively with the National Council for the Social Studies (NCSS) since 1972 to identify excellent books to be used in the teaching of social studies. The list, called Notable Social Studies Trade Books for Young People, is published each year in the May/June issue of *Social Education*, and archived lists are also available at the NCSS website, at www.ncss.org/resources/notable/. According to information at this site, the NCSS/CBC selection committee looks for the following:

> Books that emphasize human relations, represent a diversity of groups and are sensitive to a broad range of cultural experiences, present an original theme or a fresh slant on a traditional topic, are easily readable and of high literary quality, and have a pleasing format, and, when appropriate, illustrations that enrich the text. (NCSS/CBC 2008, unpaged).

Eleven of the 43 books that are both Children's Choices and Teachers' Choices have also been selected by NCSS as notable social studies trade books, such as *The Last Princess: The Story of Princess Ka'iulani of Hawai'i* (Stanley, 1991), heir to the throne, who was denied the right to rule when the monarchy was abolished and Hawaii was annexed by the United States—a story often missing from social studies textbooks. *Leah's Pony* (Friedrich, 1996) makes the difficulties of the U.S. Great Depression (Leah sold her pony and used the money to bid on her father's tractor, which was being auctioned off) much more accessible to children than most descriptions of it. *How Ben Franklin Stole the Lightning* (Schanzer, 2003) includes some of Franklin's original drawings on its endpapers, and *If the World Were a Village: A Book About the World's People* (Smith, 2002) makes global ideas much more understandable by imagining the population of the

TABLE 13.1

Books Selected as Both Children's Choices and Teachers' Choices

Year	Title	RWT	Author	Illustrator	Language Arts	Science	Social Studies
1989	Her Seven Brothers		Paul Goble	Paul Goble			
	Park's Quest		Katherine Paterson				
1990	Beyond the Ridge		Paul Goble	Paul Goble			
	If You Made a Million		David M. Schwartz	Steven Kellogg			
1991	The Empty Pot		Demi	Demi	√		
	The Place My Words Are Looking For: What Poets Say About and Through Their Work		Paul Janeczko				
1992	The Last Princess: The Story of Princess Ka'iulani of Hawai'i		Fay Stanley	Diane Stanley			√
	Manatee on Location		Kathy Darling	photographs by Tara Darling		√	
1993	Gonna Sing My Head Off! American Folk Songs for Children		Kathleen Krull	Allen Garns			√
	Goodbye, Vietnam		Gloria Whelan				
	Inside the Whale and Other Animals		Steve Parker	Ted Dewan			
	My Great-Aunt Arizona		Gloria Houston	Susan Condie Lamb	√		√
	Seven Blind Mice	√	Ed Young	Ed Young			
	Sierra Club Book of Great Mammals		Linsay Knight				
	Rising Voices: Writings of Young Native Americans	√	Arlene B. Hirschfelder & Beverly R. Singer				
	A River Ran Wild: An Environmental History	√	Lynne Cherry			√	√
	Talking With Artists		Pat Cummings		√		
1994	The Giver	√	Lois Lowry		√		
	Hiding Out: Camouflage in the Wild		James Martin	photographs by Art Wolfe		√	√
1995	Dance of the Sacred Circle: A Native American Tale		Kristina Rodanas	Kristina Rodanas			√
1996	Tops and Bottoms		Janet Stevens				

(continued)

TABLE 13.1 (continued)

Books Selected as Both Children's Choices and Teachers' Choices

Year	Title	RWT	Author	Illustrator	Language Arts	Science	Social Studies
1997	Leah's Pony		Elizabeth Friedrich	Michael Garland			✓
	Tornado		Betsy Byars	Doron Ben-Ami			
	Who Killed Mr. Chippendale? A Mystery in Poems		Mel Glenn				
1998	Chasing Redbird		Sharon Creech				
	Look to the North: A Wolf Pup Diary	✓	Jean Craighead George	Lucia Washburn			
	Seedfolks	✓	Paul Fleishman	Judy Pedersen	✓		✓
1999	Harry Potter and the Sorcerer's Stone	✓	J.K. Rowling	Mary GrandPré	✓		
	Safari		Robert Bateman & Rick Archbold	Robert Bateman	✓	✓	
2000	If You Hopped Like a Frog	✓	David M. Schwartz	James Warhola			
2001	It's Raining Pigs and Noodles: Poems		Jack Prelutsky	James Stevenson			
	Miss Alaineus: A Vocabulary Disaster	✓	Debra Frasier	Debra Frasier			
	Wemberly Worried		Kevin Henkes				
2002	Flipped		Wendelin Van Draanen				
	Fly High! The Story of Bessie Coleman	✓	Louise Borden & Mary Kay Kroeger	Teresa Flavin			
	Giraffes Can't Dance		Giles Andreae	Guy Parker-Rees			
	Martin's Big Words: The Life of Dr. Martin Luther King, Jr.	✓	Doreen Rappaport	Bryan Collier			✓
	The Secret School		Avi				
2003	If the World Were a Village: A Book About the World's People	✓	David J. Smith	Shelagh Armstrong			✓
2004	How Ben Franklin Stole the Lightning		Rosalyn Schanzer	Rosalyn Schanzer			✓
	Sacagawea		Lise Erdrich	Julie Buffalohead			
2006	Once Upon a Cool Motorcycle Dude		Kevin O'Malley	Kevin O'Malley, Carol Heyer, & Scott Goto			
2007	3-D ABC: A Sculptural Alphabet		Bob Raczka				

RWT: indicates one or more lesson plans using these books are available at ReadWriteThink.org (International Reading Association/National Council of Teachers of English)
Language Arts: Notable Children's Books in the English Language Arts (National Council of Teachers of English)
Science: Outstanding Science Trade Books for Children (National Science Teachers Association/CBC)
Social Studies: Notable Social Studies Trade Books for Young People (National Council for the Social Studies/CBC)

world as a village of 100 people—of whom 5 are from the United States, 9 speak English, and only 30 always have enough to eat.

Outstanding Science Trade Books for Students in Grades K–12

CBC also works with the National Science Teachers Association (NSTA), and the two groups have produced an annual list of Outstanding Science Trade Books since 1973. You can find their archived booklists at www.nsta.org/publications/ostb/ and when you explore, you will discover that four of the books selected as both children's and teachers' choices also appear on these lists (NSTA/CBC 2008). One of my favorites, *A River Ran Wild: An Environmental History* (Cherry, 1992), was also chosen for the NCSS list discussed earlier. Lynne Cherry's marvelous book documents the efforts of Marion Stoddart to rescue the Nashua River in New Hampshire and Massachusetts and would be a valuable addition to an environmentally themed unit that included a civics component related to taking local action. *Manatee on Location* (Darling, 1991) and *Hiding Out: Camouflage in the Wild* (Martin, 1993) combine photography with clear, accurate, and engaging text to appeal to children's seemingly endless fascination with animals. Artist Robert Bateman adds painting into the mix with *Safari* (Bateman & Archbold, 1998), which also includes some photos showing the models for Bateman's art.

Notable Children's Books in the English Language Arts

Finally, the National Council of Teachers of English (NCTE) identifies each year 30 Notable Children's Books in the English Language Arts. A committee appointed by NCTE's Children's Literature Assembly selects the books, which may deal with language explicitly or demonstrate unique or exemplary qualities (Edinger et al., 2008). Their recommendations are found in the March issue of *Language Arts*, or at the Assembly's website at childrensliteratureassembly.org (click on the red flag labeled "Notables List" when you arrive). As you can see in Table 13.1, seven of the books selected as both Children's and Teachers' Choices are also Notable English Language Arts selections. *The Place My Words Are Looking For: What Poets Say About and Through Their Work* (Janeczko, 1990) is a must for any classroom designed to encourage children as writers, as 39 different poets share their poetry and their advice with readers.

The Jackpot: Books Chosen by Children and *Lots* of Teachers

In addition to *A River Ran Wild* (Cherry, 1992) and *Safari* (Bateman & Archbold, 1998), already discussed in the science section, there are several books that appear on more than one curriculum list, as well as the Children's Choices and Teachers' Choices lists. These are worth considering very seriously for your collection, as they are potential "home run books"—books that may stimulate a lifelong reading habit (Trelease, 2001; Von Sprecken, Kim, & Krashen, 2000).

Pat Cummings's 1992 book, *Talking With Artists* (Volume 1), is recommended by both social studies teachers and language arts teachers, and was chosen for both the Children's Choices and the Teachers' Choices lists. Teachers of writing—at all grade levels—will want this book available for minilessons, for author studies, and for self-selection by children when they get hooked on a favorite author or illustrator. The glimpses it affords into the lives and times of a variety of people make it also useful to support social studies curriculum, and it very naturally supports art. Cummings profiled 14 different children's book illustrators (Victoria Chess, Pat Cummings, Leo Dillon & Diane Dillon, Richard Egielski, Lois Ehlert, Lisa Campbell Ernst, Tom Feelings, Steven Kellogg, Jerry Pinkney, Amy Schwartz, Lane Smith, Chris Van Allsburg, and David Wiesner) and includes background information, examples of adult and childhood art, and answers to the questions kids care about: Where do you get your ideas? Where do you work? Do you have pets or children? Although this volume is the only one to make our lists, writing teachers may be interested in Volume 2 (1995) and Volume 3 (1999) as well.

My Great-Aunt Arizona is Gloria Houston's (1992) biographical picture book about her father's aunt, who grew up and taught school in the Blue Ridge Mountains of the eastern United States. The poetic descriptions, and Susan Condie Lamb's illustrations, provide much fodder for conversation about the differences (and the similarities) between Arizona's time and now. Writing teachers will want this example of biography available for minilessons and genre study—perhaps inspiring young writers to collect family histories of their own. Its lyrical, repetitive language will send readers back to it over and over again.

Paul Fleischman's (1997) *Seedfolks* lends itself to supporting a variety of teaching themes: city life, communities, friendships, celebrating differences—on and on and on. It is no wonder that language arts teachers and social studies teachers recommend this book that is both a Children's Choice and a Teachers' Choice. Its chapters are narrated by 13 different voices as the ethnically diverse neighbors in a Cleveland, Ohio, USA, neighborhood turn an overgrown, garbage-strewn vacant lot into a garden that transforms them as well as the space itself.

Countless social studies topics will arise from discussing this book—immigration, civics, fairness, law enforcement, diverse backgrounds, economic resources—and writing teachers will find it a gold mine of examples of language differences, dialect differences, and shifting voices. It is truly a treasure, and some science information about plant growth and human health finds its way into the mix as well.

Lois Lowry's (1993) *The Giver*, with its futuristic, ideal-world themes, was chosen by social studies and language arts teachers, as well as being on the Children's Choices and Teachers' Choices lists—and it's a Newbery Medal winner. Clearly it's unanimous that this book is a winner. You'll want to have it available for students to choose at all times, whether it fits neatly into a curriculum unit.

Teaching Ideas: Using Books Children Love to Help Them as Writers

We know that children who are writers come to depend on the books they read for models of good writing (Graves, 1989; Harwayne, 1992), so why not capitalize on this (Gilrane, 2006) and use books that we know they love as we plan our minilessons, author studies, and genre studies? In chapter 9 of this volume, Jane Hansen shares vignettes from several writing classrooms in which children use literature as mentor texts to influence and support their own writing. Judy Davis and Sharon Hill (2003) write,

> When we set out to learn to do anything, we look to others who are expert at what we are trying to learn to do. Learning to write is no different. In teaching our students to be good writers, one of the first things we want them to be able to do is to anchor themselves to authors and texts they admire. A "mentor piece" is a short text or portion of a text used as a support

for the work they are trying to accomplish in the workshop. (p. 10)

Consider the sets of books in the sections that follow as possible mentor texts when you and your young authors are exploring the writing of biographies, of poetry, or of informational texts. You will want to share them with children in minilessons and in writing conferences, to use them as read alouds, and to have them available in the room for children to select for free reading.

Award-Winning Mentor Texts: Biography

Children are fascinated by "real-life" stories, and the variety of ways these life histories are presented will show them that there is no one, single way to compose them. Perhaps one of them will inspire one of your young authors. Every book described in the following section also employs artwork beautifully, which will be especially important to share with upper elementary (and older) writers who often believe they are "too old" for the picture books in the library.

Fly High! The Story of Bessie Coleman, by Louise Borden and Mary Kay Kroeger (2001) and illustrated by Teresa Flavin, tells the story of how Bessie Coleman beat the odds by doing what she needed to do (earning the money and learning to speak French) to get her treasured pilot's license in France when she was not allowed to in the United States. This story may lead a young writer to research and tell the story of others who have needed to go to great lengths to overcome obstacles.

In another example, *How Ben Franklin Stole the Lightning* by Rosalyn Schanzer (2003) uses humor and cartoon-like illustrations as well as incorporating some of Franklin's own drawings. The availability of many primary texts in digitized form on the Internet will make it possible for young authors to find oth-er original notes and sketches by historical persons in whom they are interested.

Martin's Big Words: The Life of Dr. Martin Luther King, Jr. by Doreen Rappaport (2001), illustrated by Bryan Collier, focuses on the important words of Martin Luther King, Jr., that Rappaport found so profound and inspirational to her own life. They are emphasized in the book by being printed in color in a very large size, compared with the rest of the text. This idea of selecting and emphasizing a critical element of a person's life is another approach to biography that students may be able to model in their own writing.

The previously mentioned *My Great-Aunt Arizona* by Gloria Houston (1992) and illustrated by Susan Condie Lamb may lead a young author to decide to interview an interesting relative, or to try to draw or paint "the old homestead" and use it to tell the story of members of the family. *Sacagawea* by Lise Erdrich (2003), illustrated by Julie Buffalohead, is a picture book biography that also includes an author's note at the beginning, and an afterword, sharing with the reader information about the subject that is missing or unclear from the record, and which the author either chose to leave out or chose to agree with one position over another in her writing. The idea of tentativeness in the historical record, and being honest about it in a piece of writing, will appeal to some young authors. Finally, by using *The Last Princess* by Fay Stanley (1991) and illustrated by Diane Stanley, as a mentor text, a young writer who believes a historical situation is unfair may be inspired to research it further and write about another point of view after reading this book.

Award-Winning Mentor Texts: Poetry

Children must be exposed to a large amount of poetry before they can be expected to write it. And many children who believe that they don't like poetry, or who think it must rhyme, have just not been exposed to the right poems yet. The texts described in this section can be used to widen their perspective.

Gonna Sing My Head Off! American Folk Songs for Children by Kathleen Krull (1992) and illustrated by Allen Garns is just the book for children who believe they don't like poetry. Use this book to help them see that music lyrics are poetry, and they will be able to find something to serve as an anchor. *It's Raining Pigs and Noodles: Poems* by Jack Prelutsky (2000) and illustrated by James Stevenson is the text for young poets who wish to emulate the fun of nonsense, wordplay, and general goofiness.

The Place My Words Are Looking For by Paul Janeczko (1990) is a collection of 63 poems by 39 contemporary poets, many of whom will be known to young authors. There are also essays from the poets sharing advice and something about themselves and their processes of writing poetry, which will inspire young poets. *Rising Voices: Writings of Young Native Americans* by Arlene B. Hirschfelder and Beverly R. Singer (1992) is a collection of poems—as well as essays and letters—written by Native American youth, and includes biographical information about each writer. The forms of the poems are varied, and the idea that poetry can be an expression of feelings that are complicated and about real life will strike a chord with young writers.

For older students, *Who Killed Mr. Chippendale? A Mystery in Poems* by Mel Glenn (1996) puts an entirely different spin on poetry than any of the others. Each free-verse poem in the book gives the reaction of a different person (colleagues, students, friends) to the murder of a teacher on the school grounds. Language and style vary with the voices of the different "poets" and offer differ-

ing emotional responses to violence, which is a concern of our young people.

Award-Winning Mentor Texts: Informational Books

I taught so many young writers over the years who were in a writing workshop for the first time and wanted to write a "report," but had no resources to draw on other than copying from the encyclopedia. Today, they would print out from the Internet, unless we show them the richness of possibilities for presenting factual information. Each of the books in the section that follows is about a favorite kids' topic—animals—but none of them is the dreaded "report," and they each offer a different way to organize and present the information that is to be shared.

In *If You Hopped Like a Frog* (1999) David Schwartz bring his "If You..." repetitive phrasing—familiar from his million-focused math books—and his love of math to the animal kingdom, using comparisons between animals and humans to illustrate the concept of ratio. The math formulas he used are shared, and young authors hooked on both math and animals may want to try their own computations.

Inside the Whale and Other Animals by Steve Parker (1992) and illustrated by Ted Dewan will be the favorite of children who are fascinated with how things work. Large pen-and-ink drawings are used to present the inner anatomy of 21 different animals, with smaller drawings or cutaway sections used to focus on special characteristics when warranted. Young writers who communicate visually will love this venue for presenting scientific information.

Jean Craighead George is already well known to young readers for her Newbery Award–winning novel, *Julie of the Wolves* (George, 1972), and in *Look to the North: A*

Wolf Pup Diary (George, 1997), illustrated by Lucia Washburn, she focuses on information about wolves over the year, using the format of a diary relating what her young readers are experiencing (e.g., Halloween, seeing baby robins in spring) to what is going on in the life of a wolf pup—telling her readers to "look to the North" to see these events. Young writers desiring to share information that develops over time may see this as an interesting way to organize their information.

Manatee on Location by Kathy Darling (1991), with photography by Tara Darling, is a photo essay representing two years of work by the author, an underwater photographer studying manatees in Florida. This book enables students to learn about the efforts of many to save these endangered animals, and presents young authors who do not feel artistic with an alternative venue for illustration.

In *Hiding Out: Camouflage in the Wild* by James Martin (1993), photographs by Art Wolfe, students can learn about camouflage in nature. Most children are, unfortunately, all too familiar with the concept of camouflage in military engagements, but they may not be as aware of its use in nature as a survival technique, both by predators and by prey. Choosing an animal characteristic and then writing about and illustrating its presence across species is another way to write an informational text, and it may appeal to some young authors.

Safari by Robert Bateman and Rick Archbold (1998) brings art firmly into the foreground, as Bateman, an acclaimed nature artist, presents paintings to serve as a guide to a safari. Facts and anecdotes are also included, as well as a few photographs showing the sub-jects of the paintings and serves as yet another way to present information for young writers to consider.

Making Sure the Books Are Always Available

Be sure that these and other books children love to read are on display and available for self-selection and free reading, and that they are not just in the classroom for a week or so during a unit of study. The very best books draw readers back again and again, and we want to allow that to happen. I can't imagine a summer when I don't reread all of Jane Austen's novels, and perhaps you have your own favorites you return to from time to time. Help young readers develop these literate habits by making books available to them constantly. The same book might draw them, with varying frequency, all year long—first, to reread until they "get" the story or feel confident in their knowledge of the information; later, perhaps to check the factual information if it's relevant to a topic of inquiry; yet again, to look closely at the author's craft or the illustrator's technique, to influence a young author's own compositions during the writing workshop. Although you will no doubt come up with many ideas for integrating these books with the teaching and learning going on in your classroom, it will also be valuable to introduce the books, make them available, and stand back and watch—being on the lookout all the time for opportunities to nudge your students to just the right text that will solve a particular problem they have identified.

REFERENCES

Davis, J., & Hill, S. (2003). *The no-nonsense guide to teaching writing: Strategies, structures, and solutions*. Portsmouth, NH: Heinemann.

Edinger, M., Austin, P., Day, D., Johnson, V.G., Levin, S., Pritchard, T.G., et al. (2008). 2007 Notable children's books in the English language arts. *Language Arts, 85*(4), 325–333.

Gilrane, C.P. (2006). Using Children's Choices to recruit young writers into apprenticeships with authors. *The Dragon Lode, 24*(2), 51–55.

Graves, D.H. (1989). *Experiment with fiction.* Portsmouth, NH: Heinemann.

Harwayne, S. (1992). *Lasting impressions: Weaving literature into the writing workshop.* Portsmouth, NH: Heinemann.

International Reading Association. (2007). Teacher's choices for 2007. *The Reading Teacher, 61*(3), 261–268. doi:10.1598/RT.61.3.7

International Reading Association & Children's Book Council. (2007). Children's choices for 2007. *The Reading Teacher, 61*(2), 175–190. doi:10.1598/RT.61.2.8

National Council for the Social Studies & Children's Book Council. (2008). *Notable social studies trade books for young people.* Retrieved March 27, 2008, from www.ncss.org/resources/notable/

National Science Teachers Association & Children's Book Council. (2008). *Outstanding science trade books for students K–12.* Retrieved March 27, 2008, from www.nsta.org/publications/ostb/

Trelease, J. (2001). *The read-aloud handbook* (4th ed.). New York: Penguin.

Von Sprecken, D., Kim, J., & Krashen, S. (2000). The home run book: Can one positive reading experience create a reader? *California School Library Journal, 23*(2), 8–9.

CHILDREN'S LITERATURE CITED

Bateman, R., & Archbold, R. (1998). *Safari.* Boston: Little, Brown.

Borden, L., & Kroeger, M.K. (2001). *Fly high! The story of Bessie Coleman.* New York: Margaret K. McElderry.

Cherry, L. (1992). *A river ran wild: An environmental history.* Orlando, FL: Hougton Mifflin Harcourt.

Cummings, P. (Ed.). (1992). *Talking with artists* (vol. 1). New York: Bradbury Press.

Cummings, P. (Ed.). (1995). *Talking with artists* (vol. 2). New York: Simon & Schuster.

Cummings, P. (Ed.). (1999). *Talking with artists* (vol. 3). New York: Clarion.

Darling, K. (1991). *Manatee on location.* New York: Lothrop, Lee & Shepard.

Erdrich, L. (2003). *Sacagawea.* Minneapolis, MN: Carolrhoda.

Fleischman, P. (1997). *Seedfolks.* New York: HarperCollins.

Frasier, D. (2000). *Miss Alaineus: A vocabulary disaster.* San Diego, CA: Harcourt Brace.

Friedrich, E. (1996). *Leah's pony.* Honesdale, PA: Boyds Mills.

George, J.C. (1972). *Julie of the wolves.* New York: Harper & Row.

George, J.C. (1997). *Look to the North: A wolf pup diary.* New York: HarperCollins.

Glenn, M. (1996). *Who killed Mr. Chippendale? A mystery in poems.* New York: Lodestar.

Hirschfelder, A.B., & Singer, B.R. (1992). *Rising voices: Writings of young native Americans.* New York: Scribner.

Houston, G. (1992). *My Great-Aunt Arizona.* New York: HarperCollins.

Janeczko, P. (1990). *The place my words are looking for: What poets say about and through their work.* New York: Bradbury Press.

Krull, K. (1992). *Gonna sing my head off! American folk songs for children.* New York: Knopf.

Lowry, L. (1993). *The giver.* Boston: Houghton Mifflin.

Martin, J. (1993). *Hiding out: Camouflage in the wild.* New York: Crown.

Parker, S. (1992). *Inside the whale and other animals.* New York: Delacorte.

Prelutsky, J. (2001). *It's raining pigs and noodles: Poems.* New York: Greenwillow.

Rappaport, D. (2001). *Martin's big words: The life of Dr. Martin Luther King, Jr.* New York: Hyperion.

Schanzer, R. (2003). *How Ben Franklin stole the lightning.* New York: HarperCollins.

Schwartz, D.M. (1989). *If you made a million.* New York: Lothrop, Lee & Shepard.

Schwartz, D.M. (1999). *If you hopped like a frog.* New York: Scholastic.

Smith, D.J. (2002). *If the world were a village: A book about the world's people.* Tonawanda, NY: Kids Can Press.

Stanley, F. (1991). *The last princess: The story of Princess Ka'iulani of Hawai'i.* New York: Four Winds Press.

Reaching Beyond the Classroom Walls to Support Literacy and Learning

As curriculum and high-stakes testing demands continue to grow, it is imperative that we seek support from resources beyond our classroom walls. The goal of this section is to make the teacher's job easier. The strategies presented here will help you work more effectively and efficiently with one of your strongest links to quality literature, the librarian. Ways to motivate families to become supportively involved with the classroom community will also be explored.

Librarians can serve as ready sources of the literature you need for your classroom. But do teachers know how to best connect with them? Chapter 14 explains methods such as "curriculum mapping" and "virtual collaboration" as productive, time-efficient ways to work with your librarian.

Studies provide evidence that exposing students to children's and young adult literature that reflects the diversity of students in their classroom helps to connect students and their families to the classroom. Chapter 15 provides effective ways to get parents involved in the classroom. Ideas include having a potluck event in which each family brings a dish that represents their culture or ethnicity, or planting a communal garden in which everyone learns to grow together.

CHAPTER 14

Teacher and School Librarian Collaboration: Imagine a Partner

Gail Bush

Both the art and the science of teaching are in flux in this rapidly expanding information universe, and it should come as a comfort to the classroom teacher to know that the school librarian is a ready and willing instructional partner. Accomplished teachers seem to have a natural capacity for that flow between a foundational skill set of instructional methodologies and the intuitive inclination toward differentiation and accommodation. Nevertheless, it takes savvy educators working together to identify quality literature, informational texts, and emerging technologies that will inspire students to engage in authentic learning experiences. Allow your imagination to conjure up this eager partner ready for your next unit of study.

Each partner is an expert in his or her own domain: the teacher knows his or her students, the curriculum, learning goals, and student objectives; the librarian knows the literature, the resources, the information literacy skills as they relate to the curriculum, and the value of inquiry as a critical thinking and learning disposition. Although this proposition seems logical, it is often fraught with misconcep-

tions and retreats back into the safety of the classroom. An illustrative project that served to affect perceptions and practices might pave the way for your own collaborative journey. In this chapter, you will learn about the Libraries, Literacy, and Learning project and discover how this project demonstrates that having specific outcomes for educator collaboration benefits our students by connecting the strengths of both the teacher and librarian in a shared purpose. The focus on multicultural literature allows for creative applications to many disciplines and grade levels.

Libraries, Literacy, and Learning: Educator Collaboration in Action

A prime example of educator collaboration in action comes from a pilot project developed by the Advanced Reading Development Demonstration Project (ARDDP), a joint partnership between the Chicago Public Schools (CPS) and local Chicago-area universities, sponsored by The Chicago Community Trust, and initiated in the 2003–2004 school year. In 2006 an issue that surfaced in the

---

Children's Literature in the Reading Program: An Invitation to Read (third edition), edited by Deborah A. Wooten and Bernice E. Cullinan. © 2009 by the International Reading Association.

Literacy Partners ARDDP project was the "lack of capacity within at-risk schools to develop culturally responsive literacy instruction using thematic text sets" (Blachowicz, Buhle, Correa, Frost, & Ogle, 2006, p. 1). Paul K. Whitsitt, CPS Director of Libraries and Information Services, identified an important department goal of supporting school librarian and classroom teacher collaboration. CPS Area Instructional Officers also indicated that this initiative fit within and enhanced their area school goals (Blachowicz & Yokota, 2006).

The goal of the Libraries, Literacy, and Learning (LLL) project was to develop internal capacity in designated CPS to deliver effective multicultural literacy instruction to a diverse student population. Not only does this seem like a worthy goal in urban and many suburban school districts, this goal is recurring as our student demographics continue to change. This project's specific objectives were as follows:

- Develop strategies between school librarians and classroom teachers for collaborative planning, instruction, and assessment

- Connect state learning standards to multicultural and informational texts; build capacity for using multicultural themes to strengthen information literacy instruction by developing the participants' knowledge base

- Build on existing curriculum mapping to identify areas of intergrade collaboration and plan for student collaborative projects

- Build on existing curricula by infusing multicultural literature and information literacy research skills into units highlighting digital and community access to resources

- Strengthen the multicultural literature and informational text collection of the participating schools

- Develop venues for sharing work including modules within and beyond the schools

Nine schools participated by enlisting a librarian and at least one second-grade teacher to attend a series of professional development sessions spread across the school year. These sessions were used to develop participant knowledge, to plan for infusing multicultural literature and information literacy research skills into the second-grade curricula, to work together on developing strategies for student collaboration, to order materials to support instruction, and to field test, share, and refine work on instruction resulting from the planning (Blachowicz & Yokota, 2006).

The idea of collaboration between school librarians and classroom teachers was recognized as important by CPS principals, but all the usual obstacles to collaboration including funding, timing, perceptions, and school culture were present and thriving (Foerster, 2004). There is a common misconception that collaboration occurs only when educators are standing side-by-side joined at the hip and co-teaching. But there are many forms that collaboration might take and collaborative planning is a critical element in teacher and librarian partnerships; it enhances instruction in both the classroom and the library and benefits student achievement by making connections among the lessons.

Collaboration Between Teachers and Librarians for Effective Reading Instruction

School librarians appreciate the challenging task of the teacher to engage each student at just the right interest, ability, and motivational level. The goal of the school library resource collection is to support the teacher by providing materials at all these levels for each student for every aspect of the curriculum including fostering a love of reading for personal pursuits. This is no small task. Additionally, it has become apparent to school librarians that it is no longer sufficient to assume that students will in fact engage in text just because a likely resource is placed before them. The 2004 American Association of School Librarians (AASL) Fall Forum focused on "Collaboration and Reading to Learn," where literacy scholars including Peter Afflerbach, Donna Ogle, and Stephen Krashen shared their perspectives on reading instruction and free voluntary reading and the role of the school librarian in supporting his or her colleagues in the classrooms (Bush, 2005).

School librarians stand ready to help cultivate student learning through resources regardless of format. Collaboratively planning with librarians ensures that classroom content is reinforced throughout the library lessons. Comprehension strategies and vocabulary used before, during, and after read-alouds help students connect classroom instruction to the stories they hear in the independent learning environment of the library. The following are a few favorite, simple ways librarians may reinforce classroom lessons in the library, all of which were used by participants in the LLL project (Bush, 2005):

- Prepare to model and explain the comprehension strategy using the text you have chosen (in collaboration with the teacher). Remember that a key to successful strategy instruction is making the invisible visible for students. Get comfortable with the idea of thinking aloud for (and with) students.

- Collaborate with the classroom teacher to provide guided and independent work that will allow students to practice and apply comprehension strategies they have learned.

- Partner with the teacher to help repeat exposure to vocabulary. Focus on both word meaning and concept development.

- Use the vocabulary that is being studied and encourage students to use it as they interpret meaning from images in informational texts and respond to literature. When you are reading aloud and discussing illustrations, be sure to elicit vocabulary that is being studied.

- Assuming you were engaged with teaching prior units of study, activate prior knowledge by using vocabulary from recent units while reinforcing the study of new vocabulary.

Most elementary school librarians are former classroom teachers. They appreciate the opportunity to directly connect their instructional role with the curriculum covered in the classroom. In many instances all that is required is a relaxed approach to a small and friendly beginning to educator collaboration. Starting with one lesson within one unit in one discipline is just about the right size. There is a natural confluence that does occur and interdisciplinary units are a likely outcome, but the best bet for a successful start is planning one collaborative lesson within one unit.

Collaborative Planning With Standards

The scheduling practices of school libraries varies widely from completely fixed schedules—where librarians have classes scheduled into the library on a weekly basis, to flexible schedules—where teachers reserve the library based on curricular needs. This scheduling phenomenon seems to act as a linchpin to collaborative planning. Those librarians with fixed schedules are the least accessible to teachers during the teachers' planning periods; in fact, the librarians often provide the opportunity for the teachers to have their "preps" as do the art, music, and possibly the physical education teachers. The classroom teacher contracts in many districts dictate a specific amount of preparation time during the school day which translates into the students attending "specials" while their teachers have prep periods. So the "specials," as the music, art, special education, (sometimes physical education), and library resource specialists are often called, find themselves in the catch-22 of knowing that they need to collaborate with classroom teachers to benefit student learning but not having the availability in their schedules because of contractual or common scheduling practices within their school cultures. Many grant-funded projects are written to provide common planning time as was the case with the LLL pilot project. It was that time carved out of each professional development workshop that allowed the participating librarians and teachers to collaboratively plan their multicultural units.

The good news is that change is possible. Principals who see the outcomes of collaborative planning between classroom teachers and librarians become more creative with their scheduling. They might use block scheduling for specials on a biweekly basis. Sometimes principals find financial incentives in the forms of honoraria or allotting funds to the classroom and school libraries to support collaborative units. In other school districts, the specials who do not attend the same meetings as the classroom teachers make the time to collaborate so that their curricula are jointly supporting the general curriculum.

A good beginning to collaboratively planning lessons is to use a curriculum mapping strategy. Look ahead in your calendar and select an upcoming unit that has a natural connection to using library resources. Within that unit you will find a lesson that seems like it is ripe for the picking. However, understand that it might take some time to acquire or borrow relevant current materials and to identify the best online resources including databases and web-based links. One common pitfall is the teacher who approaches the librarian and has an expectation of an immediate and miraculous full offering of a variety of resources in multiple formats. Chances are there will be some uneven choices. Librarians, for their part, do their best to estimate need and support of the curriculum. Without direct collaboration with classroom teachers or a stand-alone curriculum map of what is actually taught in the classroom, this is a best guess and therefore may be hit or miss. The librarian should welcome the opportunity to improve the collection but wants to feel supported in this effort and not defensive about the time or resources needed to make this happen.

In a perfect world classroom teachers might not assume that the librarian also has a curriculum map and that you are both looking for a match. In the void of having that accurate curriculum map of what is happening in the classrooms, librarians again are left in the position of making an estimate based on holidays, months celebrated, and the customary grade level units—ancient Egypt in one grade, capital cities in another. And in this void, a library curriculum has emerged. In every instance, that content curriculum should be replaced by actual classroom goals and objectives where possible. It is the process curriculum of information literacy skills and strategies that the librarian will use to enhance the content curriculum through collaborative planning with the classroom teacher.

One simple recommendation for approaching the small and friendly beginning to collaboration is this—ask your librarian about collaboratively planning a lesson. Go ahead, start a revolution. But when you meet for the first (or second) time, come prepared with not only your curriculum goals, objectives, and calendar, but also your national and state standards in mind. Together you will discover that there are many—International Reading Association (IRA), National Council of Teachers of English (NCTE), state student learning standards, and the AASL "Standards for the 21st-Century Learner" with common goals. In fact, of the nine common beliefs that form the foundation of the AASL student learning standards, the first common belief is as follows:

> Reading is a window to the world.
> Reading is a foundational skill for learning, personal growth, and enjoyment. The degree to which students can read and understand text in all formats (e.g., pictures, video, print) and all contexts is a key indicator of success in school and in life. As a lifelong learning skill, reading goes beyond decoding and comprehension to interpretation and development of new understandings. (AASL, 2007, n.p.)

Think about your most familiar standards that support your curriculum and your teaching. Consider how comfortably these four standards fit into your goals (AASL, 2007, n.p.):

Learners use skills, resources, and tools to:

1. Inquire, think critically, and gain knowledge.
2. Draw conclusions, make informed decisions, apply knowledge to new situations, and create new knowledge.
3. Share knowledge and participate ethically and productively as members of our democratic society.
4. Pursue personal and aesthetic growth.

Within each standard are four habits of mind each explicated with a key question (AASL, 2007, n.p.):

1. Skills—Key Question: Does the student have the right proficiencies to explore a topic or subject further?
2. Dispositions in Action—Key Question: Is the student disposed to higher-level thinking and actively engaged in critical thinking to gain and share knowledge?
3. Responsibilities—Key Question: Is the student aware that the foundational traits for 21st-century learning require self-accountability that extends beyond skills and dispositions?
4. Self-Assessment Strategies—Key Question: Can the student recognize personal strengths and weaknesses over time and become a stronger, more independent learner?

Classroom teachers who realize the changing nature of our students as millennial learners, the rapid multiplication of information, and the necessary elements required to build knowledge will appreciate the efforts of the school librarians to encapsulate this change and provide forward-thinking learning standards. The library as a center of learning for 21st-century learners might not only fulfill the vision of school librarians, it might also provide a comfort zone for teachers to become empowered around this changing landscape. Teachers do not need to recognize every book title, database, or emerging technology. Librarians do not need to remember the content of every unit of study for every class in the school. However, through collaborative planning that focuses on the prevailing standards, the teacher and librarian make a mighty team to better serve our students with an authentic, inquiry-based curriculum that engages even our toughest critics.

Essential Questions

Essential questions are necessary to the development of both critical thinking and the imagination. Skillfully framed essential questions act as catalysts for learning through inquiry and bring to bear problem-solving strategies. An essential question is a meaningful question that inspires inquiry of a big idea or concept. Age, experience, and education deepen the inquiry but the essential question might remain constant throughout a learner's life. Finely honed essential questions bring forth problem-finding questioning and allow students to differentiate their own learning based on their level of interest, ability, and motivation.

Essential questions can begin a unit of study and are based upon the concepts that teachers want their students to understand and apply. The best essential questions center on major concepts, problems, interests, or themes relevant and authentic to students' lives and to their surroundings. Good essential questions are open-ended, nonjudgmental, meaningful, motivational, filled with emotion, and invite further exploration. They also encourage collaboration among students, teachers, and the community. In addition, good essential questions integrate technology to support the learning process (adapted from MathStar, New Mexico State University, n.d.).

At best, essential questions motivate students to question and provoke them into action. At worst, essential questions confuse students by either being too diffuse or meaningless. Consider yourself as a lifelong learner. Reading a news magazine or watching a news report we exercise habits of mind that frame our own essential questions: What is the American Dream? How is technology changing society (and should we just because we can)? What does it mean to live in a global economy? How is citizenship in the global community having a local impact?

As we age and add experience to education, we question the nature of our society:

What is a hero? What is a friend? How do we balance privacy and the needs of our society? What is truth and beauty, and why are they important? And on and on. Once we recognize our own disposition toward essential questions we become more comfortable with the role of big ideas and essential questions to guide learning. The simple distinction between what we are learning and why we are learning this helps to put us into the habit of mind of essential questions. Teachers and school librarians find that essential questions guide collaborative lesson planning and allow for students to benefit from both learning environments; connections are made between what is taught in the classroom and explored and discovered in the library, with the essential question providing the link between the two ways of learning.

In 1989, Kathleen Cushman, then the editor of the school reform journal *Horace*, published a seminal list of essential questions for educators to consider as they reflect and plan instruction (Cushman, 1989, n.p.):

Essential Questions to Shape a School's Curriculum
In every class and every subject, students will learn to ask and to answer these questions:

From whose viewpoint are we seeing or reading or hearing?

From what angle or perspective?

How do we know when we know?

What's the evidence, and how reliable is it?

How are things, events, or people connected to each other?

What is the cause and what is the effect?

How do they fit together?

What's new and what's old?

Have we run across this idea before?

So what?

Why does it matter?

What does it all mean?

Essential questions must be grounded in real-world accountability to be eligible for consideration by educators as they reflect and plan instruction. Surprisingly to critics of any national or state guidelines, standards serve to make that connection between essential questions and units of study. Learning standards have that unfortunate connotation with national and state standardized assessments. Looking at learning standards with fresh eyes allows us to view them as big ideas that are indeed worthwhile learning. The progression then leads to framing essential questions to guide our learning. How do we take that next step? We take the standard and rephrase it into a question that captures the essence of the issue at hand. If every standard were rephrased into an essential question, inquiry would become the center of learning and students would have greater ownership over their own learning processes.

In the LLL pilot project, our teams of librarians and second-grade teachers grappled with the task of framing essential questions and allowing those questions to guide the inquiry and the lesson planning. It is a healthy exercise for educators to make the connection between essential questions, then unit questions, then lesson plans. The following is a prime example of moving from standard to essential question to unit question by educators as they collaboratively planned for the Young Explorer's Club:

> *Illinois Student Learning Goal 17*: Understand world geography and the effects of geography on society, with an emphasis on the United States.
> *Why This Goal Is Important*: The need for geographic literacy has never been greater or more obvious than in today's tightly interrelated world. Students must understand the world's physical features, how they blend with social systems and how they affect economies, politics and human interaction. Isolated geographic facts are not enough. To grasp geography and its

effect on individuals and societies, students must know the broad concepts of spatial patterns, mapping, population and physical systems (land, air, water). The combination of geographic facts and broad concepts provides a deeper understanding of geography and its effects on individuals and societies.
> 17A. Locate, describe and explain places, regions and features on the Earth.
> *Illinois Student Learning Goal 18*: Understand social systems, with an emphasis on the United States.
> *Why This Goal Is Important*: A study of social systems has two important aspects that help people understand their roles as individuals and members of society. The first aspect is culture consisting of the language, literature, arts and traditions of various groups of people. Students should understand common characteristics of different cultures and explain how cultural contributions shape societies over time. The second aspect is the interaction among individuals, groups and institutions. Students should know how and why groups and institutions are formed, what roles they play in society, and how individuals and groups interact with and influence institutions.
> 18A. Compare characteristics of culture as reflected in language, literature, the arts, traditions and institutions. (Illinois State Board of Education, 1997)

> *ESSENTIAL QUESTION:* How does your journey to different countries make you think about the world?

> *UNIT QUESTION:* How was going to school alike/different for your family members?

> *LESSON QUESTIONS:* From what continent did your family originate? What are Ellis Island and the Statue of Liberty? What do you do with a passport?

Curriculum Design and Collaborative Models

Collaboration with the school librarian is independent of any particular model or strategy. Districts adopt models, drop models, and some just seem to lose steam as time goes on.

Curriculum design, however, is the larger context within which the models reside. Curriculum design seems to have remained constant since Ralph W. Tyler published *Basic Principles of Curriculum and Instruction* in 1949, a publication which grew out of a course syllabus from the University of Chicago. Tyler posits four fundamental questions which must be answered in developing any curriculum and plan of instruction:

1. "What educational purposes should the school seek to attain?" *What is worthwhile learning? What is the scope?*

2. "What educational experiences can be provided that are likely to attain these purposes?" *How should it be taught? How shall instruction be planned? What is the sequence?*

3. "How can these educational experiences be effectively organized?" *When should it be taught? What is the instructional implementation?*

4. "How will we evaluate it?" *What is the evidence of learning? How will understanding be measured?* (1949, p. 1)

These questions underlie all effective curriculum models. They also mirror the ubiquitous Understanding by Design curriculum philosophy of backward design (Wiggins & McTighe, 2005). What is worthwhile learning—the big idea—guides the essential question, which leads to the unit question. From the unit question, assessments are developed that will provide evidence that demonstrates learning relevant to the unit. And finally, lessons are planned that optimally use instructional strategies for deep student engagement. This curriculum planning model is counterintuitive to the teachers who feel that they are trapped or scripted into their classroom curricula with no purpose to the lessons they must teach and no sense of their individuality as an educator.

However, there is much room for passionate teachers to collaborate with their librarians to provide a broader approach to learning that is more readily accommodated and differentiated and that invites innovative teaching practices. The library is in the school to support curriculum and to ensure that all students have equal access to the general curriculum. Teachers who develop a collaborative partnership with their librarians find that they are able to serve all their students better by providing a wide range of support materials. And the teachers then respond to the greater learning environment with creative assessments that are developmentally appropriate for their students and that use the breadth of the resources available.

APACA

A collaborative model was developed in Chicago in 2004 by researcher Patrice N. Foerster. Ask Plan Acquire Co-teach Assess, or APACA, marked the beginnings of an effort to prepare elementary school librarians and classroom teachers to collaborate effectively despite the obstacles to collaboration previously mentioned. Foerster's collaborative model is successful in schools where both teachers and librarians feel that time and resources are scarce. APACA is simple and elegant and does not presume that the teachers and librarians are available for synchronistic co-teaching in the library or classroom. It is a real-world solution to the collaboration phenomenon that educators sometimes feel is an unrealistic expectation within their circumstances.

The components of APACA are as follows (Foerster, 2004):

Ask—The librarian *asks* a colleague teacher to work collaboratively to enhance an existing unit of study.

Plan—The classroom teacher and the librarian *plan* during whatever blocks of time they can find, so that the unit can be reformulated to include information literacy components and other learning enhancements. The two also work to identify additional resources that should be added to the library collection to support this unit.

Acquire—The new resources are *acquired* for the school's library.

Co-teach—The collaborative unit is taught by the classroom teacher and the librarian. The *co-teaching* can be done by special arrangement with both individuals together with students, or it can be done in tandem when they each individually have the students in the classroom or the library.

Assess—Student products from the unit are *assessed* and if possible, compared with products and results from previous years; the collaborative methodology used by the librarian and classroom teacher is also *assessed* for possible improvement.

The LLL pilot project teachers and librarians were selected by their administrators (Ask); were given time to collaboratively plan through the grant funding (Plan); new resources were acquired through matching grants with the CPS Department of Libraries and Information Services (Acquire); units were co-taught by the librarian in the library and the teacher in the classroom because the librarians are on fixed schedules (Co-teach); and assessments varied greatly depending on the units taught but in all cases both the librarian and the teacher partnered in assessing student work (Assessment).

Assessment

In the backward-design *Understanding by Design* (Wiggins & McTighe, 2005) curriculum model, assessment is ongoing and is educative (Wiggins, 1998). It is much more akin to a coach on a sports or extracurricular team observing students, offering immediate feed-back, and adjusting the training based on the learners' needs. It is evaluation that is summative and comes as a culmination of the learning experience. Classroom activities should be focused on tasks that will help students find answers to essential questions. The design of individual assessments during the course of the unit is based on students answering these types of questions, the most relevant of which were written by the students. Social learning extends to assessment when student groups are continually monitoring their progress. Project benchmarks might work better for one group than another; individual reporting on progress might suit another group. Differentiation in educative assessment supports student learning through guidance and readjustment rather than final evaluation of an end product.

The participants of the LLL project were asked, How will you measure understanding? This open-ended question allowed educators to collaborate on their assessment as well as their units of study. In the case of our Young Explorers' Club, the team responded: "Authentic artifacts are created and assessed during the entire exploration. Students maintain a Young Explorer folder which possesses all the materials for this project." There are many pieces of student work along the way to the conclusion of this unit. By maintaining the folder, or portfolio, students might revisit past artifacts and continue to improve their representations of learning. Student ownership of the artifacts also serves to give the students responsibility over their learning. Formative assessment, when shared with student learners, encourages metacognitive habits of mind that are transferable skills. Opportunities for peer review might suit one class and not another.

The AASL Standards for 21st Century Learners includes a "Self-Assessment Strategies" category. Some of those highlighted strategies include the following (AASL, 2007, n.p.):

1. Inquire, think critically, and gain knowledge:
1.4.1. Use interaction with and feedback from teachers and peers to guide own inquiry process.
1.4.4. Seek appropriate help when it is needed.

2. Draw conclusions, make informed decisions, apply knowledge to new situations, and create new knowledge:
2.4.2. Reflect on systematic process, and assess for completeness of investigation.
2.4.4. Develop directions for future investigations.

3. Share knowledge and participate ethically and productively as members of our democratic society:
3.4.1. Assess the processes by which learning was achieved in order to revise strategies and learn more effectively in the future.
3.4.3. Assess own ability to work with others in a group setting by evaluating varied roles, leadership, and demonstrations of respect for other viewpoints.

There is always cause for rubrics, checklists, and exit tickets. Teachers and librarians have favorite ways to check in with students as they work on research projects. The benefit of educator collaboration regarding assessment is the one-two punch as it were. Encouraging students to reflect on their progress from different vantage points enriches the learning experience. Both the content and the process bear formative assessments to guide learning. Beginning with the end in mind as directed by backward design actually fosters the development of incremental checkpoints for understanding. Harada and Yoshina (2005) include well-developed assessment tools applicable to elementary through high school including the following examples:

- Elementary grades—Resource Matrix: Matrix for identifying resources (p. 72)

- Middle grades—Assessment for generating questions (p. 84)

- Secondary grades—Website evaluation tool (p. 96).

In each of these cases, both teachers and librarians could adjust the assessments for any grade level.

There is a fundamental concept that underlies much of these assessments that requires discussion. Students are asked to reflect on the process of their learning and the content as based on the curricular context. Teachers and librarians are in a position to support student learning but that stance is built on a foundation of trust and respect of the student as learner. Certainly some students will be more self-aware than others; some students will be more openly honest about abilities and challenges within the bounds of the project at hand. As all accomplished educators believe, the best approach to effective teaching is knowing your students. In any circumstance, the well-being and learning of the students comes first.

Perhaps the librarian is not familiar with a particular class of students and the teacher feels much more comfortable in the role of assessing student reflections. Of course, it is possible that the librarian has known each student for many years but not within the context of the current year of study. This knowledge of the students throughout their years in a school places the librarian in an interesting position when considering that the teacher knows the students from the current year of schooling only. Conversely, perhaps the teacher is not familiar with the nature of online resources that are employed in research and therefore the students' reflections regarding evaluation are better assessed by the librarian. Educator collaboration is a balance of partnership often with alternating partners in the lead; sometimes the best leading is stepping aside to let others charge ahead. This point has critical importance when considering that the trust and respect of each student as learner is always firmly in our sights.

Next Steps—Virtual Collaboration

Perhaps the term *virtual collaboration* is new to you, but the concept should feel like a natural progression from educator collaboration. Educators, like all busy professionals, have increasing connectivity through technology. Here is where personal computing habits intersect with professional relationships. Common communication tools such as e-mail and chat (e.g., iChat or instant messaging) are particularly useful considering teachers' and librarians' daily schedules. Virtual collaboration, or collaboration across virtual space, also relates to communication embedded in technology-enhanced student projects. The technologies favored by a school district might vary, but the principles underlying the collaboration stay constant. Online communities of practice take advantage of technology capabilities; success is measured by participation, and participation is increased when the technology falls within the educator's comfort zone.

In the philosophy that we are all in this together, nothing inspires our coming together as we stretch outside our comfort zones more than the desire to serve our students best. Another way of understanding this learning curve is that we are creating our own educators' zone of proximal development possibly with changing roles of expert and novice depending on the technology and our personal experiences. In one school, educators might develop wikis to collaboratively develop lessons—wiki software allows for all participants to construct and edit text. In another school, educators might post essential questions around curriculum development on a blog with comments posted in a more linear fashion. Social networking is a natural state of being for some educators and they are considering the feasibility of using emerging technologies for teaching. Virtual collaboration is a recommended first step which allows teachers and librarians to become more comfortable communicating in a new dimension. For inspired collaborative partners, it will flow toward embedding online communication tools in learning. In fact, it is possible that at last, we are able to imagine a partner who speaks to us in a way that is meaningful in today's technological universe. As we continue to embed technologically enhanced social learning as appropriate based on curriculum goals, students will feel that their education is relevant within the context of their lives outside of school.

Imagine a Partner

Teachers and librarians come to educator collaboration with some differences and many similarities. Consider citizens of your home country from a different region: we might seem more like cousins than siblings but we have a strong tie binding us together. In the best of all possible worlds, we share an unbridled respect for each student and his or her capacity for learning and for learning to learn.

So imagine a partner who does the following:

- Knows your students—but in a different way than you do

- Helps you plan *and* teach *and* assess and revise *and* plan *and* teach differently to other students or the next time the unit is taught

- Knows your standards and curriculum and understands the interconnection with information literacy standards and Standards for 21st-Century Learners (AASL, 2007)

• Provides a learning environment and outcomes that cannot be experienced in the classroom and that you could not achieve alone

Welcome to our world. Let's be patient with one another, take small steps, and understand that by our learning together, it will be our students who ultimately stand to gain the most.

Acknowledgments

The Libraries, Literacy, and Learning National-Louis University Project Directors Dr. Gail Bush and Dr. Junko Yokota would like to express gratitude to the Shaw Fund for Literacy and The Chicago Community Trust. Our gratitude to Chicago Public Schools extends to the Department of Libraries and Information Services, which not only supported this project but also highlighted the participants in a Back-to-School Professional Development Day Collaboration Showcase; the Office of Literacy; and Area 2 Central Office administrators and principals at the participating schools. Special thanks to librarian Mark Laske and teachers Marti Remon-McMaster and Judy Wenger from Stone Academy for permission to use the "Young Explorer's Club" curriculum materials.

REFERENCES

American Association of School Librarians. (2007). *Standards for the 21st-century learner.* Chicago: American Library Association.

Blachowicz, C.L.Z., Buhle, R., Correa, A., Frost, S., & Ogle, D. (2006). *2006 report to the Chicago Community Trust.* Unpublished document.

Blachowicz, C.L.Z. & Yokota, J. (2006). *Needs identified by CPS and ARDDP report to the Chicago Community Trust.* Unpublished document.

Bush, G. (2005). *Every student reads: Collaboration and reading to learn.* Chicago: American Association of School Librarians.

Cushman, K. (1989). Asking the essential questions: Curriculum development. *Horace, 5*(5).

Foerster, P.N. (2004). *Ask. Plan. Acquire. Co-teach. Assess (APACA): A simple, low-cost model of classroom teacher/librarian collaboration* (IMLS National Research Grant Final Narrative Report). Kent, OH: Institute for Library and Information Literacy Education.

Harada, V.H., & Yoshina, J.M. (2005). *Assessing learning: Librarians and teachers as partners.* Westport, CT: Libraries Unlimited.

Illinois State Board of Education. (1997). Illinois Learning Standards. Retrieved March 25, 2008, from www.isbe.net/ils

New Mexico State University (n.d.). *What are essential questions and how are they created?* MathStar. Retrieved March 25, 2008, from www.lth3.k12.il.us/inquiryhouse/Essential_Questions.htm

Tyler, R.W. (1949). *Basic principles of curriculum and instruction.* Chicago: University of Chicago Press.

Wiggins, G.P. (1998). *Educative assessment: Designing assessments to inform and improve student performance.* San Francisco: Jossey-Bass.

Wiggins, G.P., & McTighe, J. (2005). *Understanding by design* (2nd ed.). Alexandria, VA: Association of Supervision and Curriculum Development.

RESOURCES COLLABORATIVELY SELECTED BY THE LIBRARIAN AND CLASSROOM TEACHER FOR THE YOUNG EXPLORER'S CLUB (SECOND GRADE)

ESSENTIAL QUESTION: How does your journey to different countries make you think about the world?

UNIT QUESTION: How was going to school alike/different for your family members?

LESSON QUESTIONS: From what continent did your family originate? What are Ellis Island and the Statue of Liberty? What do you do with a passport?

Ancona, G., Ada, A.F., & Campoy, F.I. (2006). *Mis Fiestas/My Celebrations* (Somos Latinos/We Are Latinos). New York: Children's Press.

> Author–photographer includes both festivals and family stories.

Bierman, C. (2005). *Journey to Ellis Island: How My Father Came to America*. New York: Hyperion.

> Ocean voyage from Russia and arrival at Ellis Island in 1922.

Curlee, L. (2003). *Liberty*. New York: Aladdin.

> Art historian tells the full story of our American landmark.

Kinkade, S. (2006). *My Family*. Watertown, MA: Charlesbridge.

> Photo essays of a diverse world of families. A portion of the royalties go to SHAKTI, a program of the Global Fund for Children.

Maestro, B. (1996). *Coming to America: The Story of Immigration*. New York: Scholastic.

> Broad introduction to the history of immigration.

Mara, W. (2005). *The Seven Continents*. New York: Children's Press.

> Photos, maps, and text, "Do you know you live on a continent?"

Montanari, D. (2004). *Children Around the World*. Toronto, ON: Kids Can Press.

> Meet 12 children from different countries.

Scillian, D. (2003). *P Is for Passport: A World Alphabet*. Chelsea, MI: Sleeping Bear Press.

> Alphabet used to organize universal common experiences.

Stojic, M. (2002). *Hello World! Greetings in 42 Languages Around the Globe!* New York: Scholastic.

> International salutation with pronunciations and origins.

Stuve-Bodeen, S. (2000). *Mama Elizabeti*. New York: Lee & Low.

> Elizabeti watches little brother Obedi in their African village.

SUGGESTED CHILDREN'S BOOKS

Beaty, A. (2007). *Iggy Peck, architect*. New York: Abrams.

Chen, C-Y. (2001). *On my way to buy eggs*. La Jolla, CA: Kane/Miller.

Judge, L. (2007). *One thousand tracings: Healing the wounds of World War II*. New York: Hyperion.

Onyefulu, I. (2007). *Ikenna goes to Nigeria*. London: Frances Lincoln.

Resau, L. (2007). *Red glass*. New York: Delacorte.

Sís, P. (2007). *The wall: Growing up behind the Iron Curtain*. New York: Farrar, Straus and Giroux.

Smith, H.A. (2008). *Keeping the night watch*. New York: Henry Holt.

Tan, S. (2006). *The arrival*. New York: Arthur A. Levine.

Woodson, J. (2001). *The other side*. New York: Putnam.

Zimmer, T.V. (2007). *Reaching for sun*. New York: Bloomsbury.

CHAPTER 15

Using Literature to Build Home and School Connections

Sophie C. Degener

The connection between family influences and literacy attainment, for all ethnic and socioeconomic groups, has been well documented. Multiple research studies (e.g., Beals, DeTemple, & Dickinson, 1994; Purcell-Gates, 1996; Snow, 1993; Taylor, 1983) have revealed that parents' literacy practices and the ways that parents interact with children around literacy have a direct effect on the literacy achievement of their children. Teachers have long known that getting parents to support their children's literacy development at home is critical to children's achievement, but they have also found that getting parents involved in their children's schooling is easier said than done, particularly for their most marginalized students. This chapter will look at home–school connections and discuss ways that teachers can use children's literature to reach out to all families to maximize the achievement of all of their students.

Getting Started: Books About Families

One of the most important things teachers can do to connect with all of their students and their families is to ensure that the literature they use reflects the diversity of students in their classrooms. There is an abundance of quality multicultural literature available that represents any number of perspectives and points of view. The more that children and their families see themselves and their situations in the books they read, the more they can see the relevance and importance of literature in their lives. Whether teachers choose to have a formal program dedicated to family literacy or they choose to approach home–school connections in their classrooms, a good place to begin forging those connections is by sharing lots of high-quality literature about diverse families. Books such as *I Got a Family* by Melrose Cooper (1993) and *All Families Are Special* by Norma Simon (2003) are great for embracing the different kinds of families that our students may come from.

I Got a Family (Cooper, 1993) is a brightly illustrated book that goes through all the special members of a family, from Great-Gran to Grampy, Uncle and Auntie, to Mamma, Daddy, and Kitty. This book demonstrates the important role that different family members play in the life of one little boy. This book would be a great way to initiate a discussion

Children's Literature in the Reading Program: An Invitation to Read (third edition), edited by Deborah A. Wooten and Bernice E. Cullinan. © 2009 by the International Reading Association.

about families. Upon completing the book, students could orally share the important members of their own families. After reading *I Got a Family*, ask students to respond to the following prompts:

- Name one important member of your family.
- Why is that person so important to you?
- Name three things that are special about that family member.

Write down their answers on chart paper and post in the classroom. Encourage students to either draw a picture of that family member or bring in a photograph to share. Create a bulletin board that pays tribute to those important people.

The book *All Families Are Special* (Simon, 2003) is an appropriate follow-up to *I Got a Family* (Cooper, 1993), as it looks at the many different forms that families can take. There is often a bias toward the nuclear family within school curricula, which can be seen during discussions of holidays and Mother's Day and Father's Day activities. The truth is, children's families are much less likely to reflect our perception of the norm, and children can be made to feel like their families are less than ideal unless we emphasize and accept the different forms families can take. *All Families Are Special* establishes as normal a variety of different family situations, including two-parent families, adoptive families, single-parent families, foster families, divorced families, blended families, and same-gender parents. Similarly, Todd Parr's (2003) *The Family Book* uses humorous pictures and text to make the point that while families can be very different, there are many commonalities as well. After reading these books, teachers can ask students to create a picture of their own families, labeling each member and, if they are able, writing a short description of what makes their family unique and special.

Children's literature has rich examples of different kinds of families facing different kinds of situations. Doing a themed study of families through children's literature will allow students to see different kinds of hardships that can be overcome by diverse families as well as everyday events faced by different kinds of families. *A Chair for My Mother* is a heartwarming book with gorgeous illustrations by Vera B. Williams (1982) that looks at a working class single-parent family and how they overcome an apartment fire that temporarily displaces the family. Melrose Cooper's (1998) *Gettin' Through Thursday* looks at an African American family, who each week has to scrimp and save to get to Friday and their mother's pay day. Patricia Polacco's (1995) *My Ol' Man* examines the difficulty faced by a white working class family when a father loses his job and almost loses his special car as well. Ezra Jack Keats's (1967) *Peter's Chair* highlights the challenges faced by a little boy when his little sister is born and he feels displaced. Books such as these can be an important uniting force within a classroom, as children realize that they are not alone when it comes to the kinds of difficulties that can threaten a family's well-being.

Other books look at everyday moments that highlight the connections between family members. *Dad and Me in the Morning* by Patricia Lakin (1994) tells the story of a hearing-impaired boy and his father as they wake up early to watch the sunrise. Cynthia Rylant's (1993) *The Relatives Came* describes what happens during an annual summer get-together, when large numbers of relatives drive in and fill the house with people and activity. Patricia MacLachlan's (1994) *All the Places to Love* tells the story of the farmland that will always be a special place for the family described therein. Books such as these evoke images of the endearing and simple love that families have for one another and can help children to think of the simple but special times that their own families share.

Books About Grandparents

Many children's books about family discuss the relationship children have with their grandparents, and this can be a wonderful theme to share in the classroom. Donald Crews's (1991) *Bigmama's* involves an African American man reminiscing about his family's annual trip to visit his grandmother's home in rural Florida. With colorful, vivid pictures, the book provides sensory-rich details about the long train ride, the thrill of returning to Bigmama's house, and the joys to be encountered while exploring outside. For many children, the rural world depicted in this book may be new to them. However, though they may never have seen a chicken coop or a well before, they can certainly relate to the following:

> Everybody sitting around the table that filled the room—Bigmama, Bigpapa, Uncle Slank, our cousins from down the road, and all of us. We talked about what we did last year. We talked about what we were going to do this year. We talked so much we hardly had time to eat. (p. 27)

> The night was jet black except for millions of stars. We could hardly sleep thinking about things to come. (p. 29)

Eve Bunting's (1996) book *Going Home* describes a Mexican American family's trip back to Mexico to visit their grandparents. It is the first time the children have met their grandparents. Although the story reflects an entirely different family experience than *Bigmama's* (Crews, 1991), the similarities are clear: "Grandfather and Aunt Ana hug us. They don't feel like strangers. That night, everyone in La Perla comes to Grandfather's house. The walls bulge with talk and rememberings. I have never seen Mama and Papa so lively" (pp. 17–18).

Teachers can start exploring children's relationships with their grandparents by reading these books and asking children to reflect on the memories they may have about visiting grandparents, or someone else very special (uncles or aunts, or a special friend). After reading additional books about children's relationships with grandparents (see the list of recommended books about grandparents at the end of this chapter), teachers could do a class language experience activity or create a big book about grandparents, with each child responding to the prompt "I remember..." and sharing a special memory about a grandparent or other special person.

To involve the entire family, children could brainstorm questions that they would like to ask their grandparents (or if their grandparents have passed away or are far away, to ask their parents). The teacher could record a list of questions and then send those questions home with student "reporters." This is a wonderful opportunity to engage families in meaningful ways. Students are excited to talk to their family members about questions they have created, and parents and grandparents are given an opportunity to share information about themselves with their children, and in turn, with their children's school and teacher. This sends a powerful message to families that their experiences are important and valued within the school. This is also a family literacy experience, in that the project is initiated by reading books about grandparents (which teachers should consider sending home with students), students have to interview their grandparents and write down the responses, perhaps with the help of another family member, and then share those responses in the classroom. Students could bring in photographs of their grandparents or draw pictures, and those pictures could be posted, with the interviews, around the classroom. A wonderful culminating event would be to invite grandparents to the school to see the pictures and interviews and to meet each other. This is a nonthreatening, welcoming way for teachers to honor the special people in their students' lives. Figure 15.1 provides a sample letter that teachers could send home to inform families of the unit on grandparents and ways they can get involved.

Family Pictures/Cuadros de Familia

A beautiful bilingual book by Carmen Lomas Garza (1990), a Mexican American artist, is *Family Pictures/Cuadros de Familia*. This book includes pictures painted by the artist of her memories of growing up in Texas, on the Mexican border. In addition to colorful, detailed pictures that are filled with images of family life from the everyday to special occasions, there are also the author's explanations of the pictures in both English and Spanish. Each picture contains the author at different ages, and her reminiscences include a description of the event and what she was doing in the picture. For example, on the page entitled "Birthday Party," there is a brilliantly colored picture of a family gathered outside around a piñata, watching as a little girl hits it. Garza writes:

> That's me hitting the *piñata* at my sixth birthday party. It was also my brother Arturo's fourth birthday. My mother threw a big birthday party for us and invited all kinds of friends, cousins, and neighborhood kids.

FIGURE 15.1
Sample Letter to Introduce Grandparents Unit

Dear Families,

We have just begun a unit on grandparents and other special people in your children's lives. **Because you and your children are the experts on your own families, we are asking for your help in the following ways:**

- With your child, read the books about grandparents and other special people that we will send home each day. Share your own memories about your parents, grandparents, and your childhood. Children love to hear about family traditions and family stories, and making connections between their lives and the stories they read is an important part of their growth as a reader.

- Your child will be bringing home a class-created list of "interview" questions to ask a grandparent or special friend. Help them to read these questions and record the answers.

- Send in photographs you may have of your child's grandparent(s) or special friend. Put your child's name on the back so that we can return them after the unit.

- Mark the following date on your calendar: On this day, we will be having a celebration for grandparents and special friends. We also invite you to attend to share a special treat and to read the grandparent interviews that will be posted throughout the room.

We are so excited about this unit and can't wait to learn more about you and your family! Sharing family stories is an important way to connect your child's experiences at home with the classroom community.

You can't see the *piñata* when you're trying to hit it, because your eyes are covered with a handkerchief. Here my father is pulling the rope that makes the *piñata* go up and down. He will make sure that everybody has a chance to hit it at least once. Somebody will end up breaking it, and that's when all the candies will fall out and all the kids will run and try to grab them. (p. 10)

Another page shows the family out on the front porch eating watermelon on a summer night and the author writes, "It was fun to sit out there. The light was so bright on the porch that you couldn't see beyond the lit area. It was like being in our own little world" (p. 24).

The book captures the essence of family—the simple things that we do together that make individual families unique, yet also the universalities that we can all relate to. Reading this book aloud to children is a pleasure, because it is a visual treat—children can look at the pictures and talk about everything they see. The details are extraordinary. Then the teacher can read the simple descriptions (in English, in Spanish, or in both languages) so

that children know the story that goes with each picture. This book can be read to children slowly, perhaps just a few pages at a time to savor it. Children should be encouraged to compare the pictures they see with their own lives and memories. What are the similarities and what are the differences between Garza's childhood and their own?

Upon completing the book, teachers should have students create their own "Family Pictures" books. Students can work with their parents to find photographs at home, or even draw their own detailed pictures, of those events that help define their family experiences. Teachers should encourage children to talk with their parents about the pictures and then, with their parents' help, create their own short written descriptions of the events. If parents do not speak or write English well, this is a perfect opportunity to honor their home culture by encouraging them to write in their first language (or in two languages, if the children are more proficient in English). Figure 15.2 provides a sample letter that teachers could send home to seek parent

---

FIGURE 15.2
Sample Letter Seeking Parent Help for Family Picture Books

Dear Parents/Guardians,

We have just read a book in class called *Family Pictures/Cuadros de Familia* by Carmen Lomas Garza. The book shows paintings from the author's childhood with descriptions of those paintings in English and Spanish. The children have enjoyed reading the book and talking about their own memories of their childhood. They will now be creating their own Family Pictures books, and we are asking for your help with this project.

- Please go through family photographs and choose several of your child involved in family events.

- If you cannot find photographs, your child can draw pictures of special family times.

- Once you have chosen photographs or drawn pictures (or both), please help your child to write a description of each picture. If you speak a language other than English, please write the description in that language, too.

Your children will work on this book at school, and once it is complete, we will have an author's celebration in the classroom. We will send out more information about this soon.

help for family picture books and suggesting ways they can get involved.

Although this may be a project that starts at home, teachers may also want to build in time to work on them at school. In-class writing time could be provided to work on revising and editing the descriptions of pictures, because the end goal would be to "publish" the children's books and to include them in the classroom library. Having an author's event, where the children can share their books with one another, and to which parents can be invited, would be another way to let families know how important they are in our classrooms.

Using Food to Connect Home and School

A common approach to reaching out to families is to hold a schoolwide potluck event where families are encouraged to bring in a dish representing their culture or ethnicity. Generally, this is a very popular event and a good way to involve families. Because there are so many wonderful children's books about family and food, it is easy to imagine how teachers could provide classroom opportunities to read about food while also planning a classroom or schoolwide feast.

Norah Dooley has written a series of books (*Everybody Cooks Rice*, 1991; *Everybody Bakes Bread*, 1996; *Everybody Serves Soup*, 2000; and *Everybody Brings Noodles*, 2005) that show the universality of the foods we eat. In each book, Carrie and her little brother, Anthony, explore the neighborhood and discover that each of their neighbors, though ethnically diverse, use rice, bread, noodles, and soup in their cooking. Each book has recipes at the end, which highlight the diverse foods represented in the book. It would be fun for classrooms to create extensions of each book by compiling recipes for rice

and noodle dishes, bread, and soup that the children's families share.

There are many other books that celebrate family and food. *Feast for 10* by Cathryn Falwell (1993), is a simple counting book that shows an African American family going shopping for "2 pumpkins for pie, 3 chickens to fry" and other foods, and then preparing the food together. The pictures are warm and show the love these family members have for one another as they create a meal. Similarly, *Too Many Tamales* by Gary Soto (1993) shows a family preparing tamales for Christmas dinner and the drama that ensues when one of the children thinks she has rolled up her mother's ring in one of the tamales.

Char Siu Bao Boy by Sandra S. Yamate (2000) tells the story of a Chinese boy who loves the Chinese barbecued pork buns (char siu bao) that his grandmother makes and brings them to school in his lunches. His friends think char siu bao are terrible and encourage him to conform to their tastes by bringing sandwiches instead. Though he does, he misses his char siu bao and ultimately solves his problem by asking his friends to try his food before they condemn it. They do and realize how good the char siu bao are. Finally, Ina R. Friedman's (1984) book *How My Parents Learned to Eat* tells the story of a little girl's parents. Her mother, who was Japanese, and her father, who was an American sailor stationed in Japan, had to overcome cultural differences when they fell in love, including the difference in eating implements (knife and fork versus chopsticks). All of these books, and many more like them, demonstrate the diversity of eating experiences, and the wonder of learning about new cultures and new foods. These books can and should be used in conjunction with schoolwide potlucks or international night celebrations. Figure 15.3 provides a sample letter that teachers could send home to seek parent involvement in the creation of a schoolwide cookbook.

Calling All Gardeners

An additional way to think about using literature to unite home and school is to consider a common cause that would simultaneously help the school while using the expertise of families. Many schools find themselves with school grounds that need maintenance but lack a budget to maintain them properly. When this situation arises, schools can reach out to parents to use their expertise in planning and executing a school beautification plan. Beginning in the classroom, teachers can read books about gardens such as Lois Ehlert's (1988) *Planting a Rainbow*, Kathy Henderson's (2004) *And the Good Brown Earth*, and Eve Bunting's (1994) *Flower Garden*. Although the settings and illustrations of these books are different, they each use simple text and beautiful pictures to show families working together to create a garden. Sarah Stewart's (2007) *The Gardener* would also be a great

choice, as it tells the story of a little girl who is sent to live with her baker uncle during the U.S. Great Depression, and how by creating a garden on his apartment's rooftop, she brings hope and joy into both of their lives.

Barbara Pollak's (2004) *Our Community Garden*, Erika Tamar's (1996) *The Garden of Happiness*, and DyAnne DiSalvo-Ryan's (1994) *City Green* each tell a story about gardens created by the community. *Our Community Garden* shows diverse children each planting something that represents themselves, how they work in the garden, and then how they use what they grow to create dishes that the neighborhood comes together to enjoy. *The Garden of Happiness* and *City Green* each show how community members come together to create beauty in a blighted part of the neighborhood. *City Green* even provides information on starting a community garden, which would be a great way to initiate the idea of starting a garden on the school grounds. Figure 15.4 provides a sample letter that teachers could send home to seek parent volunteers for the community garden.

Creating a community garden at the school is an opportunity, again, to combine literature, literacy, and parent involvement. By reading books in class like the ones previously mentioned and sending them home for students to share with their parents, teachers can initiate a schoolwide community discussion about gardens. After that, students can work with their teachers to create a letter to take home to parents, soliciting their help and expertise (see Figure 15.4). Because creating a garden on the school grounds is a highly motivating event, it is not difficult to get children excited about sharing this with their parents. Teachers and parents could work together to plan a "school greening day" at which the school grounds can be prepared for a garden. Removing rocks, overgrown bushes, and sticks to make room for plants; digging the soil to prepare it for new plants and seeds; reading about and purchasing plants and seeds; and so on, could all be part of this day. There are multiple ways that literacy and literature could be part of a day like this. There could be

a place for story reading, so that while their parents work, children could listen to stories about gardens. There could be a table set up with different gardening catalogs, where parents and children could read through plant descriptions to decide what their garden should include. Or there could be an area for creating signs to label the plants that are included in the garden. After the garden is created, parents and teachers could work together to create care instructions for the different plants, so that classes can know best how to maintain the garden year after year.

Once we begin to reconsider how we involve parents in their children's literacy development—using literature and literacy in ways that are meaningful to our school communities—the ideas begin to flow. Imagine a schoolwide recycling effort or a community clean-up day. There are many great children's books that devote themselves to such community-based efforts (see the list of recommended books about schoolwide recycling efforts at the end of this chapter) and which

---

FIGURE 15.4
Sample Letter Seeking Parent Volunteers for Community Garden

Dear Families,

We've been reading all about plants and gardens, and we've decided that we should create a garden at our school. We could really use your help in the following areas:

☐ Removing rocks, branches, and trees from the garden areas

☐ Preparing the soil for new plants (by mixing the old soil with new top soil)

☐ Reading through gardening catalogs to select easy-care plants that would work well in our garden

☐ Sharing a car or truck with lots of cargo space to bring plants and bushes from the gardening center

☐ Installing our new plants and bushes

☐ Creating signs to label the new plants and bushes

☐ Creating care instructions so that each class will know how to maintain the garden

Please check the areas where you would like to help. This is a big task for the school, but we think it will really improve our school's exterior. We can't do it without you! Thanks so much!!

would make a great jumping off point for such efforts within a school. After reading many such books in the classroom, teachers and students can brainstorm ideas for instituting a recycling program at the school or planning a Green Day event that involves families.

Using Literature to Connect School, Family, and Community

The ideas included in this chapter provide a sampling of ways teachers can use literature to connect what they do in school to their students' families and communities. Each school needs to consider its own needs as well as the needs and abilities of students' families, to create literacy events that are directly meaningful and relevant. It is important to remember that when we show families how literature and literacy can be just as relevant out of school as in school, we are more likely to create bridges between our classrooms and our students' families, and in so doing better support the literacy development of each of our students.

REFERENCES

Beals, D.E., De Temple, J.M., & Dickinson, D.K. (1994). Talking and listening that support early literacy development of children from low-income families. In D.K. Dickinson (Ed.), *Bridges to literacy: Children, families, and schools* (pp. 19–40). Cambridge, MA: Blackwell.

Purcell-Gates, V. (1996). Stories, coupons, and the *TV Guide*: Relationships between home literacy experiences and emergent literacy knowledge. *Reading Research Quarterly, 31*(4), 406–428. doi:10.1598/RRQ.31.4.4

Snow, C.E. (1993). Families as social contexts for literacy development. In C. Daiute (Ed.), *The development of literacy through social interaction* (pp. 11–24). San Francisco: Jossey-Bass.

Taylor, D. (1983). *Family literacy: Young children learning to read and write.* Portsmouth, NH: Heinemann.

CHILDREN'S LITERATURE CITED

Bunting, E. (1994). *Flower garden.* San Diego, CA: Harcourt.

Bunting, E. (1996). *Going home.* New York: Joanna Cotler.

Cooper, M. (1993). *I got a family.* New York: Henry Holt.

Cooper, M. (1998). *Gettin' through Thursday.* New York: Lee & Low.

Crews, D. (1991). *Bigmama's.* New York: Greenwillow.

DiSalvo-Ryan, D. (1994). *City green.* New York: HarperCollins.

Dooley, N. (1991). *Everybody cooks rice.* Minneapolis, MN: Carolrhoda.

Dooley, N. (1996). *Everybody bakes bread.* Minneapolis, MN: Carolrhoda.

Dooley, N. (2000). *Everybody serves soup.* Minneapolis, MN: Carolrhoda.

Dooley, N. (2005). *Everybody brings noodles.* Minneapolis, MN: Carolrhoda.

Ehlert, L. (1988). *Planting a rainbow.* San Diego, CA: Harcourt.

Falwell, C. (1993). *Feast for 10.* New York: Clarion.

Friedman, I.R. (1984). *How my parents learned to eat.* Boston: Houghton Mifflin.

Henderson, K. (2004). *And the good brown earth.* Cambridge, MA: Candlewick.

Keats, E.J. (1967). *Peter's chair.* New York: HarperCollins.

Lakin, P. (1994). *Dad and me in the morning.* Morton Grove, IL: Albert Whitman & Company.

Lomas Garza, C. (1990). *Family pictures/Cuadros de familia.* San Francisco: Children's Book Press.

MacLachlan, P. (1994). *All the places to love.* New York: HarperCollins.

Parr, T. (2003). *The family book.* Boston: Little, Brown.

Polacco, P. (1995). *My ol' man.* New York: Philomel.

Pollak, B. (2004). *Our community garden.* Hillsboro, OR: Beyond Words.

Rylant, C. (1993). *The relatives came*. New York: Aladdin.

Simon, N. (2003). *All families are special*. Morton Grove, IL: Albert Whitman.

Soto, G. (1993). *Too many tamales*. New York: Putnam.

Stewart, S. (2007). *The gardener*. New York: Square Fish.

Tamar, E. (1996). *The garden of happiness*. San Diego, CA: Harcourt Brace.

Williams, V.B. (1982). *A chair for my mother*. New York: Greenwillow.

Yamate, S.S. (2000). *Char siu bao boy*. Chicago: Polychrome.

SUGGESTED BOOKS ABOUT GRANDPARENTS

Berka, E.C. (2000). *Halmoni's day*. New York: Dial.

Bunting, E. (1989). *The Wednesday surprise*. New York: Clarion.

Cheng, A. (2000). *Grandfather counts*. New York: Lee & Low.

DiSalvo-Ryan, D. (2000). *Grandpa's corner store*. New York: HarperCollins.

Dorros, A. (1991). *Abuela*. New York: Dutton.

Dorros, A. (1995). *Isla*. New York: Dutton.

Flournoy, V. (1985). *The patchwork quilt*. New York: Dial.

Grambling, L.G. (2002). *Grandma tells a story*. Watertown, MA: Charlesbridge.

Greenspun, A.A., & Schwarz, J. (2003). *Grandparents are the greatest because....* New York: Dutton.

Hamanaka, S. (2003). *Grandparents song*. New York: HarperCollins.

Johnston, T. (1996). *Fishing Sunday*. New York: HarperCollins.

MacLachlan, P. (1983). *Through Grandpa's eyes*. New York: HarperTrophy.

Mora, P. (1994). *Pablo's tree*. New York: Simon & Schuster.

Park, F., & Park, G. (2005). *The have a good day café*. New York: Lee & Low.

Polacco, P. (1998). *Chicken Sunday*. New York: Philomel.

Saenz, B.A. (1998). *A gift from Papa Diego/Un regalo de Papa Diego*. El Paso, TX: Cinco Puntos.

Say, A. (1993). *Grandfather's journey*. Boston: Houghton Mifflin.

BOOKS TO SUPPORT SCHOOLWIDE RECYCLING EFFORTS

Dr. Seuss. (1971). *The lorax*. New York: Random House Books for Young Readers.

Gibbons, G. (1996). *Recycle! A handbook for kids*. Boston: Little, Brown.

Green, J. (2005). *Why should I recycle?* Hauppauge, NY: Barron's.

Madden, D. (1993). *The Wartville wizard*. New York: Aladdin.

Murphy, S.J. (2004). *Earth day—Hooray!* New York: HarperCollins.

Showers, P. (1994). *Where does the garbage go?* New York: HarperCollins.

Van Allsburg, C. (1990). *Just a dream*. Boston: Houghton Mifflin.

Wallace, N.E. (2006). *Recycle every day!* New York: Marshall Cavendish.

Wyeth, S.D. (2002). *Something beautiful*. New York: Dragonfly.

INDEX

Note. Page numbers followed by *f* or *t* indicate figures or tables, respectively.

A

ADVANCED READING DEVELOPMENT DEMONSTRATION PROJECT, 143–144
AESTHETIC READING, 100–101
AFFLERBACH, P., 30, 101
AGENCE FRANCE-PRESSE, 47
AHRENS, M.G., 61
ALLEN, C.A., 89
ALLINGTON, R.L., 31, 48, 80
ALVERMANN, D.E., 15, 123
AMBIGUITY: in postmodern picture books, 29
AMERICAN ASSOCIATION OF SCHOOL LIBRARIANS, 147, 152
AMERICAN LIBRARY ASSOCIATION, 15
ANDERSON, M.C., 127
ANDERSON, R.C., 63–64, 121, 127–128
ANDERSON, V., 33
ANSTEY, M., 26, 30
APACA MODEL, 150–151
ARMBRUSTER, B.B., xii
ASH, G.E., 85
ASSESSMENT: librarian collaboration and, 151–153
AUTOMATIC WORD RECOGNITION: series books and, 61

B

BADER, B., 7, 78
BALES, R.J., 105
BARRON, R.F., 127
BEALS, D.E., 156
BEAN, T.W., 127
BECK, I.L., 121
BENNETT-ARMISTEAD, V.S., 121
BENTON, M., 100, 105
BIOGRAPHIES: layers in, 37–44; as mentor text, 137; picture books, 115–116; recommended, 23
BISHOP, R.S., 67, 71–72
BITZ, M., 18
BLACHOWICZ, C.L.Z., 144–145
BLEED, 6

BLINDNESS: cultural, 69
BOLING, C.J., 121
BOOK(S): availability of, 139; role in students' lives, 66–67
BOOK COVERS, 7–8; example of, 9–10, 9*f*
BOOK DUMMY, 12
BOOK NOOKS, 82, 82*f*
BORDERS, 6–7
BOTZAKIS, S., 18
BROWN, R., 33
BRUCE, B.C., 127
BUHLE, R., 144–145
BUSH, G., 145

C

CAI, M., 67
CALKINS, L.M., 123
CAPPELLI, R., 89
CARR, E.M., 101
CARY, S., 16
CHANDLER-OLCOTT, K., 89
CHANGE: radical, term, 24
CHAPTER TITLES: in series books, 62
CHICAGO COMMUNITY TRUST, 143
CHICAGO PUBLIC SCHOOLS, 143–144
CHILDREN'S BOOK COUNCIL, 131–132, 135
CHILDREN'S CHOICES: overlap with Teachers' Choices, 133*f*–134*f*; and text selection, 130–131
CHILDREN'S LITERATURE: evidence on uses in classroom, 83–84; history in classroom, 78–79; surreptitious role of, 77–87; value of, 84–85
CHOMSKY, C., 61
CIRCLES, 82
CLARK, E.R., 89
CLARK, K., 83
CLEAVELAND, L.B., 89
COLLABORATION: with school librarians, 143–155; virtual, 153
COLOR: example of, 11; in picture books, 5
COMIC BOOKS, 15–23

COMMUNITY GARDEN, 162–164, 163*f*

COMPARE AND CONTRAST: with graphic novels, 20, 21*f*

COMPREHENSION INSTRUCTION, 99–109; librarian collaboration and, 145; problems with, 99–100

CONNECTIONS: chart of, 125, 125*f*; comprehension method with, 121–129; sharing, 124–125; writing, 122–124

CONTENT AREA LEARNING: children's books and, 110–120; graphic novels and, 18–19, 23; picture books and, 111–119; poetry and, 51

CONTEXTUAL INFORMATION: in graphic novels, 16

CONVENTIONS OF READING: series books and, 62–63

COOPERATIVE CHILDREN'S BOOK CENTER, 22

CORREA, A., 144–145

COSTELLO, B., 112, 116

COUTU, R., 53

CRITICAL THINKING: questions for, 147–149

CRYSTAL, D., 47

CULHAM, R., 53

CULLINAN, B.E., xviii, 45–48, 51, 85, 121, 123

CULTURAL BLINDNESS, 69

CULTURALLY DIVERSE LITERATURE, 66–73

CUMMINS, J., 4

CURRICULUM DESIGN: challenges to, 77–87; and librarian collaboration, 149–153

CURRICULUM MAPPING STRATEGY, 146

CUSHMAN, K., 148

D

DANIELS, H., 122

DANSEREAU, D.F., 126–127

DAVIS, J., 136

DE TEMPLE, J.M., 156

DEWITZ, P., 101

DIALOGUE: in series books, 63

DICKINSON, D.K., 156

DIGITAL NATIVES, 47; term, 24

DIME NOVELS, 57–58

DIMINIO, J., 101

DIRECT EXPLANATION, 100

DIVERSITY: adult understanding of, 70; denial of, 69; literature on, 66–73; scaffolding student thinking on, 68–69

DOLE, J.A., 30

DORFMAN, L.R., 89

DRESANG, E.T., 24

DUFFY, G.G., 30, 100

DUKE, N.K., 100, 103–104, 121

E

EDINGER, M., 135

ELLIS, L., 122–123

ENDPAPERS, 8–9; example of, 10–11

ENGAGEMENT: with postmodern picture books, 33

EVANS, W.H., 121

EXEMPLARY CLASSROOMS: children's literature in, 77–87

F

FALK, L., 112

FAMILY: books on, 156–158; children's literature and, 156–165; picture books on, 159–161, 160*f*

FANTASY: graphic novels, 23

FAWCETT, G., 50

FICTION: emphasis on, in postmodern picture books, 26–28

FIELDING, L., 63

FISCHER, D., 16

FITZGERALD, J., 30

FLORES, B.B., 89

FLUENCY: series books and, 61

FOERSTER, P.N., 144, 150

FOOD: and home–school connections, 161, 162*f*

FORMAT: in graphic novels, 17; mentor texts and, 88, 90–92, 91*f*; in postmodern picture books, 28

FOX, D.L., 67

FRAMING: example of, 11; in picture books, 6–7

FRAZEE, C., 127

FREPPON, P.A., 85

FRESCH, M.J., 49, 52

FREY, N., 16

FROST, S., 72, 144–145

FULL-BLEED ILLUSTRATION, 6

G

GALDA, L., 85, 99, 105

GAMBRELL, L.B., 85, 105

GARDENING: and home–school connections, 162–164, 163*f*

GEORGE, M.A., 92

GERSTEN, R., 101

GILRANE, C.P., 136

GIORGIS, C., 4

GIOIA, D., 45

GLASSER, W., 124

GLAZER, S., 15

GOLDSTONE, B.P., 25, 28

GOODNOW, C., 15
GRANDPARENTS: books on, 158–159, 165; letter on, 159f
GRAPHIC NOVELS, 15–23; format of, 17; as mentor texts, 89; recommendations on, 17–20; use in class, rationale for, 16
GRAPHIC ORGANIZERS: with graphic novels, 18, 19f
GRAVES, D.H., 136
GROLNICK, W.S., 121
GUTTERS, 16

H
HAGOOD, M.C., 15
HALL, S., 113
HAMILTON, A.M., 20
HAMPTON, J.M., 85
HANSEN, J., 91, 101
HARADA, V.H., 152
HARRIS, V.J., 66, 72
HARRISON, D., 47, 49–51, 53
HART, B., 61
HARWAYNE, S., 136
HAYES, D.P., 61
HEARD, G., 50
HELLMAN, P., 30
HEROES: books on, 87; character features of, 81, 81f
HILL, S., 136
HISTORY: books, layers in, 37–44; children's books on, 111; picture books on, 117
HOLDERITH, K., 49, 51, 53
HOLLEY, C.D., 126–127
HOME–SCHOOL CONNECTIONS: children's literature and, 156–165
HOPKINS, L.B., 51
HUEY, E., 78
HYDE, A.A., 122

I
ILLINOIS STATE BOARD OF EDUCATION, 149
ILLUSTRATED JOURNALS, 18
ILLUSTRATIONS: in picture books, 3–14
ILLUSTRATORS: study of, 12
IMAGING. See visualizing
IMMIGRATION: mentor texts on, 92–96, 94f–95f
INFERENCES: with graphic novels, 17; with postmodern picture books, 33–34
INFORMATIONAL BOOKS. See nonfiction books
INTERNATIONAL LITERATURE, 66–73; definition of, 66; evaluation and selection of, 67; issues in, 67–70; versus multicultural literature, 69; next steps in, 71; problematic understandings of, dealing with, 68
INTERNATIONAL READING ASSOCIATION, 131–132
INTERTEXTUALITY: in postmodern picture books, 30

J
JACOBS, D., 17
JANECZKO, P., 51
JAYANTHI, M., 101
JOAG-DEV, C., 128
JOHNSON, D.D., 20
JOHNSON, N.J., 30
JONES, S., 89
JOURNALS: illustrated, 18
JURSTEDT, R., 113

K
KARAIM, R., 47
KAROLIDES, N.J., 128
KEY, D., 92
KHURANA, S., 18
KIEFER, B., 4
KIM, J., 135
KOLODZIEJ, N.J., 112, 116
KOUTRAS, M., 113
KRASHEN, S., 135
KUHN, M.R., 20, 61

L
LABBO, L.D., 24
LADSON-BILLINGS, G., 68
LAMINACK, L.L., 89
LANGER, J.A., 85, 127
LANGUAGE ARTS: picture books for, 113; text selection for, 135–136
LARKIN, J.H., 126
LEGENDS: and history, 38–39
LEHR, F., xii
LESTER, J., 78
LEWIS, P., 51
LIANG, L.A., 99
LIBRARIANS: school, 143–155
LIBRARIES, LITERACY, AND LEARNING (LLL), 143–144
LIBRARY: classroom, 81–82, 82f
LINE: in picture books, 4
LITERATURE CIRCLES, 82

M
MAHAR, D., 89

MANDATES: for classroom approaches, 79–80
MANDLER, J.M., 30
MANGA, 15
MAPS: sequence, 19–20, 21f
MARCUS, L.S., 78
MARSH, J., 122–123
MARTINEZ, M.G., 67, 78
MARZANO, R.J., 121
MATH: children's books on, 111; picture books on, 115–116
McCALLUM, R., 25, 27, 30
McCLELLAND, K., 24
McCLOUD, S., 16
McGEE, L.M., 78
McGREGOR, T., 34
McINTYRE, E., 85
McKECHNIE, L., 58
McKEOWN, M.G., 121
McMANUS, R., 20
McTIGHE, J., 150–151
MEANING: Writing and Sharing Connections and, 127–128
MELTON, D., 48
MENTOR TEXTS, 88–98; selection of, 136–139; support for use of, 88–89; uses of, 90–96
MODELING: librarian collaboration and, 145
MONAGHAN, E.J., 78
MOON, J.S., 15
MOORMAN, M., 15
MORROW, L.M., 85
MUI, Y.Q., 15
MULTICULTURAL BOOKLIST COMMITTEE, 71
MULTICULTURAL LITERATURE, 66–73; definition of, 66; evaluation and selection of, 67; versus international literature, 69; issues in, 67–70; next steps in, 70–71; problematic understandings of, dealing with, 68
MYTHS: and history, 38–39

N
NARRATION: in series books, 63
NARRATOR: in postmodern picture books, 27
NATIONAL COUNCIL FOR THE SOCIAL STUDIES, 132
NATIONAL INSTITUTE OF CHILD HEALTH AND HUMAN DEVELOPMENT, 83–84, 99–100
NATIONAL SCIENCE TEACHERS ASSOCIATION, 135
NEGATIVE REACTIONS: to multicultural literature, dealing with, 68, 70; to postmodern picture books, supporting, 32–33
NEGATIVE SPACE, 5

NEWKIRK, T., 89
NEW YORK STATE EDUCATION DEPARTMENT, 110
NEW YORK TIMES, 59
NO CHILD LEFT BEHIND ACT, 83
NONFICTION BOOKS: layers in, 37–44; as mentor texts, 90–91, 91f, 138–139
NONLINEARITY: in postmodern picture books, 28–29
NORTON, B., 15
NOTES: in Writing and Sharing Connections, 125–126

O
OGLE, D., 144–145
OKAZAKI, S., 93
OSBORN, J., xii

P
PAGE TURNS: example of, 11–12; in picture books, 7
PAIRED READERS, 50
PANTALEO, S., 25–26, 29
PARENTS: children's literature and, 156–165
PARIS, S.G., 101
PARODY: in postmodern picture books, 29–30
PARTICIPATION: in poetry discussion, 47
PATBERG, J.P., 101
PEARSON, P.D., 20, 30, 83, 85, 100–101, 103–104, 121
PERSPECTIVE: example of, 11; in picture books, 6
PETERSON, D.P., 85
PETIT, A., 91
PHELPS, S.E., 123
PICTURE BOOKS: for content area learning, 111–119; creation of, 9–12; definition of, 4; design characteristics of, 6–7; of family, 159–161, 160f; physical aspects of, 7–9; of poetry, 53; postmodern, 24–36; visual images in, 3–14
PLANNING: librarian collaboration and, 145–147
PLEASURE: reading for, series books and, 58
PODCASTS: as mentor texts, 89
POETRY, 45–56; as mentor text, 91–92, 137–138; rationale for, 45–46; for two voices, 50–51; and visualizing, 105–107
POETRY HAMS, 49
POETRY JAMS, 49–50
POETS: rationale for, 45–46; and reader, 47–48
POLITICS: picture books on, 117
POSITIVE SPACE, 5

POSTMAN, N., 77
POSTMODERN PICTURE BOOKS, 24–36; characteristics of, 25–30; definition of, 25; integration into curriculum, 30–33; negative reactions to, supporting, 32–33
PREDICTING, 101–105, 103*t*; suggested books for, 109
PRENSKY, M., 24
PRESSLEY, M., 30, 33, 83–85, 99
PURCELL-GATES, V., 85, 156
PUTNEY, L.G., 127

Q
QUESTIONS: for curriculum design, 150; librarian collaboration and, 147–149; standards and, 147
QUINTERO, E., 92

R
RABINOWITZ, P., 62–63
RADICAL CHANGE: term, 24
RAND READING STUDY GROUP, 99
RANKIN, J., 84
RASINSKI, T., 50
RAY, K.W., 89
RAYBURN, S., 105
READER-RESPONSE INSTRUCTION, 99–109; versus comprehension instruction, 99–100; predicting and, 101–105; visualizing and, 105–107
READING: for pleasure, series books and, 58; time spent on, and proficiency, 63–64, 63*t*
READING ALOUD, xiii; in content areas, 117–118; librarian collaboration and, 145; paired, 50; poetry, 46; talk and, 89; time for, 48–49; Writing and Sharing Connections and, 121–129
READING INSTRUCTION: school librarians and, 144–149
RECOMMENDED LITERATURE. *See* suggested books
RECYCLING: books on, 165
REFLECTION: librarian collaboration and, 152
REPETITIONS: in series books, 62–63
REVISING: poetry, 53–54
RHYME: in poetry, 52
RIOJAS-CORTEZ, M., 89
RISLEY, T.R., 61
ROBB, L., 46, 51, 121–123
RODRIGUEZ, M.C., 85
ROEHLER, L.R., 30
ROHMANN, E., 3
ROMANO, T., 92

ROSENBACH, A.S.W., 78
ROSENBLATT, L.M., xvii, xviii, 99, 122, 127
ROSENBLATT, R., 53
ROSER, N., 78
ROSS, C.S., 57–58
ROTHBAUER, P., 58
RUMELHART, D.E., 30
RYAN, R.M., 121

S
SCAFFOLDING: and multicultural and international literature, 68–69
SCALA, M., 51
SCHEDULING: librarian collaboration and, 145–147
SCHON, I., 71
SCHOOL BEAUTIFICATION PROJECT: and home–school connections, 162–164, 163*f*
SCHOOL LIBRARIANS, 143–155
SCHRODER, V., 51
SCHUDER, T., 33
SCHWANENFLUGEL, P.J., 20
SCIENCE: children's books on, 111; graphic novels on, 23; mentor texts on, 90–91, 91*f*; picture books on, 113–115, 114*f*–115*f*; text selection for, 135
SCIENCE FICTION: graphic novels, 23
SCIESZKA, J., 48
SEALE, D., 71
SELF-ASSESSMENT: strategies for, 151–152
SELZNICK, B., 7
SEMANTIC FEATURE ANALYSIS, 20, 21*f*
SEQUENCE MAPS, 19–20, 21*f*
SERAFINI, F., 4, 32
SERIES BOOKS, 57–65; popularity of, 58–61, 59*t*
SHAPE: in picture books, 5
SHORT, K.G., 67
SIMON, H.A., 126
SINGER, H.K., 127
SIPE, L.R., 6–8, 25, 33
SLAPIN, B., 71
SMITH, H.L., 89
SMITH, H.M., 71
SNOW, C.E., 156
SOCIAL ACTIVITY: series books and, 58
SOCIAL CONSCIENCE: mentor texts and, 92–96
SOCIAL STUDIES: children's books on, 111; graphic novels on, 23; picture books on, 116–119, 118*f*–119*f*; text selection for, 132–136
SORTER, J., 127
SPACE: in picture books, 5

SPIEGEL, D.L., 30
SPIRO, R.J., 127
STAHL, S.A., 20, 62
STANDARDS: librarian collaboration and, 145–147
STANZI, L.C., 105
STEFFENSEN, M.S., 128
STELTER, B., 59
STICKY NOTES: writing connections on, 122–124
STONE, V.F., 127
STORYTELLING: importance of, 89
STRATEMEYER, Edward, 58
STRUGGLING READERS: Writing and Sharing Connections and, 121
STUDENT TALK: and postmodern picture books, 31–32
SUGGESTED BOOKS: graphic novels, 23; on heroes, 87; for home–school connections, 165; international literature, 73; mentor books, 97–98; multicultural literature, 72; nonfiction, 43–44; picture books, 14; picture books for older readers, 120; poetry, 55–56; postmodern picture books, 36; for predicting, 109; series books, 65; for visualizing, 109; for Writing and Sharing Connections, 129
SWISTAK, L., 89
SYMBOLISM, 113, 114f

T
TALK: in classroom, 82–83; and postmodern picture books, 31–32; and read-alouds, 89
TAYLOR, B.M., 83–85
TAYLOR, D., 156
TEACHERS: and school librarians, 143–155
TEACHERS' CHOICES: overlap with Children's Choices, 133f–134f; and text selection, 131–132
TEALE, W., 85
TEMPLE, C., 67
TERRY, C.A., 46
TEXT SELECTION, 130–140; multicultural and international literature, 67; picture books, 112–113; poetry, 46–47
TEXTURE: in picture books, 5–6
THORNDYKE, P., 30
TIME: for reading aloud, 48–49; spent on reading, and proficiency, 63–64, 63t; for writing, 81–82
TIMELINE: student-driven, 126–127, 126f
TINGLEY, S., 22
TITLE PAGE, 9

TOLERANCE: and diversity, 70
TOPPING, D., 20
TRAIT CHART, 83, 83f
TRANSITIONS: in graphic novels, 16
TRELEASE, J., 46, 135
TURNER, M., 15
TYLER, R.W., 150
TYPOGRAPHICAL FEATURES: in series books, 63

U
UNDERSTANDING BY DESIGN MODEL, 151

V
VACCA, J.L., 111
VACCA, R.T., 111
VAN METER, P., 33
VAN'T HOFFT, M., 89
VARDELL, S., 45
VEEN, W., 24
VINCENT, T., 89
VIRTUAL COLLABORATION, 153
VISUAL DESIGN: elements of, 4–6
VISUAL IMAGES: in picture books, 3–14; versus text, 112
VISUALIZING, 105–107; suggested books for, 109
VISUAL PERMANENCE: in graphic novels, 16
VOCABULARY: librarian collaboration and, 145; series books and, 61–62
VON SPRECKEN, D., 135
VRAKKING, B., 24
VYGOTSKY, L.S., 32, 122–123

W
WADSWORTH, R.M., 89
WALMSEY, S.A., 77
WALPOLE, S., 83
WEBB, T.B., 30
WEINER, S., 15, 22
WEINGARTNER, C., 77
WHARTON-MCDONALD, R., 85
WHEATON, A., 49, 52
WHITE, E.B., 47
WHITSITT, P.K., 144
WIGGINS, G.P., 150–151
WILHELM, J., 121
WILSON, P.T., 63
WINK, J., 127
WOOTEN, D.A., 121, 123, 126–127
WORD RECOGNITION: series books and, 61
WORTHY, J., 15

WRITING: mentor texts and, 88–98; picture books for, 113; poetry, 51–54; text selection for, 136–139; time for, 81–82

WRITING AND SHARING CONNECTIONS, 121–129; steps for, 121–127; student-driven timeline in, 126–127, 126*f*

Y
YANG, G., 16

YOKOI, L., 84
YOKOTA, J., 67, 69, 72, 144
YOSHINA, J.M., 152

Z
ZEMELMAN, S., 122

CHILDREN'S LITERATURE AUTHOR INDEX

Note. Page numbers followed by *f* or *t* indicate figures or tables, respectively.

A

ADDY, S., 81
ANNO, M., 116
ARCHAMBAULT, J., 81
ARCHBOLD, R., 135, 139
AZUMA, K., 17

B

BANG, M., 5
BATEMAN, R., 135, 139
BENNETT, J., 51
BENSON, K., 116
BERNER, R.S., 115
BIERMAN, C., 118
BORDEN, L., 137
BRETT, J., 7
BROWNE, A., 29
BUNTING, E., 112, 117, 158, 162

C

CARLE, E., 5
CHARLIP, R., 7
CHERRY, L., 114, 135
CHILD, L., 29–30, 32
CLEARY, B., 63
COLE, J., 60*t*
COLLINS, B., 48
COOPER, M., 156–157
CRAN, W., 47
CREWS, D., 158
CULLINAN, B., 45–46
CUMMINGS, P., 135–136

D

DAHL, R., 82
DARLING, K., 135, 139
DiCAMILLO, K., 102
DiSALVO-RYAN, D., 162
DOBSON, M., xvi
DOOLEY, N., 161
DOTLICH, R., 51

E

EDMONDS, W., xi, xiii

EHLERT, L., 5, 162
ENZENSBERGER, H.M., 115
ERDRICH, L., 132, 137
ESBENSEN, B.J., 107

F

FALCONER, I., 5
FALWELL, C., 161
FEELINGS, T., 116
FLEISCHMAN, P., 50–51, 107, 136
FLEISHER, P., 111
FLEMING, C., 8
FLEMING, D., 6–7, 114
FRASIER, D., 132
FRIEDMAN, I.R., 161
FRIEDRICH, E., 132

G

GALVIN, J., 111
GARZA, C., 159
GEORGE, J.C., 138
GEORGE, K.O., 106
GIBLIN, J.C., 37–43
GIOVANNI, N., 116
GLENN, M., 138
GRAVETT, E., 27
GUTMAN, D., 81

H

HADDON, M., 111
HARPER, C.M., xvi
HARRISON, D., 48–51, 53–54
HASKINS, J., 116
HEARD, G., 50
HEIM, M.H., 115
HENDERSON, K., 162
HESSE, K., 88, 91
HILLS, T., 8
HIRSCHFELDER, A.B., 138
HOPKINS, L.B., 51
HOSLER, J., 19
HOUSTON, G., 136–137
HUDSON, W., 80

J

Janeczko, P., 107, 135, 138
Jenkins, S., 7
Jiménez, F., 88, 94
Johnson, J.W., 116
Jonas, A., 5
Junger, S., 116

K

Keats, E.J., 104, 157
Kooser, T., 47
Krakauer, J., 111
Kroeger, M.K., 137
Krull, K., xvi, 122–123, 126, 132, 138

L

Lakin, P., 157
Lasky, K., 115
Lee-Tai, A., 88, 92
Lehman, B., 6, 26, 33
Levine, E., 116
Lewis, J., 51
Lorbiecki, M., 112
Lowry, L., 91, 136

M

Macaulay, D., 26, 31–32, 113–114
MacLachlan, P., 157
MacNeil, R., 47
Martin, B., Jr., 7, 53, 81
Martin, J., 135, 139
McClafferty, C.K., xvi
McGill, A., 123, 124
Meachem, J., xii
Medina, J., 51
Mills, L.A., 82
Muntean, M., 25
Muth, J.J., 6
Myers, W.D., 111

N

Na, A., 68

O

Obiolis, A., xvi
O'Connor, G., 18
Olaleye, I., 51

P

Parker, S., 138
Parr, T., 157
Pfetzer, M., 111
Pilkey, D., 60t, 61–63
Polacco, P., 5, 157

Pollak, B., 162
Prelustky, J., 46, 52, 138

R

Rappaport, D., 137
Riordan, R., 59
Rocco, J., 4
Rohmann, E., 6, 9–12
Rumford, J., xvi
Rylant, C., 157

S

Say, A., 117
Schanzer, R., 132, 137
Schwartz, D.M., 132, 138
Sciezska, J., 26–27, 115
Seeger, L.V., 4
Selznick, B., 7
Sendak, M., 7
Seuss, D., 11
Shulevitz, U., 4
Sidman, J., 107
Silverstein, S., 46
Simon, N., 156
Singer, B.R., 138
Sís, P., 115, 117
Smith, D.J., 132
Smith, L., 26–27
Soto, G., 161
Spiegelman, A., 15–16
Spinelli, J., 68
Stanley, F., 132, 137
Steen, S., 9
Stewart, S., 8, 162
St. George, J., 117
Storace, P., 81
Sutton, S., 6
Sweet, M., 6

T

Tamar, E., 162
Tan, S., xvi
Tang, G., 115
Teague, M., 8–9
Thomson, S., xvii

V

Van Allsburg, C., xv, 6, 11
Van den Bogaert, H.M., 18
Vander Zee, R., xvi

W

Washington, B.T., 81, 82
Watt, M., 28

WEATHERFORD, C.B., 51, 81, 116
WHATLEY, B., 29
WIESNER, D., 6, 8, 26, 29–30, 33–34
WILCOX, L., 26
WILLEMS, M., 8
WILLIAMS, V.B., 157
WILSON, A., 113
WISNIEWSKI, D., 81
WOOD, A., 5

WOODRUFF, E., 94
WOODSON, J., 113
WORTH, V., 51, 106

Y
YAMATE, S.S., 161
YANG, G., 15
YOLEN, J., 6
YORINKS, A., 8

CHILDREN'S LITERATURE TITLE INDEX

Note. Page numbers followed by *f* or *t* indicate figures or tables, respectively.

A

ALL FAMILIES ARE SPECIAL (SIMON), 156–157
ALL THE PLACES TO LOVE (MACLACHLAN), 157
ALL THE SMALL POEMS (WORTH), 51, 106
AMERICAN BORN CHINESE (YANG), 15
AMERICAN LION: ANDREW JACKSON IN THE WHITE HOUSE (MEACHEM), xii
AND THE GOOD BROWN EARTH (HENDERSON), 162
ANNO'S MATH GAMES (ANNO), 116
ANNO'S MYSTERIOUS MULTIPLYING JAR (ANNO), 116
THE ARRIVAL (TAN), xvi

B

BECAUSE OF WINN-DIXIE (DICAMILLO), 102
BEETLE BOP (FLEMING), 7
THE BIG BANG (FLEISHER), 111
BIGMAMA'S (CREWS), 158
BLACK AND WHITE (MACAULAY), 26, 28f, 31–32
BOUND FOR AMERICA (HASKINS & BENSON), 116
BROWN BEAR, BROWN BEAR, WHAT DO YOU SEE? (MARTIN), 7, 53
BUGS: POEMS ABOUT CREEPING THINGS (HARRISON), 54

C

CAPTAIN UNDERPANTS AND THE WRATH OF THE WICKED WEDGIE WOMAN (PILKEY), 62
CAR WASH (STEEN & STEEN), 9
CASEY BACK AT BAT (GUTMAN), 81
CASTLE (MACAULAY), 114
CASTLES: OLD STONE POEMS (LEWIS & DOTLICH), 51
CATHEDRAL: THE STORY OF ITS CONSTRUCTION (MACAULAY), 114
THE CAT IN THE HAT (SEUSS), 11
A CHAIR FOR MY MOTHER (WILLIAMS), 157
CHAR SIU BAO BOY (YAMATE), 161
CHESTER (WATT), 28, 29f
THE CIRCUIT: STORIES FROM THE LIFE OF A MIGRANT CHILD (JIMÉNEZ), 88, 94

CITY: A STORY OF ROMAN PLANNING AND CONSTRUCTION (MACAULAY), 114
CITY GREEN (DISALVO-RYAN), 162
CLAN APIS (HOSLER), 19, 20f
CONNECTING DOTS: POEMS OF MY JOURNEY (HARRISON), 48
THE CURIOUS INCIDENT OF THE DOG IN THE NIGHT-TIME (HADDON), 111

D

DAD AND ME IN THE MORNING (LAKIN), 157
DALI AND THE PATH OF DREAMS (OBIOLIS), xvi
DELIGHTS AND SHADOWS (KOOSER), 47
DETECTIVE LARUE: LETTERS FROM THE INVESTIGATION (TEAGUE), 8–9
THE DISTANT TALKING DRUM: POEMS FROM NIGERIA (OLALEYE), 51
DOG AND BEAR: TWO FRIENDS, THREE STORIES (SEEGER), 4
DO NOT OPEN THIS BOOK! (MUNTEAN), 25
DON'T LET THE PIGEON STAY UP LATE! (WILLEMS), 8
DO YOU SPEAK AMERICAN? (MACNEIL & CRAN), 47
DUCK, DUCK, GOOSE (HILLS), 8

E

EMMA KATE (POLACCO), 5
ERIKA'S STORY (VANDER ZEE), xvi
EVERYBODY BAKES BREAD (DOOLEY), 161
EVERYBODY BRINGS NOODLES (DOOLEY), 161
EVERYBODY COOKS RICE (DOOLEY), 161
EVERYBODY SERVES SOUP (DOOLEY), 161

F

FALLING DOWN THE PAGE: LIST POEMS (HEARD), 50
FALLING FOR RAPUNZEL (WILCOX), 26
THE FAMILY BOOK (PARR), 157
FAMILY PICTURES/CUADROS DE FAMILIA (GARZA), 159
FARMER'S DOG GOES TO THE FOREST (HARRISON), 53

FARMER'S GARDEN (HARRISON), 53
FEAST FOR 10 (FALWELL), 161
FENCES (WILSON), 113
THE FIRST DAY OF WINTER (FLEMING), 6
FLOTSAM (WIESNER), 8, 29
FLOWER GARDEN (BUNTING), 162
FLUSH: THE SCOOP ON POOP THROUGHOUT THE AGES (HARPER), xvi
FLY HIGH! THE STORY OF BESSIE COLEMAN (BORDEN & KROEGER), 137
THE FOLD (NA), 68
FORTUNATELY (CHARLIP), 7
THE FRIEND (STEWART), 8

G
THE GARDENER (STEWART), 162
THE GARDEN OF HAPPINESS (TAMAR), 162
GETTIN' THROUGH THURSDAY (COOPER), 157
GHOST-EYE TREE (MARTIN & ARCHAMBAULT), 81
THE GIVER (LOWRY), 91, 136
THE GLORY FIELD (MYERS), 111
GOING HOME (BUNTING), 158
GONNA SING MY HEAD OFF! AMERICAN FOLKS SONGS FOR CHILDREN (KRULL), 132, 138
GRANDFATHER'S JOURNEY (SAY), 111
THE GRAPES OF MATH: MIND-STRETCHING MATH RIDDLES (TANG), 115
GREEK GRIME (DOBSON), xvi

H
HENRY'S FREEDOM BOX (LEVINE), 116
HEY, AL (YORINKS), 8
HIDING OUT: CAMOUFLAGE IN THE WILD (MARTIN), 135, 139
HONEY...HONEY...LION! (BRETT), 7
HOW BEN FRANKLIN STOLE THE LIGHTNING (SCHANZER), 132, 137
HOW MY PARENTS LEARNED TO EAT (FRIEDMAN), 161

I
I, MATTHEW HENSON: POLAR EXPLORER (WEATHERFORD), 81
IF THE WORLD WERE A VILLAGE (SMITH), 132
IF YOU HOPPED LIKE A FROG (SCHWARTZ), 138
IF YOU MADE A MILLION (SCHWARTZ), 132
I GOT A FAMILY (COOPER), 156–157
IMAGINE A PLACE (THOMSON), xvii
INSIDE THE WHALE AND OTHER ANIMALS (PARKER), 138
INTERRUPTED JOURNEY: SAVING ENDANGERED SEA TURTLES (LASKY), 115

IN THE SMALL, SMALL POND (FLEMING), 114
IN THE TALL, TALL GRASS (FLEMING), 114
INTO THIN AIR (KRAKAUER), 111
THE INVENTION OF HUGO CABRET (SELZNICK), 7
ISAAC NEWTON (KRULL), xvi
IT'S RAINING PIGS AND NOODLES (PRELUTSKY), 138

J
A JAR OF TINY STARS (CULLINAN), 45–46
JOURNEY INTO MOHAWK COUNTRY (VAN DEN BOGAERT & O'CONNOR), 17–18
JOURNEY TO ELLIS ISLAND (BIERMAN), 118
JOYFUL NOISE: POEMS FOR TWO VOICES (FLEISCHMAN), 50, 107
JULIE OF THE WOLVES (GEORGE), 138
JUMANJI (VAN ALLSBURG), 11
JUST ONE FLICK OF A FINGER (LORBIECKI), 112

K
KAMISHIBAI MAN (SAY), 111
A KITTEN TALE (ROHMANN), 9–12
KNUFFLE BUNNY: A CAUTIONARY TALE (WILLEMS), 8

L
THE LAST PRINCESS: THE STORY OF PRINCESS KA'IULANI OF HAWAI'I (STANLEY), 132, 137
LEAH'S PONY (FRIEDRICH), 132
THE LIBRARIAN WHO MEASURED THE EARTH (LASKY), 115
THE LIFE AND DEATH OF ADOLF HITLER (GIBLIN), 37
LIFT EVERY VOICE AND SING (JOHNSON), 116
A LIGHT IN THE ATTIC (SILVERSTEIN), 46
LOOK TO THE NORTH: A WOLF PUP DIARY (GEORGE), 138
LUCKY JAKE (ADDY), 81
LUNCH (FLEMING), 7

M
THE MAGIC FINGER (DAHL), 82
MAMA CAT HAS THREE KITTENS (FLEMING), 6
MANATEE ON LOCATION (DARLING), 135, 139
MANIAC MAGEE (SPINELLI), 68
THE MAN WHO MADE TIME TRAVEL (LASKY), 115
THE MANY RIDES OF PAUL REVERE (GIBLIN), 37, 40–43
MARTIN'S BIG WORDS: THE LIFE OF DR. MARTIN LUTHER KING, JR. (RAPPAPORT), 137
MARVELOUS MATH: A BOOK OF POEMS (HOPKINS), 51
THE MATCHLOCK GUN (EDMONDS), xi, xiii

MATH CURSE (SCIESZKA), 115
MAUS: A SURVIVOR'S TALE (SPIEGELMAN), 15–16
THE MAZE OF BONES (RIORDAN), 59
THE MEMORY COAT (WOODRUFF), 94
THE MIDDLE PASSAGE: WHITE SHIPS/BLACK CARGO (FEELINGS), 116
MISS ALAINEUS: A VOCABULARY DISASTER (FRASIER), 132
MOLLY BANNAKY (MCGILL), 123, 124
MONARCHS (LASKY), 115
MOSES: WHEN HARRIET TUBMAN LED HER PEOPLE TO FREEDOM (WEATHERFORD), 81, 116
THE MOST BEAUTIFUL ROOF IN THE WORLD (LASKY), 115
MUNCHA! MUNCHA! MUNCHA! (FLEMING), 8
MUSIC FOR ALICE (SAY), 111
MY FRIEND RABBIT (ROHMANN), 6, 9
MY GREAT-AUNT ARIZONA (HOUSTON), 136–137
MY NAME IS JORGE ON BOTH SIDES OF THE RIVER (MEDINA), 51
MY OL' MAN (POLACCO), 157

N
THE NAPPING HOUSE (WOOD), 5
NOISY POEMS (BENNETT), 51
THE NUMBER DEVIL (ENZENSBERGER, BERNER, & HEIM), 115

O
OLIVIA (FALCONER), 5
THE OTHER SIDE (WOODSON), 113
OUR COMMUNITY GARDEN (POLLAK), 162
OWL MOON (YOLEN), 6

P
PASS IT ON: AFRICAN AMERICAN POETRY FOR CHILDREN (HUDSON), 80
THE PERFECT STORM (JUNGER), 111
PETER'S CHAIR (KEATS), 157
PIE IN THE SKY (EHLERT), 5
PIRATES (HARRISON), 51
THE PLACE MY WORDS ARE LOOKING FOR (JANECZKO), 135, 138
A PLACE WHERE SUNFLOWERS GROW (LEE-TAI), 88, 92
PLANTING A RAINBOW (EHLERT), 162
THE PURCHASE OF SMALL SECRETS (HARRISON), 49

R
THE RAG COAT (MILLS), 82
RAIN, RAIN RIVERS (SHULEVITZ), 4

RAMONA THE PEST (CLEARY), 63
THE RANDOM HOUSE BOOK OF POETRY FOR CHILDREN (PRELUTSKY), 46, 52
THE RED BOOK (LEHMAN), 6, 26, 33
REEKING ROYALS (DOBSON), xvi
THE RELATIVE CAME (RYLANT), 157
RICKY RICOTTA'S MIGHTY ROBOT (PILKEY), 61–62
RISING VOICES: WRITINGS OF YOUNG NATIVE AMERICANS (HIRSCHFELDER & SINGER), 138
A RIVER RAN WILD (CHERRY), 114, 135
ROADWORK (SUTTON), 6
ROSA (GIOVANNI), 116
ROUND TRIP (JONAS), 5

S
SACAGAWEA (ERDRICH), 132, 137
SAFARI (BATEMAN & ARCHBOLD), 135, 139
SAILING ALONE AROUND THE ROOM (COLLINS), 48
SCIENCE VERSE (SCIESZKA), 115
SECRETS OF THE SPHINX (GIBLIN), 37–40
SECTOR 7 (WIESNER), 6
SEEDFOLKS (FLEISCHMAN), 136
SEQUOYAH: THE CHEROKEE MAN WHO GAVE HIS PEOPLE WRITING (RUMFORD), xvi
SIDEWALK CHALK: POEMS OF THE CITY (WEATHERFORD), 51
SMOKY NIGHT (BUNTING), 112
THE SNOWY DAY (KEATS), 104
SOMETHING OUT OF NOTHING: MARIE CURIE AND RADIUM (MCCLAFFERTY), xvi
SOUNDS OF RAIN: POEMS OF THE AMAZON (HARRISON), 51
SO YOU WANT TO BE PRESIDENT? (ST. GEORGE), 117
STARRY MESSENGER (SÍS), 115
THE STINKY CHEESE MAN AND OTHER FAIRLY STUPID TALES (SCIESZKA & SMITH), 26–27
STONE BENCH IN AN EMPTY PARK (JANECZKO), 107
SUGAR CANE: A CARIBBEAN RAPUNZEL (STORACE), 81
SUNDIATA: LION KING OF MALI (WISNIEWSKI), 81
SURTSEY: THE NEWEST PLACE ON EARTH (LASKY), 115

T
TALKING WITH ARTISTS (CUMMING), 135–136
THE THREE PIGS (WIESNER), 26, 27f, 30, 33–34
TOASTING MARSHMALLOWS: CAMPING POEMS (GEORGE), 106

Too Many Tamales (Soto), 161
Top Cat (Ehlert), 5
Tupelo Rides the Rails (Sweet), 6
Two Bad Ants (Van Allsburg), 6

U

Underground (Macaulay), 114
Up From Slavery: The Autobiography of Booker T. Washington (Washington), 81, 82

V

The Very Hungry Caterpillar (Carle), 5
Victorian Vapours (Dobson), xvi
Vile Vikings (Dobson), xvi
Voices in the Park (Browne), 29

W

Wait! No Paint! (Whatley), 29
The Wall: Growing up Behind the Iron Curtain (Sís), 117
The Wall (Bunting), 117
The Way Things Work (Macaulay), 113
What Do You Do with a Tail Like This? (Jenkins), 7
When Cows Come Home (Harrison), 53
When Sophie Gets Angry—Really, Really Angry... (Bang), 5

Where the Wild Things Are (Sendak), 7
Who Killed Mr. Chippendale? A Mystery in Poems (Glenn), 138
Who's Afraid of the Big Bad Book? (Child), 29–30, 32
Wild Country (Harrison), 51
Wilma Unlimited: How Wilma Rudolph Became the World's Fastest Woman (Krull), 122–123, 126
Within Reach: My Everest Story (Pfetzer & Galvin), 111
Witness (Hesse), 88, 91
Wolf! Wolf! (Rocco), 4
Wolves (Gravett), 27
A Woman for President: The Story of Victoria Woodhull (Krull), xvi
Words with Wrinkled Knees (Esbensen), 107
The World According to Dog: Poems and Teen Voices (Sidman), 107

Y

Yotsuba&! (Azuma), 17

Z

Zen Shorts (Muth), 6
The Z Was Zapped: A Play in Twenty-Six Acts (Van Allsburg), xv